THE EAGLES' WAR

THE SAGA OF THE EAGLE SQUADRON PILOTS 1940–1945

VERN HAUGLAND

JASON ARONSON
New York • London

To the memory of those Eagles who have folded their wings. Their number increased with the passing of Leroy Skinner in 1973, of Vernon Boehle in 1977, of Sir Michael Duff, William T. O'Regan, and Dr. Arthur B. Osborne in 1980, of Paul Salkeld, Harold H. Strickland, and William H. Nichols in 1981, and of William L. C. Jones in 1982.

Copyright © 1982 by Vern Haugland
10 9 8 7 6 5 4 3 2 1
All rights reserved. Printed in the United States of America. No part of this book may be used or reproduced in any manner whatsoever without written permission from *Jason Aronson, Inc.* except in the case of brief quotations in reviews for inclusion in a magazine, newspaper or broadcast.

Library of Congress Cataloging in Publication Data

Haugland, Vern, 1908–
The Eagles War.

Includes index.
1. World War, 1939-1945—Aerial operations, British.
2. Great Britain. Royal Air Force. Eagle Squadron—History.
3. Fighter pilots—United States.
4. Fighter pilots—Great Britain.
I. Title.
D786.H35   940.54′4941   82-1766
ISBN 0-87668-495-9   AACR2

Manufactured in the United States of America.

CONTENTS

CONTENTS

It is a good many years since the end of the Second World War and even longer since it started. Memories are naturally more receptive to the dramatic events before the final victory while the circumstances leading up to the outbreak of war and the very considerable uncertainties of its early days tend to be forgotten.

The massive involvement of the U.S. Army Air Force in the final stages of the war naturally overshadowed the gallant and vital contribution of the Eagle Squadrons during the critical days of the Battle of Britain.

Forty years may be a long time to wait, but sooner or later the story of the Eagle Squadrons had to be written. This account of the volunteers from the United States who felt strongly enough about the issues at stake to commit their skills and their lives to the struggle against the aggressor cannot fail to stir the blood. It is a timely reminder that there will always be more to be admired in altruism and sacrifice than in the pursuit of security and self-interest.

PREFACE

Vern Haugland has made many great contributions to the literature on fighter flying and fighting in World War II. In this book, he brings together everything that he has acquired in his long experience as a war correspondent, writer, and researcher. It is an important addition to the historical record. Many of us who flew in World War II are finding that even though hundreds of thousands of words have been written about those experiences, many things remain to be related before the story is completely told.

The Eagle Squadrons formed an extremely unusual group. In fact, only once before had such an "organization" been put together and that was made up of Americans who volunteered to go to France and fly in the Lafayette Escadrille. The Eagle Squadrons were made up of American pilots who wanted so badly to fly and fight in World War II that they couldn't wait for the rather uncertain entry of their country into the conflict. They went to England and joined the Royal Air Force.

They ranged in age from a boy of 14, who had to bluff his way in, to the oldest, who was called the elder statesman of the group at 38. Most of these young men had very little flying time and practically none of them had flying time in anything with large engines or resembling the Hurricanes and Spitfires which they flew for the RAF. The pay wasn't worth talking about, but these men wanted to help wage war against Hitler.

These were the first Americans to fight the Axis powers. Eventually they became the foundation for the 4th Fighter Group of the Eighth Air Force. Many of these American young men became aces, and they not only flew over the continent of Europe fighting the Nazis but over the Mediterranean, the North Atlantic, and, in fact, wherever they were called on to go.

Some 243 pilots participated as Eagles from the summer of 1940 until the end of 1942, when the United States became actively engaged in the air war in Europe. Almost one-third of these young Americans were killed in action.

Anyone interested in aviation is going to enjoy this book. It is written in a style that brings the whole story to your eyes and into your consciousness. You can actually feel what these men were doing—in the cockpit, sitting around the ready room, worrying about aircraft, worrying about tactics, and doing what every fighter pilot in the history of aviation has done: swear the next day is going to be his best.

SENATOR BARRY M. GOLDWATER

ACKNOWLEDGMENTS

Heartfelt thanks to the good men and women of the Eagle Squadron Association. Thanks for their generous response to the call for input for this informal and strictly unofficial record—photographs, anecdotes, reminiscences—and for their willingness to spend personal resources for the furtherance of Eagle Squadron research. Thanks, too, for their forbearance and patience, for their constant support, and for their faith and friendship.

There were too many helpers in this project to mention each by name. However, special credit should go to the men who pushed the effort along during their three-year terms as presidents of the ESA: Carroll McColpin, Chesley Peterson, Richard Alexander, Reade Tilley, and Edwin Dale Taylor. Perhaps even more deserving of gratitude are their wives: Joan McColpin, Audrey Peterson, Marilyn Alexander, and Edith Taylor.

As a matter of special good fortune, Norbert Slepyan, editorial director at Jason Aronson, was principal editor of this second volume about the Eagles. With his previous experience as editor of *The Eagle Squadrons*, perhaps no one else could have accomplished the fine tuning of *The Eagles' War* as deftly as he has done. Thanks are offered also to other members of Jason Aronson's team—Jack Putnam, editor of the *Flying Book News*, and Joyce Noulas, production editor—for their expert and intelligent guidance.

Finally and emphatically, thanks to the one who expects it the least and deserves it the most, my loyal and understanding fact checker, researcher bloodhound, and cointerviewer, my dear wife Tess.

INTRODUCTION

This book has a common objective with its predecessor, *The Eagle Squadrons*: to lay before the public for the first time the complete and true story of a richly variegated, highly unorthodox, and most resourceful band of World War II fighter pilots, the members of the three American Eagle Squadrons of Britain's Royal Air Force.

The Eagle Squadrons: Yanks in the RAF 1940-1942 deals essentially with the recruitment and training of the 243 American volunteers and their two years of combat flying for the RAF. This volume sheds more light on the Eagles' RAF career and follows them through their transfer into the United States Army Air Forces, late in 1942, to the end of the war.

Most of the Yanks who volunteered to aid in Britain's defense in the dark days before the United States entered the war were very young—barely into their twenties—and inexperienced. Few were accustomed to military discipline. At the beginning, their performance in general was so poor that at one point the RAF was faced with the embarrassing prospect of having to disband the entire group and send it back to America.

Instead, in time and with excellent leadership, the Eagles' performance became something extraordinary within the RAF and a kind of model for the American units who followed them into combat after Pearl Harbor.

Many were the scrapes and scrambles, the mixes and melees, that these pilots were caught up in in the various theaters of war. The firsthand accounts of their thoughts and experiences assembled here provide a unique close-up of the phases of World War II. Cross-checking of individual narratives with official records and with versions from other persons has made for a high degree of accuracy. (It also has led unexpectedly to the exposure, as largely fraudulent, of a book that has been accepted as true for almost forty years. That work is discussed in an appendix to this book.)

While *The Eagles' War* is roughly chronological in its organization, the chief intent is to create a realistic sense of the Eagles' experiences in the war: choosing to fight "someone else's war," being essentially lightplane pilots learning to do battle in high-performance planes like the Hurricane and Spitfire. The book portrays these pilots as they faced the first shocks of combat, terror, and loss; as they found new friends and allies; and as they coped in the RAF and USAAF with the bizarre fortunes of war for which no one can ever be adequately trained.

In broad outline, this is a history of military units; in essence, it is a story of men, and of boys who became men, pursuing one of the most demanding tasks ever asked of warriors—mortal combat in fighter airplanes. If the chronology at times seems disjointed, the reader is asked to remember that warfare is disjointed; its events take on an order of their own, often far removed from clocks and calendars.

It has been said that the Eagles do not want to be called heroes. Very well, if they were not heroes, they also were not mercenaries, weaklings, or cowards; nor were they unfeared by their enemies or unaccomplished under the stresses and terrors of battle. They were not cruel or vicious, or disloyal to the values for which they fought. Maybe in *their* eyes they were not heroes—but no suitable way of defining them can be found without the use of that compelling word.

PROLOGUE

GREATER LOVE

From the Holy Gospel according to John, chapter 15, verse 13: "Greater love than this no man has, that one lay down his life for his friends."

Consider the fighter squadron commander, a major, who offers to bail out of his own plane into the English Channel if necessary to save one of his pilots from drowning. The latter, a lieutenant, has been hit by antiaircraft fire and temporarily blinded by hot engine oil. It appears likely that he will have to take to his parachute over the water. This occurs during history's greatest invasion, the Allied landings along 50 miles of the German-held Normandy coast on June 6, 1944—D-Day.

Consider this major one week later, daring to land his heavy Thunderbolt fighter on an emergency strip at Omaha Beach, at the eastern base of the Cherbourg Peninsula, in an attempt to rescue a fallen squadron mate—if he is alive—or to recover his body before it can be bulldozed into a mass grave. The major's intent is to load his friend, dead or alive, into his single-seat P-47 and fly him back to England, to a hospital or a decent burial.

The major is Edwin Dale Taylor, 24 years old, commanding officer of the 406th Fighter Bomber Squadron, 371st

Fighter Bomber Group, United States Ninth Air Force. He is known as Jessie to his fellow pilots. Part Choctaw Indian, part Irish, part German, Taylor is an alumnus of 133 Eagle Squadron of the British Royal Air Force.

D-Day covers Normandy. The rocky shore has been divided into Utah and Omaha beaches, for the American landing units, and Juno and Red beaches for the British. The night before, a preliminary force of 18,000 troops landed in darkness by parachute and glider at the village of Sainte-Mère-Église, to secure the eastern and western ends of the beachhead.

As Taylor and his colleagues suit up in the morning for the day's flying, an awesome drama is about to unfold. Some 5,000 ships will carry 185,000 Allied soldiers across the Channel. Naval guns will hammer coastal key points and 11,000 Allied planes will take part in the assault. Within 24 hours there will be 10,000 Allied casualties—more than 6,500 Americans, and close to 3,000 British and almost 1,000 Canadian soldiers. Close to 3,400 Americans will be dead or listed as missing in action, in addition to almost the same number wounded. In the end, the Allies will have a firm grip on the edge of the Continent, which Hitler's forces have long controlled.

Taylor's recollection of the scene conveys the immediacy of swiftly mounting crises.

"As we get to the target, on the first of four strafing missions I am to lead across the beachhead this day, our Navy is throwing an intense barrage of heavy ordnance into the Nazi entrenchments directly behind Omaha Beach. To avoid getting hit by friendly fire from off shore, I pull the squadron out of the first strafing run a little higher than I had planned.

"On the second run, we get down closer, to suppress enemy ground fire that we saw on the first run. It is obvious that the enemy guns are concentrating on our attack. I have never seen the sky so full of tracers and light flak.

"Just as we are pulling out of the run, one of my pilots, Lieutenant Samuel B. Kennedy, of Berwyn, Pennsylvania, radios, 'I'm hit. I'm losing oil. I can't see.'

"An oil line has been shattered, and his cockpit canopy and windscreen are completely covered over with black oil. He is dropping through the heavy barrage the Navy is putting up from the Bay of the Seine. As we both descend through the barrage, I am fearful that I may not be able to catch up with him before he augers in. When I do catch him, he is only seconds away from crashing.

"'Sam,' I call. 'Can you hear me?' He replies that he can.

"'Can you see me? Do you know where I am?'

"'No.'

"'I am 20 feet off your left wing. Your prop is still turning okay. I'm right with you. Calm down. Hang on and we will make it.'

"It is essential that I encourage him and try to steer him out over the Channel, away from the invasion area. I must assess the damage done to his P-47 and get him into a position to bail out if necessary. The damage looks severe. Black oil is spraying from the engine, directly behind the propeller, and prop wash showers the thick fluid back over the cowling. But there is no trace of smoke. Fire is my biggest worry.

"I keep talking to him, giving him guidance. Just as I get him leveled out and under control, he opens the canopy. Hot oil sucks into the cockpit, covering the instrument panel and burning his hands, face and eyes. Now a pilot who has been flying blind, at 300 miles an hour, is an injured pilot. We must gain altitude quickly. Bailing out may be the only way to save him. He knows, and I know, that if fire breaks out, at one touch of flame his oil-drenched body will become a blazing torch. I begin to wonder if I have the mental and manual skills to save him.

"We are too close to the enemy coast at this point for him to bail out. Air-Sea Rescue will be unable to get in to help him. The tone of his voice tells me he is close to panic, and I try to soothe him. 'You'll be all right,' I tell him. 'You're doing fine. Just don't rub your eyes.'

"Later, 'Your left wing is down a bit. Let's level it out.' Then I tell him we have to gain altitude, so that he can use his parachute if need be. 'You're going to be okay,' I assure him, 'but if you have to bail out, I'll stay with you. If your engine should quit, I'll be in my chute right beside you. You know I'm a strong swimmer. I will be there to help you into your dinghy if you need me. Now let's start our climb, and then we'll turn to the left.'

"Kennedy's engine still seems to be running properly, and the P-47 appears normal except that the oil gives it the look of having two coats of black paint all over. We are at an altitude of about 1,000 feet, and we move up into an overcast. I have to start flying by instruments, but I don't tell him that. I tell him not to change the throttle setting, mixture or prop pitch, and I keep talking to him, or having him talk, almost constantly. I set my course for England, about 90 miles away, and start flying time, speed and distance in order to calculate when we'll be over land if we remain in the overcast.

"This is the most trying piece of formation flying I have ever experienced—and what a strange position to be in. I am flying behind Kennedy in order to keep track of him, flying in the number two position to lead a blind and injured pilot, flying by instruments on a time and distance course, not knowing how long it will be before his oil-starved engine freezes and dies, or fire breaks out. And reassuring him, 'Your prop is turning good. Don't change the pitch. Leave the throttle where it is.'

"We climb out of the overcast at about 3,500 feet, an overcast that has seemed more like 25,000 than 2,500 feet thick. I can certainly relate to what Kennedy is going through in that cockpit, blind and all alone, because two years earlier, in combat over France, a German bullet had shot away part of my foot and another had creased my forehead, stunning me and temporarily blinding me. I had managed to keep control of my Spitfire, and after a short period of panic, my sight came back in one eye. Almost the toughest problem at this point is to keep Kennedy talking so that I can tell from the sound of his voice how great his tension is. His mind must be controlled; he cannot be allowed to panic. He does not have much front-line flying experience, but he knows that his squadron commander is an old hand in the combat zone, so he trusts me.

"Now we are near the British coast. I know fairly well where the emergency grass landing strip is. We have to lose altitude. If I tell him to throttle back and the engine freezes, he can still bail out; but if we try for a landing and pull the plane in with power, and then the engine freezes, I will lose him—and that will haunt me to my grave.

"The airstrip comes into sight, a tiny piece of real estate on which to land a sick Thunderbolt with a blind pilot. I know I am taking liberties with a man's life. Sam *could* bail out. But I decide to go for it; Kennedy will stay with the plane and land it. Should I have him put the gear down, or make a belly landing? If he puts the gear down, braking the plane, can he maintain control at the slower speed? He cannot be asked to make a 180-degree approach, so it has to be a straight-ahead landing. Should we try to use just flaps, and belly in? Questions, questions.

"As Kennedy starts to ease back on the throttle, the engine coughs and back-fires. That is our answer; we cannot depend on the engine any longer. Kennedy's voice now is almost a scream. He wants to know how high we are and how far from landing.

"I lie to him and say we are about to start our approach into a great big smooth grass field. My final decision is: put the landing gear down, no flaps, cut power completely and dead-stick it. I'll use my judgment of height, speed, glide angle and distance, and we'll go straight into the grass strip. If my judgment is wrong, there'll be no alibis.

"'Crank down your wheels, Sam,' I tell him. Then I have him kill the engine and cut the switches at about 1,400 feet. His tail wheel takes off the top wire of the fence, and he bounces once, then rolls straight ahead across the grass field. Welcome a 23-year-old pilot back to the land of the living. What a tribute this is to his stamina and ability to follow orders and to our Training Command for producing a flier so well trained and disciplined. After I land and we face each other, and I see how burned and frightened he is—the tears, the embrace—then I know that he knew how close it had been."

On the practical side, once the two men had regained control of their emotions, Taylor prepared to hurry back to base. "If you weren't covered with oil, Sam," he said, "I'd take you home piggyback. I'll call Control and have them come over for you."

Lt. Gen. Lewis H. Brereton, Commander in Chief of the Ninth Air Force, later visited the Squadron and awarded Taylor the Distinguished Flying Cross. The citation said, in part:

> Major Taylor, by reassuring the pilot and expertly guiding and directing his every move, gave him his courage and led him from the beachhead home across the channel. Major Taylor's assistance was in the noblest tradition of the Army; his expert flying and leadership prevented the loss of a pilot and an aircraft, conserving them for future vital operations.

Taylor had sent a recommendation to Group Head-quarters for an award to Kennedy.

"I thought the DFC should have gone to Sam Kennedy rather than to me," Taylor said later. "You have to be well disciplined to do what Sam did. He didn't panic. He followed every bit of guidance. He did things just right. A decoration for him would have been well justified."

On another strafing mission low over the embattled beachhead, seven days after the D-Day landings, Taylor saw one of his P-47s crash and burn. The pilot, 1st Lieutenant John H. Shepard, an American whose parents lived in Buenos Aires, Argentina, bailed out very close to the ground. His parachute had barely started to open when he hit.

Taylor decided to chance landing his Thunderbolt on the wire-mesh-on-sand surface of the airstrip at Omaha Beach. There was no turnaround at the end of the short strip. Taylor would need a bulldozer tow to get turned around for takeoff.

"I landed not knowing whether John was dead or alive," Taylor said. "Light spotter planes had landed there, but this was the first landing of a fighter on the beachhead in France."

Taylor's ground search of the area led him to rows of dead servicemen—English, American, German—stacked four feet high. "There must have been a thousand dead men there," he said. "It was frightening."

"Finally I found John on top of one of these rows. I got help, and we carried him out by my airplane and laid his body down on the sand under the wing. There was a bulldozer down the beach and I was afraid it was getting ready to go into action. The body had already been stripped. There was a tent nearby, and I went over to see if I could get John's personal effects. This proved to be a mistake. I explained to a lieutenant in the tent that I had found the body of one of my pilots and would like to get his wallet, watch and other personal items to send to his parents in Argentina. The lieutenant said he could not release them."

"'At least let me have his MIT ring,' I said. It was a beautiful class ring from his days at Massachusetts Institute of Technology, and he was very proud of it.

"The man in the tent refused, and asked what I was doing with the body. I told him I intended to put it in my Thunderbolt and fly it to England for a decent burial, with a grave that his family some day could visit. I would have to leave my parachute here, because there just wouldn't be enough room in the plane for it."

"I am the graves registration officer," the Lieutenant said. "That body has been registered. It is not to be removed."

"I told him the hell with registration—I was going to take the body. I was the dead man's commanding officer and had the right.

"The Lieutenant said that if the body had not already been registered, something might have been worked out. Now it was too late. The body would stay on the beach."

Taylor insisted; the graves registration officer stood firm. When Taylor moved to pick up the dead pilot anyhow, the Lieutenant drew his sidearm and pointed it between the squadron commander's eyes. Realizing that his plan was hopeless, Taylor climbed into his P-47, frustrated and furious.

"It was touch and go whether I would get airborne from that emergency strip," Taylor said later. "A Thunderbolt with full throttle through the gate, full flaps and in a stall, is really a handful.

"I had no gun, or I might have challenged the lieutenant. I had a knife with a seven-inch blade strapped to my left leg just below the knee. I could have killed him. But at that time I was sick of death. It was all around me, in every direction. Besides, I might not have been able to get away with it. I wound up with a censure and with the knowledge that I could have been court-martialed. I made a point of flying over the site again the next morning. The rows of bodies were still there. For several days the weather was overcast. The next time I saw the place there was no sign of the dead."

Part I

RAF

1

SQUADRON FORMATIONS

In Europe, the Nazi offensive had rolled forward with brutal force. France bowed before her enemy in June 1940, only weeks after the German invasion, and Western Europe now belonged to Hitler. Only Britain remained free, and in July and August, an invasion of the British Isles appeared imminent. A deluge of air raids on Britain had begun, climaxing in the great Blitz on London. Increasingly, the Germans were bombing out of frustration, for as the Battle of Britain progressed during that bloody summer of 1940, it was becoming ever more clear that the Royal Air Force would not be destroyed and that the British could not be induced to sue for terms.

On September 15, the Germans threw virtually everything they had into a succession of raids on London and surrounding areas. The Luftwaffe intended the attacks to be a monument to Nazi superiority. A commemorated occasion it did become —Battle of Britain Day, the day when the most the Germans could do was not enough. The day belonged to the fabled Few, of whom Winston Churchill spoke, the RAF fighter pilots who began the turning of the tide.

Still, by nightfall, no one in Britain or the rest of the world could know the significance of the past hours. Indeed, the bombings went on and on, for many months.

In America, the public watched in awe and horror, with no small amount of admiration for the British people and their warriors. They knew of the heroism at Dunkirk, the deep sadness of Coventry, the image of the dome of St. Paul's stark against the fire-dashed London sky. There were some who favored Germany and many who favored official American neutrality, being for "America first" and "too proud to fight." But by and large, public sentiment was sympathetic to the British and the Commonwealth.

Some Americans could not let it go at that. As the Battle of Britain raged, a trickle of young American pilots was already on its way into the RAF. In fact, some were already serving His Majesty. Four days after the September 15 Nazi onslaught became such a day of British triumph, three Yanks reported to their RAF commanding officer at Church Fenton to begin the fleshing out of the first Eagle Squadron. In time, the number of Yanks flying as Eagles would swell to 243. The number of Eagle squadrons would grow to three, and their battle record would be outstanding.

The concept of an all-American squadron of fighter pilots for the RAF had first been proposed by Charles Sweeny, a wealthy and socially prominent young American businessman working in London. Sweeny and his famed golfing brother, Bobby, were noted in the British capital for their beautiful and elegant female companions. At the time, Bobby was escorting the Countess Reventlow, the former Barbara Hutton. Meanwhile, the beauty of Charles Sweeny's wife, Margaret—later, after their divorce, to become the Duchess of Argyll—had inspired Cole Porter to write in a song, "You're the top, you're Mrs. Sweeny; you're the top, you're the great Houdini."

When Britain went to war, Sweeny had helped to organize Americans living in England into a motorized machine gun unit attached to the London area headquarters of the British home defense system. In June 1940, he proposed in a letter to the British Air Ministry the establishment of an "American Air Defence Corps" of volunteer United States pilots. The corps was to be commanded by his uncle, Colonel Charles

Sweeny, a celebrated adventurer, whose exploits as an international soldier of fortune had dazzled the younger Charles.

Colonel Sweeny's career had been colorful in the extreme. He had been the hero of peasant uprisings in Mexico, Venezuela, and Nicaragua, a soldier of the French Foreign Legion fighting in France in World War I, a colonel in the American Expeditionary Force in the same war, an aide to the French General Weygand supporting the Poles against the Bolsheviks in the Battle of Warsaw in 1920, an advisor to Kemal Ataturk in the Greco-Turkish War in 1922, again a Foreign Legionnaire, this time fighting a Berber revolt in the Moroccan Sahara in 1925, and a military advisor to the Republican Forces in the Spanish Civil War of the late 1930s.

Such a luminary's association with the American group would be excellent public relations, the younger Charles Sweeny argued. At first, the British military authorities frowned on the idea of a separate American command, as suggested by Sweeny, but the Secretary of State for Air approved the plan, mainly because of its propaganda value.

The Colonel's involvement did indeed become a publicity plus, though the elder Sweeney never actually exercised control over the American volunteers. Thanks to his nephew, he was made Honorary Commander of 71 Squadron and received the temporary RAF rank of Group Captain. Often, during those hectic early days of the war, reliable information was buried under dramatic but erroneous news tidbits, and the press picked up on the Colonel's participation, turning the window dressing into "leadership" and the Colonel himself into the "organizer of the Eagle Squadron," as *The New Yorker* had it in December, 1940. It would have been unlike Colonel Sweeny to play down his role, much less deny the exaggeration of it, and he stayed very much in character.

Nominated for actual command by the younger Charles Sweeny was Billy Fiske, a member of the wealthy American colony in London, who had joined the RAF as a pilot two weeks after the war started. However, Fiske suffered fatal burns in August 1940, on landing his damaged fighter at Tangmere airfield. Sweeny then proposed William E. G. Taylor for the position. Taylor, age 35, had been released from U.S. Navy pilot service to fly for the Royal British Navy, and had taken part in combat operations off aircraft carriers.

Thus, by the autumn of 1940, with the British still sorely pressed by the Luftwaffe, the beginning of a stream of American pilots was moving to join the RAF, while the necessary organizational steps were being taken in Britain to create the pilots' unit. Yet the process was not entirely smooth. Taylor had been promised the position of 71 Squadron Leader, but other arrangements were being made, even as the first pilots were en route.

That Yanks were on the way was due in no small part to the foresight of the British and Canadians and the tenacity of some concerned Americans. From the first days of the war, a mechanism had been in action to screen potential pilots from the many American volunteers that were expected to try for the RAF and Royal Canadian Air Force. To handle the operation, RCAF Vice Marshal Billy Bishop had approached Clayton Knight, an American who had flown for the Royal Flying Corps in World War I and who was an artist held in particular respect by aviation enthusiasts for his excellent depictions of aerial warfare.

Knight and an influential and hardworking friend, Homer Smith, set up interviewing and screening operations in various cities, at first clandestinely and then openly. By the time of Pearl Harbor, the Knight Committee had handled 50,000 applications and had cleared 6,700 American pilots for service with the RAF and RCAF. Of the Eagles, 92 percent were Knight Committee selections.

In anticipation of the flow of recruits from across the Atlantic, the RAF established the all-American Eagle Squadron Number 71 at Church Fenton, 180 miles north of London, near the city of York. The first men to join the squadron, on September 19, 1940, were Eugene Tobin, of Los Angeles, Andrew Mamedoff, of Connecticut, and Vernon Keough, of Brooklyn, three escapees from France. On reaching England, the three had enrolled in RAF Squadron 609 at Warmwell, in Dorset. In a month of action there, Tobin destroyed three enemy planes and damaged two, and Mamedoff and Keough shared in shooting down a Dornier bomber. Then they were sent to Church Fenton.

Ten days later, they were joined by the appointed commanding officer of the new unit, Squadron Leader Walter Myers Churchill, an English fighter pilot hero, and by another

American, Art Donahue, of St. Charles, Minnesota. In action in France during May, Churchill had shot down seven enemy aircraft. Subsequently, in England, while commanding 605 Squadron during the Battle of Britain, he scored his eighth kill. He also had helped to organize and train two squadrons of Polish volunteers for fighter pilot duty. Churchill had been awarded both the Distinguished Service Order and the Distinguished Flying Cross. Donahue had been injured in combat early in August, flying with 64 Squadron, and was just out of the hospital.

During October 1940, two more English pilots, Flight Lieutenants (the equivalent of U.S. Army Captain) Royce C. Wilkinson and George A. Brown checked into 71 Squadron with four Americans: Squadron Leader (Major) William E. G. Taylor, of Houston, Texas, who had been promised command of 71; Pilot Officers (second lieutenant) Philip Leckrone, of Illinois, and Luke Allen, of Colorado; and Flight Lieutenant Robert V. "Bobby" Sweeny, of Palm Beach, Florida.

The Squadron's first combat-ready planes, nine Hawker Hurricanes, arrived at Church Fenton November 7, 1940, along with eight more American volunteers: Mike Kolendorski, Bell, California; Byron Kennerly, Pasadena, California; James L. McGinnis, Hollywood, California; Edwin E. Orbison, Sacramento, California; Dean Satterlee, Sacramento; Richard Arthur "Jim" Moore, Fort Worth, Texas; Chesley G. Peterson, Santaquin, Utah; and Gregory "Gus" Daymond, Van Nuys, California.

Later in November, 71 Squadron was transferred to a somewhat larger base, Kirton-in-Lindsey, 40 miles southeast of Church Fenton but still in the relatively quiet Midlands defense area known as Group 12. What the Squadron was really looking forward to was a move into the active Group 11 area defending London.

Five more Americans had signed in at 71 Squadron by mid-January: Kenneth S. Taylor, Los Angeles; Victor Bono, Novato, California; Nat Maranz, Tiburon, California; William H. Nichols, Woodland, California; and James Keith Alexander, Huntington, West Virginia.

William Taylor arrived at the 71 Squadron station at Church Fenton on October 4, only to learn that the British squadron leader, Walter Churchill, had arrived there five days earlier. Puzzled pilots were told simply that they now had two squadron commanders, but it became evident that Churchill, on the basis of his squadron leadership experience and his superior combat record, was the man in charge. Taylor bowed out temporarily, transferring to another base to take special training on the new Spitfire fighter.

Meanwhile, Colonel Sweeny announced at a news conference in Ottawa that the formation of the Eagle Squadron had moved forward so well that he was retiring from his association with the unit. "The men are in good hands, and they don't need me any more," the old soldier said. In London, Charles Sweeny arranged for his brother, Bobby, to become adjutant of 71 Squadron.

Walter Churchill proved to be the ideal commander to launch 71 Squadron on its way to excellence. "He was a strict disciplinarian, but we came to love that man," said Pilot Officer Vic Bono of him. When Bill Taylor returned to 71 Squadron—now at Kirton-in-Lindsey—from Spitfire indoctrination, he found Walter Churchill still very much in charge. The American went to London to remind the Air Ministry of the assurances that had been made to him. The RAF thereupon promoted Churchill to commander of a wing, which was composed of three fighter squadrons. In January 1941, Taylor at last was in control of 71, an American leading American pilots in a British unit.

Bobby Sweeny had found at 71 Squadron a job overlap situation not unlike that involving Taylor and Churchill. British Flying Officer F. H. Tann had become Squadron Adjutant, the post that Charles Sweeny had lined up for his brother Robert. Bobby Sweeny in effect became assistant adjutant, an office that did not exist in the RAF table of organization. "I was educated at Oxford, and Air Marshal Sholto Douglas, chief of Fighter Command, thought I could keep the Squadron in line so they wouldn't break too many RAF regulations," Bobby Sweeny recalled. "What a hope!

"On their nights off, these fellows were like a pack of Sioux Indians on the warpath. I must have visited most of the jails in England bailing and talking them out wherever we were stationed, mostly in Lincolnshire.

"I left the Squadron late in 1940. After a little flight training, as I already had 150 hours, I transferred to 247 Squadron, RAF Coastal Command, flying B-24 Liberators."

Fellow Eagles recalled years later that occasionally they had given Bobby Sweeny some rough verbal bullying, in part because he was a rich man and a famous athlete, winner of the British amateur golf championship in 1937. "The fighter pilots used to give him hell, in a kidding way," Pete Peterson said. "'You can't drink with us in our bar,' they would say. 'You're not a military flier. You're just an old lounge lizard.'

"Bobby took the ragging for 30 days or so, and then got so annoyed he decided to become a combat pilot, too. He was a little over age, but had enough political pull to get into the RAF Training Command. It was a rough struggle, but finally, he got his wings and was assigned to fly B-24s in the Coastal Command."

Sweeny flew the four-engine bombers some 800 hours on operations—convoy work and antisubmarine patrols, mostly in the Bay of Biscay area. His crew attacked eight submarines, destroyed two and damaged five.

The feat for which he was principally decorated was for bringing in his heavily damaged aircraft after a particularly difficult battle with a German submarine. The return trip was through German patrols and highly dangerous. Wing Commander Clouston, Sweeny's flight commander, could hear Bobby's SOS from 800 miles out and "felt sure," as he said, "he had bought it."

Clouston recommended Sweeny for the DSO, but when the station commander objected to flight lieutenants getting DSOs for doing their duty, Clouston awarded Sweeny an immediate DFC.

Said Peterson of the event, "When Bobby went to Buckingham Palace to receive the DFC from the King, I was just about as proud as when I went there and received my own. I had always admired him."

A new squadron was declared operational by the Royal Air Force when it had completed preliminary training and was ready to engage the enemy. With Bill Taylor as its commanding officer, 71 Squadron reached combat ready status early in February 1941. In April, the Squadron moved to its third home, Martlesham Heath, in Suffolk, near Ipswich and only 65 miles northeast of London. At last, the Eagles were in an air war zone, a part of 11 Group. The pilots began to sight and pursue enemy planes, and even to fire at them, ineffectively.

In May, the Americans exchanged their Hurricane I aircraft for the improved Hurricane IIA, and they began to encounter the enemy. On a sweep over Holland, Mike Kolendorski was killed, the first Eagle to be lost in action.

The Squadron was sent in June to a central post at North Weald, near Epping, just north of London, where for the first time it would operate with two British squadrons in an RAF Wing. Squadron Leader Taylor, offered a promotion to wing commander and a transfer to a fighter training command, refused both and resigned from the RAF. He returned to the U.S. Navy and served with distinction in the Pacific.

The RAF transfered one of its battle-tested English pilots, Henry "Paddy" Woodhouse, leader of 610 Squadron, to the 71 Squadron command post vacated by Taylor. Fighter Command also appointed another Battle of Britain hero, Squadron Leader Peter Powell, to take charge of a second Eagle Squadron, number 121, being established in mid-May 1941, at the Kirton-in-Lindsey base formerly occupied by 71 Squadron. Powell was already an ace with a score of seven enemy planes shot down.

A third Eagle Squadron, number 133, came into being on August 1, 1941, at Coltishall, Essex, and soon settled in at Fowlmere airdrome, a satellite of RAF Station Duxford, five miles south of Cambridge. Its British commander, Squadron Leader George A. Brown, had been a flight leader in 71 Squadron since its establishment, and knew from experience how to work with and handle American pilots. The RAF provided 133 Squadron with newer equipment—the Hurricane IIB with the improved Merlin XX engine—than that used by the other Eagles. The Mark IIB carried twelve .30 caliber machine guns, four more than in the earlier model Hurricanes.

With the two senior Eagle Squadrons operational and beginning to score in combat—71 Squadron accounted for three Messerschmitt 109 fighters on its first engagement on July 2—the RAF decided to send 133 Squadron to Northern Ireland, to a newly-constructed station at Eglinton, eight miles from Londonderry, for further training as a unit. En route, four of the pilots—Mamedoff, Hugh McCall, Roy Stout and William J. White—crashed into hillsides while letting down through an overcast for a refueling stop on the Isle of Man and were killed.

In August 1941, the RAF started changing the Eagles over gradually from Hurricanes to the Spitfire, first with the IIA model and then the VB. In September 1942, 133 Squadron graduated to the Spit IX.

The Eagles of 71 Squadron returned from North Weald to Martlesham Heath in December 1941; 121 Squadron moved from Kirton-in-Lindsey to North Weald; and, rounding out the airbase game of musical chairs, 133 Squadron, upon completing its training tour in Northern Ireland, transferred into Kirton-in-Lindsey. In May 1942, 71 Squadron shifted over to Debden, future home of the U.S. 4th Fighter Group, and 133 Squadron moved to another great base, Biggin Hill.

Squadron rosters changed sporadically as new Eagles arrived to replace men posted elsewhere or lost in action. Paddy Woodhouse, leader of 71 Squadron, won promotion to the command of the Tangmere Wing, and was succeeded by Stanley Meares, another of the brilliant young commanding officers called in from the rolls of the RAF. Less than three months later, on November 15, 1941, Meares and one of his American pilots, Ross Scarborough, were killed in a collision during a close-formation practice flight.

The death of Meares led to the appointment of 21-year-old Chesley "Pete" Peterson as 71 Squadron Commander, the first American to lead the Eagles in combat. At 121 Squadron, Peter Powell, promoted in January, 1942, to command of the Wing at Hornchurch, was succeeded by Hugh Kennard, the able young Englishman who had been one of his flight lieutenants. Kennard was severely wounded in a July 31 engagement during a bomber escort mission over France, in which he and two other Eagles, William P. Kelly and Frank R. Boyles, each shot down a German plane, and fellow Eagles Sel Edner and Barry Mahon managed to destroy two enemy fighters each. With Kennard out of action, 121 Squadron acquired yet another English leader, Dudley Williams.

At 133 Squadron, meanwhile, the dynamic commanding officer, George Brown, had moved up the ladder in November 1941, to Fighter Command Headquarters. Another equally strong and effective English officer, Eric Hugh Thomas, succeeded him. Under the deft leadership of Thomas, the Squadron achieved some of its greatest air triumphs. In early August, however, Thomas also was promoted, to the command of the Wing at Biggin Hill. Once again, a way was cleared for an American to be an Eagle Squadron Leader: Carroll "Red" McColpin, of Albany, New York. The only man to serve in all three Eagle Squadrons and to fly combat missions in each, McColpin had also set a record for swiftness in attaining acedom, by shooting down five enemy planes within a five-week period, in October and November 1941.

With the entry of the United States into the war following the Japanese attack on Pearl Harbor in December 1941, the Eagles clamored for immediate transfer to service of their own country. It took months to be accomplished, but in time the Eagles became part of the USAAF, although some remained with the RAF for duties including combat against the Germans and Italians in the Mediterranean and Middle East and against the Japanese in the Far East. The pilots who had preceded all other Americans as a unit in the war against the Axis—beating the Flying Tigers into action—were no longer the leading edge of Yank involvement; they had become the backbone of America's massive air establishment in Europe.

2

"SOMEONE ELSE'S WAR"

Diaries, logbooks and letters home describe graphically and realistically the Eagles' experiences. They not only tell of the fliers' lives in the Royal Air Force but in some cases reveal or suggest answers to the constantly asked question: Why did they do it—why did they go off to put themselves in harm's way when their country was officially at peace?

Among the especially dedicated takers of notes was Harold Herman "Strick" Strickland. He had done 36 hours of flying as an Army aviation cadet in 1925 and had accumulated 2,129 hours in commercial flying and instructing as a federal government flight examiner before entering 133 Eagle Squadron at the age of 38. That was in August 1941, four months before Pearl Harbor decided once and for all the agonizing issue of U.S. neutrality.

Strickland meticulously calculated after the war that as an Eagle he flew more than 80 hours on 56 combat missions: 5½ hours on scrambles after enemy aircraft, 7 hours and 40 minutes in operations with minesweepers, 9½ hours with air-sea rescue boats, and 69 hours with shipping convoys. Using RAF terminology, his total numbers of combat missions by type were: Circus—large-scale combined fighter and bomber operations designed to bring enemy fighters into action—30, Rodeo—fighter offensive sweeps over enemy territory without bombers—16, Ramrod—escorting bombers against selected targets—3, Rhubarb—small-scale fighter harassing operations over enemy-occupied territory against ground targets or low-flying airplanes—3, Roadstead—escorting bombers in attacks on ships—1, combined operations—3.

Born in 1903, Strickland was one of the oldest of the Eagles when he signed up and was readily considered by them their "elder statesman." At the time of his signing, this blue-eyed redhead was a slight 5 foot 6 inches tall and weighed only 138 pounds. He had been orphaned at 16 and compelled to earn a living after only two years of high school education. At 18, Strickland enlisted in the Army Signal Corps and within four months was promoted to corporal.

Weighing the entirety of his military experience in peace and war, Strickland once said, "As Corporal of the Guard, aged 18, I thought I knew something about the 'burden of command.' Twenty years later, I could appreciate with deepest admiration the roles played by my younger British and American commanders, many in their early twenties, who had to handle life and death responsibilities as well as a few extra rugged individualists.

"I had particular admiration for the very young pilots in the Eagle Squadrons who so skillfully led flights, squadrons and wings of RAF and USAAF fighters through some of the greatest air battles of World War II. When I was their age, I thought that leading a Signal Corps squad was tough."

By mid-1940 Strickland had become District Flight Supervisor in the Civilian Pilot Training Program of the Civil Aeronautics Authority, a government-industry partnership designed to create a reserve of college-age pilots. The CPTP offered ground training at colleges and universities and flight training at established civilian flying schools.

"My CPTP district covered Indiana and parts of Ohio and Kentucky, and included about a dozen widely separated colleges and universities," Strickland recalled. "I used a Waco UPF-7 open-cockpit biplane and a Ford sedan to cover my district. I needed both to keep in regular contact with the college staffs, ground and flight instructors, and the student trainees. I lectured to the ground classes in the colleges, flew check rides with the students, licensed primary and advanced instructors and attended CAA conferences."

Frequently, after flying most of the day, Strickland would head by automobile for the next point on his schedule. On many of the long drives late at night, his only companion was the car radio. The news it poured out was always bad. Germany's Wehrmacht had rolled across Belgium, France, and Holland; the Scandinavian countries, except for Sweden, were occupied; the Luftwaffe maintained around-the-clock attacks on the United Kingdom and its coastal approaches, and German submarines prowled the Atlantic. Meanwhile, many Americans, including a number from the CPTP, were volunteering for the RAF and the Royal Canadian Air Force.

Strickland recalled, "Looking back, I think that during the Battle of Britain I must have subconsciously considered the possibility of volunteering. But it was months later that the thought actually surfaced.

"En route from Kalamazoo, I stopped at South Bend to talk with the CPTP contingent. Although it was not in my district, I always enjoyed visiting Notre Dame. After a short stay, I strapped on my parachute and took off in my UPF-7. It was late afternoon, with visibility unlimited. The skies were blue, clear and cold.

"As I levelled off, I glanced back over the tail of the Waco for another look at the golden dome of Notre Dame, brilliant in the sunlight. Then I looked ahead and began steering down the section lines by pilotage. This is extra easy and a lot of fun in familiar areas on clear days, particularly in so many areas of the Midwest, where the earth is flat and the farmland is laid out in mile-square section lines, east and west, north and south. It is in marked contrast, as I later found out, to the boundaries in the United Kingdom and other parts of Europe, which ramble along in a haphazard manner.

"Spring comes late around the Great Lakes. Most of the rich, wide farms around South Bend still looked bare and brown. Only an occasional patch of green showed here and there. As the engine purred away, I picked up familiar landmarks far out on the horizon. I think that anyone flying anywhere in the United States who looks at our bounteous land and industry would agree that this country is worth fighting for any time.

"Somewhere between South Bend and Indianapolis, the decision was made. I would resign my successful, enjoyable, well-paying and exciting job and volunteer my services to the Royal Air Force as soon as it could be arranged without interrupting the continuity of the training in my district.

"I was sufficiently mature to know what I was doing. I did not discount the physical risks. If there was any hesitancy, it was the possibility of losing my American citizenship by fighting in a foreign force, swearing allegiance to a foreign ruler."

The law in effect at that time, set forth in a 1907 statute, provided that any American citizen would be deemed to have expatriated himself when he had taken an oath of allegiance to any foreign state. According to a statement in 1980 by the Immigration and Naturalization Service, during the war, there were reciprocal agreements between most allied countries, which attempted to preserve the citizenship status of nationals serving in the foreign military. "However, there are a lot of ifs, ands and buts to these agreements," said Verne Jervis, the agency's public information officer. "Consequently, some persons lost their United States citizenship while others did not, depending on the circumstances and terms of the agreements. The United States Supreme Court in recent years has considerably modified the expatriation laws. The effect of this is that United States citizenship has since been restored to those persons who were found to have expatriated themselves by service in the foreign military of an allied nation during World War II and who had no intention of abandoning such citizenship. Those persons are now considered never to have lost their citizenship."

Through the British Embassy in Washington, Strickland got in touch with the Clayton Knight Committee. He reported, as a prospective $68-a-month pilot officer, to the RCAF advanced training center at Ottawa for a flight test in a Yale trainer.

"The instructor explained the cockpit, controls, and so on, taxied out, took off, climbed into the traffic pattern, and turned the airplane over to me. He told me to do some turns. I did. Somewhere around 3,000 feet, he took back the controls, nosed down, and opened the throttle. Then he pulled up, and looped the loop. He asked me to please do a loop.

"In the advanced CPTP program I had done hundreds of loops and other aerobatic maneuvers, but not in any high-horsepower aircraft. I nosed down, increased the power, and pulled back on the stick. The nose came up to the horizon. Then the horizon disappeared as usual in a loop, and did not reappear until we were upside-down at the top of the loop, where I began to pull into the dive, surprised that I had encountered no difficulty with the loop and the strange airplane.

"I was asked to do a snap roll. I did. Then a slow roll, which is more difficult because it requires coordination of all three controls as the airplane rolls around its longitudinal axis. Again I had no difficulty.

"The instructor asked for a three-turn tailspin. I looked below, closed the throttle, and gently pulled the nose upward into a stall; then pulled the stick all the way back, and kicked hard on the right rudder. The nose dropped suddenly in the stall, and the heavy airplane went into a slow-turning, straight-down, high-speed diving spin. I counted the turns, eased the stick forward, kicked the opposite rudder, stopped the spin, and recovered from the high-speed dive without difficulty, although there was considerable altitude loss before levelling off. Then we flew into the pattern and I landed. This completed my 30-minute check ride."

Moran Morris and Edwin Dale "Jessie" Taylor were buddies at Southeastern State College, in Durant, Oklahoma, where they learned to fly in the Civilian Pilot Training Program before going into the RAF together. Morris had difficulty distinguishing certain colors, so he asked Taylor to take his eye test for him. In return, Morris, one of the few flying cadets to have mastered shorthand, would share with his friend the copious notes he assembled during lectures. They took their operational training in England, first at Debden and then at Ashton Down, before joining 133 Squadron at Eglinton on October 15, 1941.

Chesley Gordon "Pete" Peterson was a tall, skinny kid from Utah. With six of his colleagues from the Los Angeles area, he reported to the British Air Ministry in England on July 24, 1940. According to Peterson, "We were an odd-looking bunch, still in our California civilian clothes. Within two hours we had our warrants and our orders to Hawarden airfield near Liverpool. There was an aircraft factory at one end of the field. On the operational side there were only tents. It looked like a scene from a World War I camp on the French front.

"Our Wing Commander Flying was Teddy Donaldson, one of the greatest and finest pilots I've ever known. He had led an RAF acrobatic team late in the 1930s, and was a Hurricane squadron commander in France at the start of the war. He was an ace several times over, and was one of the few pilots I've ever known to have the killer instinct. He served as a liaison officer with the USAAF in 1943 and 1944, and retired as an Air Commodore in 1950. After that he became widely known as the air correspondent for the *London Daily Telegraph*.

"The RAF did not know what to do with us, but we had to have uniforms. We went to a local store in Chester, and bought uniforms off the shelf.

"I was easy to fit, but Jim Moore, six-foot-two, was a problem. Although he was beautifully proportioned, he could not get trousers that fit. If they were long enough, they would be three times too big around the waist. After he got his uniform, he used to pull it out from his body and say, 'Look, everybody. How do you like my double-breasted jacket?'

"We arrived the Hawarden Operational Training Unit simultaneously with 50 RAF pilots who had been flying reconnaissance in France, in Lysanders, and were now to be crosstrained in Spitfires to become fighter pilots. Gene Tobin, Andy Mamedoff and Shorty Keough had been at Hawarden three weeks previously, and Phil Lechrone had just been graduated, so the RAF pilots knew Americans.

"We sat around a week, waiting for our turn to fly, and found that the Lysander pilots had priority. Teddy Donaldson, meanwhile, had been sent to the Advanced Flying School at Sealand as Wing Commander.

"I went to Teddy and said, 'We came over from America to fly, but our priority at Hawarden is so low we are not getting any flying time. You have plenty of Miles Masters at Sealand. If we could be transferred over to fly under you, you could give us priority.'

"Donaldson arranged the transfer, and we did get priority on the training planes. We flew like mad in the Masters, and made good friends at Sealand. Three weeks or a month later, in September, we returned to Hawarden where the load on the Spitfires had eased a bit."

Carroll McColpin, who became the first Eagle to attain the rank of two-star general, says, "My flying days started shortly after I was born. I can recall a photograph showing me as an infant on board a World War I Jenny in 1917. My family claimed at the time that I was the youngest passenger ever to fly in an aircraft in the Pacific Northwest. Another entry in the family album depicts my enthusiasm for flying at an early age. I was photographed with my father at the conclusion of the first automobile run from San Francisco to New York with California air in its tires—an advertising event backed by the Firestone Company. A reporter asked me what I, as a five-year-old, wanted to do when I grew up. The quote, in the Firestone booklet: 'I want to become a pilot and shoot down the Kaiser.'

"Since my father ran a nationwide business that manufactured electrical testing equipment, I grew up in cities all over the United States, from New York to Seattle and Los Angeles. My boyhood resembled those of most American youngsters except in one department, flying. I designed and built my own airplane, and taught myself how to fly.

"From 1930 to 1939, when soup lines became part of the national scene, few men were able to go to college. I was no exception. I worked at a variety of jobs to support my mother, five sisters and a brother. Despite these hard times, I always managed to get to the airfield each week for a few hours in the air. When war clouds settled over Europe and England started asking for help, I asked myself, 'Why spend good money to fly, when someone else is willing to pay you for it?'"

Leo Nomis, nicknamed "the Chief," is the son of Leo Noomis (the son subsequently dropped the second *o*), one of the most noted stuntmen in the early days of the motion picture industry. "Dad was in the Air Service in World War I, but not in the Lafayette Escadrille, as was set forth in some of the studio publicity," Nomis recalls. "He was killed in 1932 stunting a biplane. My father was part Sioux Indian."

Nomis characterizes his years before the war as "the standard—getting out of high school, hanging around airports, learning to fly, accumulating flying hours little by little, and then the golden opportunity to hit the big time with the RAF."

Eagle Bill Geiger was from an air-minded family. His father was in the Balloon Corps in World War I, and an uncle, Harold Geiger—a West Point graduate for whom Geiger Field, in Spokane, Washington, was named—received a license to fly from the Signal Corps in 1912. Bill Geiger was captain of the fencing and ski teams at Pasadena City College, in California, at the time he learned about the Eagles. "I had an Olympic coach in fencing and was trying to work up to the Olympic team when I decided I would rather fly in the RAF."

During the freighter-convoy voyage from Canada to England as an RAF volunteer, Geiger started writing a diary-type letter, adding a bit to it each day. He set down the size of the convoy and the nature of its cargo, and described the escorting naval vessels. He wrote that he was particularly intrigued by a French submarine that was carrying its own airplane.

"I mailed the letter home and about two weeks later was called on the carpet by the commanding officer of the 56th OTU at Sutton Bridge," Geiger says. "He explained the censorship rules to me in quite some detail. It just had never occurred to me that there would be a problem about that."

Geiger states that on his first RAF mission, a squadron flight, "we crossed what looked like a lot of water and then we flew in a great oval to cover some bombers coming out of France. Because we had crossed water, I thought we were over enemy territory. It turned out that all we had done was to cross the Thames estuary. We were holding over Manston, England!"

Barry Mahon says that when he entered "what was loosely called a training program" at Burbank, California, American neutrality was guarded so carefully that only civilian aircraft could be used to train pilots for combat.

"The school at Burbank was under the control of Major Mosely, who also had contracts for training American cadets at Lancaster and Ontario, California. We RAF cadets were sort of bastard children, kept separate. Not until later in the program did they combine RAF volunteers with other trainees. While I was at Burbank, no one really would admit that we existed.

"Because of the civilian nature of the training, we were not allowed any low flying, gunnery, or formation flying until we got to England. I must admit, however, that many an afternoon there was consternation among the ranch owners as beat-up yellow Stearmans buzzed their livestock at grass level heights.

"One person who complained, but in a rather good-natured way, was Clark Gable, who was to go on and join the Air Force himself as a gunnery officer and fly several missions over Germany.

"Through a friend, film agent Pat DiCicco, I arranged the appointment of pin-up favorite, Betty Grable, as honorary colonel of our Burbank RAF cadets. We also were given tours of several of the studios.

"During my training period, I went home to Santa Barbara for the weekend. At a bar an older friend took me to a back table where several men were seated and introduced me to Howard Hughes. When he learned that I was an RAF cadet, Hughes took special note. He sat there with me all evening drawing sketches of flight formations which he considered superior to those being used by the Americans. He was correct. His drawings were almost identical to the three flights of four, strung out, that we used during our offensive sweeps in the RAF in 1941 and 1942.

"One evening, Hughes came over to Burbank, picked me up, and took me down to his hangar to show me a mock-up of what was later to be the Lockheed Constellation. I found him to be an extremely interesting person. Certainly he showed no signs of eccentricity. I had the feeling that he loved planes and felt at ease with people who understood them.

"On arrival in England, we were sent to Bournemouth on the south coast, where we got used to the fact that we were RAF officers. The King and Queen paid us a surprise visit, and I happened to be in one of the front ranks in the inspection.

The Queen graciously asked me why I had volunteered. I was momentarily at a loss for words, and then blurted out, 'Because there must always be an England, Madam.' That was not exactly the reason I had volunteered, but it caused their majesties to smile.

"From Bournemouth I went to 56 OTU, at Sutton Bridge. The evening the train arrived, the local flight instructors were giving the field a beat-up in their Hurricanes, to train ground controllers. I had never seen planes flown so low to the ground and so precisely.

"We newcomers stood at the edge of the railroad platform and watched with open mouths while the Hurricanes made pass after pass across the field, only a mile or so away. The pilots noticed us and started a series of attacks on the station itself. I had never been so excited about anything in my life. Later, in combat, when I performed the same maneuvers, I felt no excitement whatever, but there on the ground, it was probably the most eventful day I had in the air force.

"Later at the airdrome, the pilots we had just seen in the air were taking off their flying gear. They walked into the officers' mess the same time we did. I experienced a large twinge of hero worship. Here they were, veterans of France, the Battle of Britain and all the things we had seen in magazines and movies.

"During the last part of our training in the Miles Master and Hurricane at Sutton Bridge, we had instruction in gunnery and formation flying. Of our class of about 30, two were killed in training, and only half of the remainder were posted to Eagle Squadrons."

"When I left Ashton Downs, my OTU, I was to report to my squadron at Castletown," writes Nicholas Dimitrios Sintetos. "I took a train from London, but when I arrived there was no airfield around—only a radio station operated by the Women's Auxiliary Air Force. They told me this was Castleton, Yorkshire, and I probably should have gone to Castletown, Cathness, in Scotland. They asked me to stay at the radio station the night over—which I did, not knowing what I was in for.

"It was a rare treat. They had a clubhouse with a record player. Here I was, a sergeant pilot, the only male around.

That night I danced with about forty different women. They all lined up to dance with me."

The next day Sintetos was on the train again, bound this time for the Cathness Castletown. At Castletown, on the northern tip of Scotland, he was dismayed to find "nothing but men, planes, barracks and sheep. In bed, I wondered what I had gotten into. This was not 11 Group, where I would have plenty of action. Here there would be only boring convoy patrols.

"Sheep! I thought about those woolly animals until I made up this story. My new CO informed me there were no women here and that any airman inclined to molest a sheep was to be turned over to the RAF police. Then he added, 'If anyone molests the sheep with the pink ribbon, he'll have to answer to me personally.' With this on my mind, I fell asleep, chuckling. The next day I got new orders to report to 121 Eagle Squadron at Rochford."

Like Sintetos, Clarence "Whitey" Martin and Ross Scarborough found themselves somewhat off the track on their way to becoming Eagles. "After 18 long days at sea, our converted White Star passenger ship, the *Allionia*, put us ashore at Reykjavik, Iceland," says Martin.

"We went by lorry to a British outpost 10 miles out of the city and stayed there for seven lonely days, surrounded for miles by lava covered ground with a little bit of grass here and there but not one visible tree. This was April—so different from springtime at home.

"At this outpost in Iceland, our latrine consisted of a bucket in a corner of our barracks. Our rations were beans on toast, kippered herring and English tea. For bathing, the only hot water we had was outside, in a seething volcanic spring and a stream flowing by the barracks."

In 1937 Martin had purchased a plane and had taken flying lessons while working for a chemical company in California's Mojave dessert. When he registered for the draft in 1940, the Army classed him 1-A. Martin rushed off to the Hollywood Roosevelt Hotel, where the Clayton Knight Committee was interviewing candidates for what they called ferry pilot jobs. "After a very brief interview and after seeing that I had 300 hours flying time, they asked me how soon I could report to the Grand Central air terminal in Glendale, where the training was taking place," Martin recalls.

"Before completing our training we were told that instead of becoming ferry pilots, we would go to Canada for more training, and then proceed to London to fly for the RAF. We would be commissioned pilot officers—the same as second lieutenants—on arrival in London. This sounded like a good deal—much better than being in the Infantry."

Joseph Ellsworth Durham, a golf professional, became involved with the RAF when circumstances led him and seven other young men to visit a room in the Baker Hotel, in Dallas, Texas, in the summer of 1940. A British officer talked of the heroic deeds of RAF pilots over occupied France and invasion-threatened England. The officer said an American Eagle Squadron was forming in England, and that American pilots with 300 or more hours of flying experience were needed. Durham's total flying time at that moment was 39 hours in 40-horsepower Piper Cubs. "It took me most of the night to enter an additional 300 hours in my flying log and make it look official," he says. "I was accepted for training without question."

"The episodes experienced by my instructors during the 36-hour training course at Love Field could best be described as hair-raising. When we would fly upside down, it would be evident that I had failed to tighten my belt sufficiently. My instructor would pound on the side of the cockpit to get my attention, and then hold his nose.

"The terribly urgent need for RAF pilots was the only possible reason I was permitted to complete this training. My instructors made this quite plain to me. Cloyd Cleavenger, our truly great aerobatics instructor, made a final appeal to me just before we entrained for Canada. His parting words were, 'Son, think about this, and go back home. Those guys over there mean business, and they have all got to be better than you. I'm afraid you'll kill yourself before you get started. There must be other ways you can help, if you must.'

"I never took his well-intended advice. He died in a crash a short time later. I often wish he could have known that the German pilots who were to fly the planes of my three con-firmed victories, and the half-dozen others credited to my score as probably destroyed, would not likely agree with his thinking that I was the world's worst pilot."

There was no mistaking Durham's fondness for golf. Standing in line with Canadian soldiers, waiting to board ship in Halifax harbor one cold morning in February, 1941, he was the only person carrying clubs. Later, on leave in Scotland, he achieved a lifelong ambition by playing the famous St. Andrews and Carnoustie courses.

In London, Durham struck up a conversation with an attractive young woman sitting alone at the bar of the Regent Palace Hotel. They had a couple of drinks and then went to her apartment for a nightcap.

"We began discussing our lives, and when she learned that I had been a professional golfer, she provided me with one of my most pleasant surprises," Durham says. "She opened a dresser drawer and presented me with a box of a dozen new golf balls. New balls were virtually nonexistent in the British Isles. The gorse and heather lined fairways of the courses I had played had very nearly claimed the few precious balls I had managed to bring from the States. The ten shillings I gave her for cigarette money seemed infinitesimal for the prize I had received."

Durham and his training-school roommate, Fred Scudday, of Sweetwater, Texas, quickly discovered that they shared similar outlooks—"We both liked women, drinking and general hell-raising"—so it was natural for them to become great friends. "We flew together as a team at every possible opportunity. Our off-duty sorties often prompted some rather stern reprimands from commanding officers, but we had little to fear from rough characters in the establishments we frequented. Fred was 200 pounds of muscle and as strong as the bulls of his beloved West Texas. I supplied an additional 200 pounds to the team, and looked down on most men from a height of 6 feet 5 inches."

Durham had been on duty with the RAF for six months when he received a letter from his father enclosing an order from the United States War Department to report immediately for induction into the armed forces. "My father wrote that, despite all his efforts to explain to the local draft board that I was already engaged in hostilities against the enemy, he had failed to convince these officials that I was not avoiding the draft. He was told that if I did not report to them within a scheduled deadline, I would be regarded as a fugitive. Perhaps I will check some day and see if I am still listed as a draft dodger in the war records of Fort Smith's one-time draft board."

Bill Dunn—Wild Bill, they called him—had a career up the military ladder from private to lieutenant colonel, back down to enlisted rank, and up once again to retire as a lieutenant colonel. He shot down two enemy planes from the ground before becoming a fighter pilot. The two German aircraft were not included among the five victories that won him recognition as the first American ace of the war.

Dunn's interest in flying had been inspired by his uncle, Larry Hammond, who shot down three or four German planes as a World War I fighter pilot and was himself shot down twice. Dunn's stepfather, Roy Harding, an aviation representative for the Texas Oil Company, also had been a fighter pilot in World War I.

"My stepfather had a Stinson Reliant monoplane, so he taught me a bit of flying in it. Then I managed to save some money, and with a loan from Roy bought a Byrd biplane with an 85-horsepower Kinner engine. It cost $500 about fifth or sixth hand, and could go 65 miles an hour.

"This was at Love Field in Dallas. Now and then I'd race my stepdad from Dallas to Forth Worth airport, about 30 miles—he in the Stinson and I in the old Byrd. He always gave me a head start, but when I got to Fort Worth, Roy would be sitting on the ground waiting for me. I wound up with maybe 150 hours of flying time in that plane, and I developed my judgment to match my limited skill. I didn't fly in bad weather or after dark, and I never damaged the airplane."

Dunn served out a 1934 enlistment in the Army's Fourth Infantry Regiment, in North Dakota, went to college and art school in Minnesota, and when war broke out tried to enlist in an Army Cooperation Squadron, which was flying Westland Lysander aircraft. The Squadron was not taking American volunteers, he learned, but the Seaforth Highlanders, a Canadian infantry outfit, was—by bending the rules. At the Seaforth barracks in Vancouver, British Columbia, the squadron recruiting officer said, "Sorry, can't take American citizens. But if you walk around the block and come back and decide you are from some place in Canada, you might be able to fill out this enlistment paper."

Dunn made a quick turn around the barracks square. When he returned, the recruiting officer asked again, "Where are you from?"

"Moose Jaw."

"Good," said the Canadian, making an entry on the recruiting form. "Now, where is Moose Jaw?"

Dunn grinned. "How in hell would I know? I just thought of it."

"It's in Saskatchewan, and don't you forget it," the officer said sternly. "You are hereby enlisted."

Dunn went to France, and then to England, with the Seaforth Highlanders. During a German Stuka raid on the Canadian unit's camp near Borden, in Hampshire, a Nazi bomber knocked out an antiaircraft gun post. Dunn rushed to the weapon from the shelter of a bunker, set the gun back in position, and fired at an oncoming Stuka. To his surprise, the plane started smoking, then smashed into the ground. A second Stuka raced toward the sandbagged emplacement. Again the machine gun bullets found their mark. The plane crashed, and exploded into flame.

The British Air Ministry invited Army men with pilot experience to transfer to the RAF. Dunn recalls, "There were two of us Americans in the battalion—the other one was Jimmy Crowley—and we both put in for the RAF. I think my shooting down two planes that way might have helped me get accepted by the Royal Air Force."

Early in 1940, Vernon A. Parker, a civilian pilot at Del Rio, Texas, tried to enlist in the RCAF, at Regina, Saskatchewan, but gave up the effort because of the red tape involved. Later, through the Knight Committee, at Dallas, he signed up for the RAF training school called BCFL—British Commission Ferrying, Ltd., at Love Field. The initial training for solo aerobatic and cross-country flights was in Fleet biplanes from Canada, an American BT-15, and two Beechcraft Staggerwing biplanes in which the instructor-pilot made the takeoffs and landings.

"We did get about 10 hours in a Link trainer and a few hours under the hood in the BT-15, which was in such bad shape that almost every flight ended in a dead-stick landing in a cowpasture somewhere," Parker writes. "Toward the end of the course, we received two Fairchild low-wing monoplanes. The entire fleet was serviced by Major Long's civilian student mechanics. With no reflection on the late Major Bill Long or his Dallas Aviation School, his would-be mechanics just barely kept the aircraft one jump ahead of the CAA inspectors.

"While practicing landings in a pasture five miles north of Love Field, I lost a wheel on a running takeoff and ended up on my back with a thoroughly washedout Fleet. Since I would have to report to a CAA inspector at Love Field terminal, I expected my budding aviation career to end right there.

"To my surprise, I was congratulated all around by all the CAA personnel. Their remarks added up to, 'Well, that's one plane we won't have to worry about any more. Now, fellows please get rid of the rest of them for us.'

"The BCFL staff told us not to worry about flying time, as we would receive an additional six months or more of training after we arrived in England. During training we received a dollar a day, with board and room provided at Love Field. Upon graduation we went by train to Ottawa. For the records, we were regarded as civilian pilots for the Canadian Air Force, but strong rumors indicated we were on our way to England.

"We stayed in Ottawa for one month, and received five dollars a day, but with no duties. We paid our own hotel and meal bills. We were entertained well and did fly a few times in AT-6 Harvard aircraft designated for the French, with French instruments. We were unfamiliar with kilometers and meters, and none of us were checked out on the French terms. Thus we never knew how fast or how high we were flying.

"We sailed from Montreal at the end of May 1941, on the British S.S. *Bayonne,* a 5,000-ton converted banana boat which never before had operated outside the tropics and was not equipped for northern routes. Also aboard were 99 Australians and New Zealanders.

"We were told in Dallas to travel light, and we did, expecting uniforms in Canada. We did not receive our uniforms until we arrived in England. Had not the Australians shared their heavy clothing with us, we would have arrived half frozen.

"The voyage was supposed to take 17 days, and the ship was stocked with just enough food for that period. There were delays waiting for a convoy to form, and then we had to cut back our speed so some tankers could keep up with us, so the trip to England took 31 days instead of 17. Food was severely rationed, and we were held to a quart of water a day each, for drinking shaving and bathing.

"We arrived in England thoroughly tired and hungry. British rations in England were not much more generous than they had been on the ship. I was still hungry when I transferred over to the Americans and had my first good meal in almost a year and a half.

"We were commissioned in the RAF the day we arrived, and started drawing regular pay as pilot officers—second lieutenants—at the equivalent rate of $80 a month. Out of this we had to pay a small mess bill, for our food and quarters. In May 1942, I was promoted to flying officer—first lieutenant— at $88 a month. As flying officers we received about two shillings a day—55 cents—more than nonflying officers."

Roland L. Wolfe—Bud, or Timber, to his friends—recalls the following about his instruction period in Canada.

"Believe me, something of a good time was had in Ottawa. The UK representative used to come to our hotel and shoot craps. We drew about $10 a day while in Canada. He got most of it back. A real fine gentleman in swallowtail coat, and striped pants, derby—down on his knees, seven come eleven! We loved that man."

Bert Stewart, a North Carolinian, recalls flying a Moth training plane at Trenton, Ontario, one day in a 60-mile-an-hour wind: "The Moth stalls at around 40 mph. I found that by opening the throttle I could fly into the wind slowly across the field. Then, with the throttle back, the wind would blow me backward 10 or 15 miles an hour above stalling speed. It was great fun, and I did it several times, in spite of evidence of great consternation on the ground."

Stewart gained considerable notoriety—and prestige— among his peers by becoming the only volunteer to smuggle himself to England to join the Eagles. He had enlisted in the RCAF as a sergeant pilot—his roommate during four months of training was Whitey Dahl, a famous figure of the Spanish

Civil War—but became disenchanted when assigned as an instructor at a New Brunswick flying station. In a railroad station waiting room en route to his new assignment, he became acquainted with two Americans, Oscar Coen and William Hall, who turned out to be on their way to board ship for England to become RAF pilot officers. Stewart promptly went AWOL from his own unit, tagged along with his new friends, walked boldly up the gangplank with them and crossed the Atlantic unchallenged. In England, he confessed to the RAF, and was accepted into the Sutton Bridge OTU on his way to 121 Eagle Squadron.

The banner headlines across the front pages of the Oakland, California *Post Enquirer* and *Tribune* on September 29, 1942, were bold and black and almost identical in wording: "Alameda Pilot Shot Down, Nazi Prisoner." Below the streamers were photographs of a handsome, wavy-haired young man who looked a lot like movie actor Dick Powell. "George Brooks Sperry, RAF Flier, Scion of Flour Family, Downed During Raid on France." One of the articles added: "The weekend which brought his name into the news saw the internment in Paris of his great aunt, Princess Poniatowski, one of a large number of Americans taken into custody, assertedly to be held as hostages by the Nazis."

The stories went on to tell how the flier's great-grandfather, Simon Willard Sperry, sailed around the Horn in his own ship in 1851, proceeded on up the San Joaquin River from San Francisco Bay to Stockton, started growing wheat, and built the flour and feed mills that became The Sperry Flour Company. Simon had one son, George, the grandfather of his namesake, the RAF pilot, and two daughters, Ethyl and Beth. Ethyl married William H. Crocker of the banking family. Beth—Elizabeth—married Prince Andre Poniatowski, a French nobleman of Polish descent. In 1928, Sperry Flour became a western division of General Mills.

"For many years I saved every scrap of paper—photographs, souvenirs of important events, and anything to do with flying," said George Brooks Sperry. "Very much like an old packrat, I placed these bits of my life in various scrapbooks and boxes. In several cases, the use of a good sized trunk came in mighty handy. Glancing through these old albums and diaries, I was surprised to realize that I could not even remember the names of over half of the oddballs I had served with in the RAF. How can one forget such memorable characters gathered all in one spot?

"I can give no good reason why I chose to go to fight someone else's war. Maybe we who did so were different from other men of our age group back in the States. Restlessness, frustration, and love of flying seemed to be the main reasons for going to England. Or maybe it was a reach for personal glory, perhaps to show others just who the hell we were.

"At the BCFL Detachment at Dallas, the chief instructor, on loan from American Airlines to provide instrument training, needle-ball-and-airspeeded me until I damn near went nuts. All checkout, crosscountry and hood flying was done with five persons aboard the Beechcraft Staggerwing—instructor-pilot and four students. It worked out quite well—four hours in the plane for every hour of actual stick time. Instead of only an instructor pilot being along to criticize mistakes, there was a whole rooting section. This made everyone stay on his toes."

Each entering Eagle had his special story and circumstances which, though briefly told in some cases, were critical in their lives.

Charlie Cook's world was confined to California, until Charlie went away to war. From the day he was born, he had lived on only two streets—Los Robles Avenue, in Pasadena, and then Dos Robles Place, in Alhambra. At 56 OTU he rolled up more than 53 hours of flying instruction before becoming an Eagle, but less than a month after his first solo in a Spitfire, he wrote in his diary, "While returning from convoy patrol P/O Nelson and myself collided in midair, damaging my starboard wing tip. I returned to base and landed safely."

Lewis Gleason, Springfield, Ohio, was 18 and in England when the war broke out. He had read about the Eagles, and volunteered. Unable to qualify for RAF pilot training because of an eye defect, he asked for and won admittance to 121 Squadron in a nonflying category. As a rigger at North Weald, he worked on Spitfire airframes and hydraulic systems.

Don Dawson Nee, of Whittier, California, had more than 200 hours of flying experience when he volunteered through the Knight Committee, and it took only a 55-minute flight check—"just chandelles, lazy eights, slow rolls and snap rolls"—for him to qualify for the RAF. After eight weeks of

Spitfire training at 53 OTU in South Wales, he was posted to 152 Squadron, which was named for its Indian sponsor, the Nizam of Hyderabad. He asked for a more active unit and wound up in 133 Squadron.

"As Americans we did not receive any special consideration regarding discipline, rank or other matters. The British were extremely kind and good to us."

Andrew J. "Steve" Stephenson, unable to realize his hopes of joining the Flying Tigers in China, took RAF training in California and joined 133 Squadron only a short time before its transformation into the USAAF 336th Squadron in 1942.

He remembers "how composed Wing Commander Duke-Woolley was on a mission with Carl Miley, Don Blakeslee and Don Nee, when we were outnumbered at least two to one by Germans above and behind us and in the sun. Duke-Woolley would say, 'Keep cool, chaps. Just wait until they get closer. Hold it; be ready to break!' And when the enemy was too close for my liking, he'd say, 'Now, chaps—break!'"

Leroy Gover, of Loveland, Colorado, graduated from the OTU at Llantwitt Major, Wales, with an above average grade, and was retained as an instructor for the next class. Among his students, George Middleton, Len Ryerson and Gil Wright went into Eagle squadrons.

"After three weeks of the blind leading the blind, I was posted to 66 Spitfire Squadron at Portreath, Cornwall," Gover says. On the day he joined the unit, the squadron leader and a sergeant pilot were killed on a mission. "I knew I was now in the real thing. Within a week, I encountered my first enemy aircraft. Two Me 109s came in on a low-level flight and strafed the streets in Redruth. I flew as No. 2 man on the interception. We made contact, and I fired away, but I was too excited and did not hit anything."

The squadron moved to Ibsley to relieve a heavily pounded unit. The Ibsley Wing had lost 11 men in the preceding 24 hours, bringing its total losses for two weeks to 50 pilots.

"We were definitely into front line action," Gover says. "We really put in the hours at Ibsley—shipping reccos, fighter sweeps, convoy patrols, interceptions—two or three every day; and night alert, which meant sitting in the aircraft at the end of the runway for two hours, then relief for two hours, then

back in the cockpit again. The tower would fire a red flare and
you had best be airborne within one minute, or you got run
over by an Me 109.

"We lost a lot of planes on convoy patrol. The weather
was pretty bad in the Channel. The Jerries could come in low,
hit a patrol plane, and be gone before they were seen."

While still with 66 Squadron, before he transferred to the
Eagles, Gover led a section of four Spitfires on a tough
mission, July 31, 1942. The Wing—three squadrons of 12
planes each—refueled at Bolt Head and teamed up with other
squadrons to escort Boston bombers to St. Malo, in France.

"Visibility was bad, and the sea so smooth there wasn't
much of a horizon. We crossed 130 miles of water, staying at
sea level until within 30 miles of the target. We used long
range tanks, and jettisoned them just before reaching St.
Malo.

"We climbed rapidly to 10,000 feet on the approach. The
Bostons dropped their eggs right on target—finest bombing I
had seen. We brought the Bostons back right along the whole
Cherbourg peninsula and out by the Jersey Islands, with Jerry
fighters swarming over us. Eleven Jerries were shot down, and
we lost eight Spitfires."

Richard "Dixie" Alexander, having enlisted in the RCAF
as an air gunner, discovered that before entering formal
training, air crew members had to do guard duty as a matter
of strict rigid discipline. "I was assigned to Ottawa, and
during this period, we did continuous guard duty—two hours
on and four hours off, 24 hours a day, seven days a week for a
period of five months. The time was winter, with the temperature ranging down to 30 below zero. A normal period of
guard duty rarely exceeded 10 weeks. When we were in our
third month, we began to wonder just what was happening.
We had started to call our island 'the Rock.'

"Through one of the Canadian lads, whose uncle was a
wing commander, we were able to locate ourselves. Our papers
had become lost. But for this discovery, we might still be on
sentry duty in Ottawa."

After six weeks of elementary flight training at a school
in Quebec, Alexander took advanced flying from RCAF pilots
in Harvards, at Aylmer, Ontario. "In both schools, discipline
was strict. The courses were tough, and, in contrast with cadet
training in the States, there was no horseplay. The empire was

at war, and it was losing. Foolishness was not to be tolerated. Pilots were a dime a dozen, but aircraft, materiel and time were not. There were more older persons here—professionals, doctors, lawyers–and all dead serious. *Esprit de corps* was high."

As they took the steps that made "someone else's war" their own, the Yanks in the RAF became known for their spirit and high dedication. Morale was high as they approached the true ordeal. The first real shocks would soon hit them.

3

BAPTISM BY HURRICANE AND SPIT

"How about scary? I'll tell you about the very first one. When I went to the Eagle Squadron, the unit was newly formed— still in an operational training status, so to speak. All the boys had come from different squadrons, and so they had to fly together for a while and get used to each other."

This is retired Air Force Lieutenant Colonel William R. Dunn speaking, to a session of the Air Force Academy's oral history program. The Eagle veteran had just been asked about some of his earlier flights in the RAF.

The very first operation I ever went on was a fighter sweep. I guess we were about midway in the Channel and flying parallel to the French coast, looking for a fight, when a German squadron came out to meet us.

Both squadrons flew parallel, about a mile or so apart, looking each other over for a couple of minutes. We were slightly higher than they were. All of a sudden, our squadron leader says on the R/T—radio telephone—"Let's go get 'em." And the first thing you know, I was sitting up there in the sky all by myself; there wasn't a soul around me. I looked down below and there was everybody milling around in a big gaggle, squirting at each other. I thought, "Well, this is kind of stupid, sitting up here by myself." So down I went.

"About the first thing that happened to me after I got down among that milling mess was that a bunch of tracers went flying over my canopy, and another bunch went flying across my nose. I shoved the throttle full forward and headed my aircraft back toward England—and went straight home, flat out.

Scared? You bet I was. First time in combat, and bullets flying all around me. On the way back, I noticed the fingers on my right hand were numb. I finally realized I was holding the control column so tight that I'd cut off all the circulation in my fingers. I got to thinking to myself, "What the hell am I doing up here, anyhow? I should be back in the Seaforths with my three-inch mortar." I think that probably if I had landed and someone had said, "Do you want to go back to the infantry?" I might have said yes. Luckily, there wasn't anybody there to make the offer. No one in the squadron seemed to notice my sudden departure from the flight—at least, no one said anything about it.

That was my first taste of aerial combat. I had never fired my guns in anger before—and I had less than a hundred flying hours with the RAF, probably about 20 hours in a Hurricane. It scared the hell out of me for the moment, because it suddenly dawned on me that I wasn't quite ready for that sort of thing.

I'll tell you one thing. I really went to work learning how to fly my aircraft. And when I wasn't on alert duty, I did a lot of air-to-air and air-to-ground firing practice. I also—and this is most important—conditioned my mental attitude to aerial warfare. I used to tell myself that the other guy was no better than I was, and he was probably just as scared. So I calmed down, and that's when I decided to use the "strike fast, fire at close range, and get the hell out" tactic. My limited skill as a fighter pilot in those days wouldn't permit me to stay and mix it up with some Kraut pilot.

At first, while we were stationed at Martlesham Heath, our main job was to escort naval and supply convoys up and down the English Channel. We escorted convoys until hell wouldn't have it. It got pretty boring flying around the ships, so periodically, we'd sort of slide away from the convoy and edge over toward the French coast to see what was going on. We had a radar defense system of sorts in those days, and damned if Ops B— that was the ground control radio operator —wouldn't call us and say, "Get back on station. You are 10 miles off your station."

Then, once in a while, when a German intruder would come in, we'd get scrambled to make an intercept on him.

That's when we got to use the British radar system and see how effective it was. One time, a Ju 88 came in to attack our convoy. There was a low cloud deck, at about 600 or 700 feet. Radar put us on this guy.

We were flying in a section of two aircraft, so I sent my wingman, Tommy McGerty, below the cloud deck, and I stayed above. Pretty soon he called me on the R/T and said the Kraut was dropping bombs down there, that he saw the Ju 88, and was opening fire on him. The 88 then popped up through the clouds and I gave him a squirt. He ducked back below the cloud, and McGerty gave him the blast. So it went—up and down through the cloud deck—each of us shooting at the 88 until we had chased him back to France. We damaged him, but didn't shoot him down. Radar kept giving us his position all the time, and when we were almost over the French coast, told us to come home as the 109s were being scrambled to take a crack at us.

After the squadron finished its operational training, we were moved to North Weald and started flying sweeps with a couple of other squadrons in our wing. A fighter sweep was designed to fly over France and get the Germans to scramble their fighters for a fight with us. So we'd go over France, get shot at by antiaircraft guns, end up in a big dogfight and scare ourselves and scare them. At first they'd come up and fight— and then after a while they figured that wasn't too practical because there wasn't any sense in shooting up ammunition, wasting fuel, and getting airplanes shot up for a bunch of our fighters that couldn't do any damage anyhow. If they didn't come up to fight, all we could do was bore a hole in the sky. Pretty soon we'd go over France, and nothing would happen, except for the flak being shot at us.

We started escorting Blenheim and Stirling bombers on what we called Circus operations. Then, of course, the enemy fighters would come up in droves, and we'd get in some pretty big fights with them. The biggest I was in had over 300 aircraft all milling about. You spent more time trying to keep from running into some other guy than shooting at each other.

After a while we started carrying bombs on our fighters, so it got to the point where the Germans didn't know, when they saw a batch of our fighters coming over to France, whether they were just fighters on a sweep, or fighter-bombers. So they'd have to scramble and engage us. If we carried bombs, we'd go first to our selected target—probably some marshalling yards or an airfield—bomb the place, and then run a sweep on our way home.

We used to pull a few intruder operations now and then. For example, we'd fly over to Holland, on the deck, across the North Sea to Walcheren, where there was a German seaplane base. We'd try to arrive just at dawn, shoot up the seaplanes, then do a turn to port and cut across a German Me 109 base on the island. You could sometimes catch the 109s being scrambled—just as they were getting off the deck. You'd take one pass at them and then head out to sea on the water, fast. You'd be long gone by the time the Krauts got off the deck to chase you. That particular intruder operation worked every time we tried it—we always caught them flatfooted. These operations were all volunteer missions. A couple of guys in the squadron would plan something of that sort, get Group's approval, and then go do it. We never took more than four aircraft on an intruder operation, and after we hit the target, it was every man for himself getting home.

The first kill is always the outstanding one. Mine happened on a fighter sweep. We mixed it up with a squadron of 109s. I dove down and got behind a 109E—about 75 feet behind him. He filled up the whole windscreen, and it's hard to miss when you're that close.

So I started firing at him, and chips flew off his aircraft, he caught on fire, and then he started down. I watched him go all the way in. He crashed near a crossroad in France. Another fellow in our squadron, Pete Provenzano, saw me shoot the German down, and he confirmed the story for me. As my old wing commander, Teddy Donaldson, used to say, "Kill the bastards before the bastards kill you."

Dunn had a couple of narrow escapes without scores. Shortly after takeoff one day, the engine of his Hurricane caught fire and he had to bail out at a dangerously low altitude. He parachuted to safety a second time after enemy fire crippled his plane over the English Channel. Picked up almost immediately, he shared the RAF rescue launch with two other RAF pilots and with two newly captured German airmen.

Since the rescue crew made note of his name and squadron, Dunn assumed that his home base would be informed of his safety. Accordingly, he took a leisurely route back, through London. When he arrived at the room he shared with his wingman, McGerty, he found that all of his clothing, including his socks and underwear, had been distributed among the other pilots. "Took me a hell of a time to get it all back," he recalls.

An essential part of Dunn's cockpit equipment, by the way, was a large fragment of dark glass—part of a broken beer bottle. Dunn drilled a hole through the glass and tied it with a string to the map case, so that he wouldn't lose it if he dropped it on the cockpit floor. He also filed off the sharp edges of the glass. The Germans liked to attack from above with the sun at their backs, so Dunn used the pieces of beer bottle as a shield for peering into the sun.

"If you looked through the glass directly into the sun," he explains, "it made any enemy aircraft there show up real black. It wasn't my idea—I got it from a Canadian pilot in 245 Squadron, and started to use it in March or April of 1941. In the latter part of 1941, the RAF came out with some new goggles that had a brown plastic shade you could turn down over the clear goggle glass. It served the same purpose."

The Hawker Hurricane was the Eagles' first mount, in most cases. The *Hurri*, as the German pilots learned to call it in the frenzy of battle—and the Hurris provided much frenzy for the Luftwaffe during the Battle of Britain and the months preceeding it—was the warhorse of the RAF until the faster Spitfire came along in real numbers. The Hawker's Merlin engine increased in power, through successive models produced over a four-year span, from 900 to 1,260 horsepower, thus advancing the Hurricane's speed from 312 to 342 mph, sharply raising the rate of climb, and extending the service ceiling to 34,200 feet and the range to 525 miles. From model to model, the aircraft weight increased from 6,600 pounds gross to 7,800. The wingspan was 40 feet; the plane's height was just over 13 feet; its length was 31 feet, 5 inches.

A major RAF way station on the route to becoming an Eagle pilot was Operational Training Unit 56, at Sutton Bridge, about 40 miles north of Cambridge. George Sperry arrived at 56 OTU with an abundance of self-confidence derived from six years of flying experience.

"My flight commander and instructor was Flight Lieutenant Bisdee, Battle of Britain ace from 609 Squadron, an amazing type with handlebar moustache and all. Within 24 hours after my arrival at Sutton Bridge, I was checked out in a Miles Master, a low-wing wood constructed aircraft powered by a 700-hp Rolls-Royce Kestrel engine. It cruised at a little better than 200 mph.

"After a 30-minute dual check ride, the instructor climbed out, and I spent the next hour shooting takeoffs and landings. I taxied back to my flight area feeling quite proud of myself and figuring that with another 20 hours in the Master, I might be ready for the Hurricane.

"Bisdee was waiting for me, smiling. 'How do you feel?'

"'Okay sir,' I replied, trying to conceal my emotion.

"'Well, old boy, we'll try you out in the Hurricane.'

"I demurred a bit, saying, 'I think I need 20 or 30 more hours in the Master.'

"'I realize that, old boy, but as you know, there is a war on. Petrol is in short supply. All you have to do is keep alert and you won't have a bit of trouble.'

"With a sinking heart, I climbed into the Hurricane Mark I. I would be flying a fighter aircraft for the first time— a rugged powerful brute lacking the beautiful lines of the Spitfire but a thoroughbred to fly, the instructor said; the plane that primarily saved the day during the Battle of Britain the summer before. She may have been outmoded by all of the newer fighters coming along, but no aircraft could turn with her or pull out a dive as readily.

"Ground Control gave me final instructions, and I tried to remember everything my flight commander had told me. I lowered the seat and, with clammy hands, slowly opened the throttle. She leaped into the air like a startled jackrabbit. Busily adjusting throttle and propeller controls for climb, I forgot all about the undercarriage until I was 10 miles away and up at 5,000 feet.

"My God, she was quick on the controls! The slightest pressures with hands or feet made her buck like a mustang. Not knowing quite where I was heading, I timidly tried a turn, eased the spade grip back slightly, and hurtled to 10,000 feet with no effort at all. I had no idea where the field lay. All I wanted to do was learn to handle this bird. As the minutes went by, I got bolder and tried a few basic maneuvers. Lord, how she reacted!

"As my confidence grew, I decided to see how she would go downhill. Easing the stick forward, I started the descent, and in a matter of seconds, the velocity changed from a normal indicated air speed of 220 mph to an IAS of 400. The ground seemed to be coming straight at me.

"Frightened by the speed, I eased slowly out of the dive. A weight drove my head into my shoulders, and pressed my back into the seat. My eyes blurred, and I started to black out. Instinctively, I released the pressure on the stick. As my vision returned, I was hurtling straight into the sky.

"Back again in level cruise, I called the ground controller for a homing vector. Several minutes later, over the field, I circled above pattern altitude. Cleared to land, I went over the cockpit procedures several times: Open the radiator wide, throttle back, change prop to high rpm, open the canopy, raise the seat and, as I approached the runway, lower the undercarriage and flaps.

"The ground flew toward me at an alarming speed. I eased back on the stick, felt the wheels touch, and with a slight bounce she was rolling on the ground nice and easy. A touch of the brakes to keep her straight down the field, and by the time I had taxied back to the flight line, I had gained complete control of my emotions. To my fellow students crowding around the wing when I shut her down I said, 'Nothing to it. Just another airplane.'

"The next six weeks were anxious ones. The flying hours accumulated daily—air-to-air and air-to-ground gunnery over The Wash, that big bay just off the Station; night flying from a flare path; more formation flying in twos, fours and twelves; dogfighting practice, basic air tactics, aircraft recognition, instrument flying. We even had a course on proper elocution for speaking over the radio.

"The procedure for instrument checkout in fighter aircraft was simple and effective. F/Lt. Bisdee gave me one check ride under the hood in the Miles Master, and then ordered me into the air in a Hurricane when the ceiling was only around 400 feet. To practice 'cloud flying,' he called it. Having done all my instrument flying—about 70 hours—in a Beechcraft Staggerwing, under a hood and with an instructor alongside me, the concept of hurling that Hurricane up through the clouds all alone left an empty feeling in the pit of my stomach. I had misgivings when I taxied out and prepared to take off into the soup hanging over the airdrome.

"Slowly applying throttle, rolling faster each moment, I went over the dials as we left the ground. By the time we hit the bottom of the overcast, the undercarriage was already retracted, climb settings were set, and I made a straight-out climb until we shot out of the clouds at 6,000 feet.

"Ground Control called every two or three minutes, giving me compass headings to steer by and allowing me to stay within the areas assigned for this type of flying. Following headings for the next hour, I cruised around in the clouds at 5,000 feet. I could, if necessary, pop out of the top of the overcast in case I happened to suffer extreme vertigo.

"I discovered, to my amazement, that instrument flying in a fighter was not a bit different from under the hood in the Staggerwing. If anything, it was much easier. As the hours stacked up in the next few weeks, so did my confidence in my ability to stooge around in the English mist. Not all of us were quite so lucky.

"One of the students spun in while attempting to let down through the weather. His funeral, with full military honors, was moving in its simplicity, but made the rest of us aware that this training to become fighter pilots was different from the weekend flying jaunts back home in California."

For whatever other reasons, these Americans had come to England to fly. Any pilot can appreciate the memories of Joe Durham, of Fort Smith, Arkansas: "It was a typical cold, cloudy day in England in late March of 1941, when the green flight flashed from the airdrome tower, signalling the start of my first ride in a Royal Air Force Hurricane fighter.

"I had dreamed for months of this day, and all the earlier fears and anxious moments seemed to slip away as I felt the force of the powerful Merlin engine driving the aircraft across the small field for takeoff. Only those men who live to fly are privileged to share the feelings of pure joy I experienced after I had slipped into the air and then landed smoothly after a wide circle of the field."

Richard "Dixie" Alexander also had vivid memories of fighter indoctrination at the OTU on The Wash. "At Sutton Bridge we were given a dual ride in a Miles Master, a couple of solo rides in the same, and ground checked on a Hurricane. Then we flew it.

"On my first circuit I flew completely out of sight of the airdrome, which was grass and camouflaged, as were all British airdromes, and took 40 minutes getting back. Not too unusual in that area, since visibility was rarely over half a mile. I had always been fascinated by instrument flying, and had logged quite a bit of Link time. It stood me in good stead now, and I continued to get as much of it as I could.

"It was at Sutton Bridge that I saw our first casualty. Al Eves, a Virginia boy, hit high tension wires while flying low, and was scattered all over the countryside. I called in the location and was ordered back to base. I landed, went to Operations, and made my report. Then I was escorted to the mess hall, given a couple drinks of whiskey, and taken back to the flight line. I was put into the air and kept there most of the day, and again, first thing in the morning. After that, I never thought about it. Too busy. All in all, we lost seven fellows from our class in OTU, flying Hurricanes.

"We had two Poles in the class, both of whom had been in the Polish Air Force. One, Zeronecky, was an officer, and the other, Pokorney, a sergeant. They had little love for each other. They would time their fights and go up and dogfight. Good and equally matched, they would make head-on passes, getting closer and refusing to give way until the last moment. Finally they waited too long, and Zeronecky was killed in the headon crash. Pokorney bailed out, and lived to be killed later over France.

"Pokorney's hatred of the Germans, like that of all the Poles I met over there, was a dedicated thing. It kept him and his colleagues from being really good pilots. Even with superior equipment, they would not hesitate to ram a foe, and while their record as a group was exceptionally good in the number of enemy aircraft destroyed, their losses through foolishness and recklessness were greater. They were never really dependable on assignment, because on the slightest excuse, they would go off individually to fight their own war."

Harold Strickland described his introduction to the Hurricane in the days at 56 OTU before his assignment to an Eagle Squadron:

"I received an hour and 20 minutes of dual instruction on the Miles Master, after which I flew an hour and 20 minutes solo, practicing landings. Following lunch, I was given a cockpit drill in the Hawker Hurricane I fighter, with a 1,030-hp Rolls-Royce engine, and then was told to practice solo circuits and landings. I found the Hurricane surprisingly easy to handle on 'circuits and bumps,' as it was referred to, especially after flying the Master. Unfortunately, four other trainees in three Hurricanes and one Miles Master cracked up that same day. Luckily, there were no fatalities or serious injuries."

There were several other accidents while Strickland was at Sutton Bridge. Two Americans who had hoped to become Eagles, Robert Wilbur of San Mateo, California, and Fred Grove of Chicago, were killed when their Miles Master's wing collapsed.

"A military funeral, Last Post, was held for Wilbur, Grove, an Australian pilot killed in a Hurricane, and two bomber crewmen who crashed on return from a mission over France. A Free French pilot was killed in a Hurricane later found to have been shot down at a high altitude. Four days later Sergeant Pilot Mills was killed in still another Hurricane accident, and on that same day, three Hurricanes and one Boulton Paul Defiant cracked up. The following day, two Hurricanes collided at 10,000 feet, but both American pilots stayed with their damaged planes and maneuvered them to a safe landing.

"Accidents in operational training were attributable to a mixture of unlucky factors, such as mechanical failure, weather, and pilot error. For example, Pilot Officer Glenn Coates, of San Francisco, belly landed his Miles Master without injury when the undercarriage stuck partially open. Glenn and I practiced air attack maneuvers and dogfighting with our Hurricanes, but the next day, Glenn was killed in a *motorcycle* accident."

On the plus side, Jimmy Nelson, of Denver, was at low altitude when his Hurricane's engine quit. He had to crash land in a small field practically surrounded by stone fences. He performed excellent emergency piloting by fishtailing and stalling the plane so that he pancaked in at relatively low speed. He walked away from the wreck with minor injuries and shook up, but essentially okay.

Clarence "Whitey" Martin's "fit" into the Hurricane was not entirely congenial.

"My first flight in a Hurricane was horrifying. These were vintage airplanes, and to operate the landing gear and flaps, you had to use a hand pump on the right side of the seat. Since I am only five and a half feet tall, I had to lower the seat to the bottom of the cockpit. By the time I had the landing gear up and had raised the seat, I was at 2,000 feet and miles from the airport."

Martin joined 121 Eagle Squadron at Kirton-in-Lindsey on July 1, 1941, and was assigned to B Flight as wingman to Mac McColpin. Martin remembered his new leader particularly for the way he would light up a cigar before getting into the Link Trainer at the Polaris school, in Glendale, and then fill the Link room with cigar smoke as they simulated cloud flying.

"Mac literally took me under his wing. He always had this passion for instrument flying. When regular flights were cancelled due to bad weather, he would say, 'Come on, Whitey. Let's do some cloud flying.' And off we would go for an hour or so in the murk.

"After endless squadron formations and convoy patrols in the Channel, we finally got our chance to escort bombers into France. In order to do this, we had to fly to southern England to refuel, and then set out for France.

"While refueling on our first mission of this kind, Mac said, 'Stick with me, Whitey, and I think we will get some action. We'll see if we can't get an Me 109 on our first time out.'

"We couldn't find the enemy, so our CO gave the order to make a 180-degree turn left and take a heading for England. Instead of going left, Mac and I turned right. By the time we completed the turn, our companions were out of sight.

"We stooged around for a few minutes, and then Mac said, 'Let's go home.' Soon we saw eight planes off to our right and above us. Thinking they were the rest of our squadron, we flew toward them. At that moment the planes turned toward us and Mac yelled, 'Let's get the hell out of here! They are 109s.'

"They had the advantage of height, they outnumbered us four to one, and we were short on fuel, so we did not fire our guns. Luckily we were just above an overcast. 'Close in,' Mac ordered. 'We are going into the clouds.'

"After what seemed an hour, but actually was about 10 minutes, I lost Mac completely and was on my own, in very turbulent clouds. When I thought I must be over the Channel, I let down, broke into the open out over the water, and could see the English coast about 10 miles away.

"In our training, we were taught not to fly a straight course, but to keep weaving and looking for other aircraft. Our mentors always told us, 'You never see the guy that shoots you down.' I did a sharp turn to my right, and there was a plane right on my tail.

"What a relief when I saw *R. Robert* on the fuselage and knew it was Mac.

"We were still over water, and very low on fuel. As we got over land we saw other planes circling over an airfield. It was Biggin Hill.

"Never again did we leave our squadron to go looking for action."

"OTU was a wonderful experience," Jessie Taylor remembers. "The only thing I could find wrong with it was that it didn't last long enough. Operational training was so easy and so much fun it was almost as though I had done it before and this was a refresher course.

"Flying airplanes was the nourishment my ego was feeding on at that time. The more hours I had in the air, the better I liked it. They called airdrome defense and coast patrols 'training,' even though our guns were live. The same kind of flying later would have been classed operational. The only person who knew I flew actual operations with the instructor was Lucky Miner, who flew some formations with us."

Taylor flew operational missions with the 43rd Night Fighter Squadron at Drem, Scotland, for five weeks. "We flew four-cannon Hurricanes and went out every night that the weather would permit," he says.

Not yet battle tested, the pilots went on patrols in the Irish Channel, kept guard on convoys in the North Sea, and sometimes went on shipping strikes in the English Channel. "I liked strafing barges, minesweepers, small armed trawlers and other shipping, because you could always see the results," Taylor says. "Some of the pilots griped about the monotony of convoy patrols. I never found them to be boring at any time. There was always so much to do—watching for bandits, checking weather, listening to Operations, monitoring engine performance. Chances of surviving a maintenance failure were almost nil.

"Most patrols were flown in low ceiling conditions, in weather that served as a cover for German aircraft hunting convoys. At low altitude, radio-telephone range was fairly short. This meant that the pilot had to be constantly on the alert for changes in wind direction, in navigation, and in the weather. It took ability and intense concentration to do the job well."

Brewster Morgan, from Hawaii, had less than five hours in the Hurricane in England when his class was ordered, with its instructors, to fly to Scotland's Tealing airdrome, north of Dundee. The weather forecast was unfavorable. Heavy cloud conditions might be encountered on the border of Scotland. Morgan recalls, "We were into the soup just south of the border. I had had little formation flying experience, and I dreaded the thought of a collision, so I broke away, telling my instructor that I would go on alone.

"I was down to the water on the east coast of Scotland. The clouds were on the cliff-tops; if they came any lower I would be forced to set down on the water. I tried to turn back, but visibility was worse than ever. I headed north, hoping for some kind of an improvement.

"Suddenly, a miracle! I rounded a point of land, and there was a river winding inland. Banking my plane sharply around the point and up the river, I saw that I could not go far. The rising land was disappearing under a heavy cloud bank. But there, just under me, was a large plowed field. I turned steeply just a few feet off the ground, surveyed the situation, and started a sharp turn into the wind and a short final approach. It was a rough but successful landing. It was a miracle that in the deeply plowed field the Hurricane did not go over on its back.

"I mopped my brow, climbed out of my parachute and the cramped cockpit, and jumped to the ground. Back down my landing path where my wheels had hit, there were two deep wheel marks, and then no more. The tail wheel had not hit once until I came to a full stop at the corner of the field not 50 feet from the fence line.

"I felt like I had just awakened from a bad dream, and my body began to shake uncontrollably. To settle my nerves, I jumped up on the wing, reached into the cockpit for my helmet, turned on my radio, and tried to contact the flight. There was no answer.

"Greatly depressed, I leaned against the wing, and watched the approaching rain. Then a staff car appeared, and a British Army major came up, waving as he saw me. 'Arr ye all right lad?' he called. I saluted smartly, and he embraced me like a brother."

Later, at an officers' club, Morgan called his station and learned that of 30 planes that had departed from Sutton Bridge, seven had crashed. Back at Sutton Bridge, the Commanding Officer scolded him for landing with his gear down. "After all," he said, "we can always build an aircraft, but pilots are hard to find." He added that if it were peacetime and this had happened, Morgan would have been court-martialled.

Baptism into warplanes and fighter operations meant exploring one's own personal "envelope"—physical and mental. In September 1941, after years of flying experience, Harold Strickland was still testing himself.

"One clear day, I climbed the Hurricane to 24,000 feet, and did some tight turns with maximum power. I wanted to find out for myself whether I would black out. In all of my advanced aerobatic flying, I had never had a blackout, but much had been written about the subject for high-horsepower aircraft.

"After three or four maximum-power, steep, shaking turns, I could detect no symptoms of a blackout, so I leveled off, inhaled oxygen, and pushed over into a screaming vertical dive. The altimeter needles were turning like a propeller. When the Hurricane started some shaking, I pulled back hard on the stick. I don't remember the airspeed, nor could I guess the maximum Gs that were exerted on the aircraft structure and my cardiovascular system. Again I was surprised. No blackout!

"I had assumed that a 38-year-old fighter pilot would be more susceptible to blackouts than a 28-year-old. I don't know how the flight surgeons would explain it. Perhaps, at age 38, some individuals already have narrowed, unelastic arteries, while younger pilots have clean elastic arteries that permit too much blood to flow toward their feet in high-G turns."

The Hurricane was an airplane of high performance. The Spit—the Supermarine Spitfire—was even more so. Born of a line of fine racing planes and the genius of designer Reginald Mitchell, the elegant Spitfire was, at the time, an unparalleled fighter, a machine the young Americans approached with respect, even awe.

After five weeks with 133 Squadron, Strickland was transferred to 71 Squadron, which was equipped with the Spitfire VB.

"I had a cockpit check and then flew the Spitfire locally for about an hour. The minute I took off and climbed toward the clouds, I understood why every pilot who had ever flown that plane loved it.

"The Spitfire was no longer an inanimate object. It was an interceptor with quick reaction time, two 20-mm cannon and four machine guns; but for all practical purposes, it was a living thing, a part of the pilot, an extension of his own hands, feet, eyes and brain. It was sheer joy climbing, practicing stalls, whipping around in steep turns and pull-outs, and the hour passed before I knew it. I didn't want to land, but after an hour and ten minutes, I reluctantly lowered the flaps and wheels, landed, and taxied to the revetment."

James Edward Griffin, of Tucson, Arizona, had been with 121 Squadron about a month when orders came transferring him to 71. Peter Powell, the CO, disliked the idea of 121 serving as a training squadron for 71. There was rivalry between the two squadrons at that time—with 121 being the poor relations flying Hurricanes on the Scottish border, while 71 was flying Spits outside London. According to Griffin, "A few days after the transfer, I was in the 71 dispersal hut at North Weald. I didn't know any of the members. Pete Peterson was soon to become squadron leader, and an Englishman was my flight leader.

"The Englishman, a flight lieutenant, asked me if I'd ever flown a Spit, and I told him I'd never been within 10 feet of one. He called in one of the pilots and told him to give me a cockpit check and send me up for an hour of touch-and-go landings and a sector reconnaissance.

"Many of the features of the Spitfire differed from those of the Hurricane. The controls were situated differently. The warning systems were not the same. At 59 Operational Training Unit, Crosby-on-Eden, before we took a Hurricane up for the first time, we practiced on one mounted on jacks until we knew every instrument and its function by heart and could work every control automatically. Then, when ready to fly, we were reminded of the old RAF axiom—that for the first 20 or 30 hours, the airplane would be flying the pilot.

"The Spitfire checkout that day at North Weald was a little different. After I was in the cockpit, the young pilot officer reached in, touched the control column and said, 'This is the stick; you know what that is.' Touched the throttle, 'This is the throttle—oh hell! You know what everything is. Go fly it!'

"With the help of a mechanic I got the engine started, taxied out to the end of the runway, received permission to take off, and gave it full throttle. One of the things I didn't know about the Spit—a feature the Hurricanes didn't have— was that it was equipped with emergency boost. Push the throttle through a gate and you had extra power that could be used for 10 seconds. Of course, I pushed the throttle through the gate and climbed straight up.

"Aside from the hectic takeoff, the sector recco was uneventful. Spitfires undoubtedly were one of the nicest flying airplanes ever built. They had no bad characteristics.

"When I got back to the field and into the landing pattern, I began to wonder about the transcontinental radio towers that were at one end. They had looked pretty high when viewed from the door of the dispersal hut, but the Pilot Officer who had checked me out said that they were only a couple of hundred feet tall. No problem.

"The fact was that they were sitting on a hill, and the actual height was 700 feet above the field. They were no problem once you got used to them, you simply made a tighter circuit. This time, however, I flew too far downwind, and when I turned into the crosswind leg, they kept getting closer and closer. I selected 'wheels down,' then had to gun the engine to clear the tops of the towers.

"I never did find out if the warning system had worked properly. Of course, it didn't really matter. I never should have become so absorbed in the towers, turning into the final approach, and sideslipping to lose altitude so that I didn't notice the landing gear hadn't come down.

"The first hundred yards after touching down was a nice, smooth ride, because of the Spitfire's duck belly. Then the nose settled, and the prop and one wing-tip dug into the grass.

"The pilots at 121 kidded me later—deliberately crashing to get back to Kirton-in-Lindsey and thereby setting a record for the shortest tour of duty with 71 Squadron, they said. But it didn't seem particularly funny that day, sitting there waiting for a half-dozen crash trucks and Jeeps to converge. An unintentional wheels-up landing was about the most embarrassing mistake a pilot could make. My head had smashed into the gunsight, and a good tunic was covered with blood. There was no serious injury—just anger and embarrassment.

"The English flight lieutenant was no help. He was one of the first to arrive. He jumped onto the wing and started giving me hell for wrecking the Spit.

"The Spitfire I had landed on its belly was a Mark II. The next morning, Pete Peterson, who was also a flight lieutenant at that time, took me out to a new Mark V, gave me a proper checkout, patted me on the back and told me to take it up, 'But please don't forget the wheels, Sarge. It's my personal plane.'

"Pete was a nice guy, a good leader, and after almost 40 years, I can still remember his grin and friendly wave as I taxied out to take off for another sector recco.

"These were my only flights with 71, and a few days later I was back with 121. I don't know if the transfer was cancelled because Peter Powell had raised so much flak, or because I had crash-landed a Spit, or because I had called a flight lieutenant a son-of-a-bitch for ignoring the fact that I might have been hurt, and for worrying more about a plane than a pilot. I rather think it was the latter."

Denver E. "Lucky" Miner, of Racine, Wisconsin, considered himself fortunate to train at the prestigious Spartan School of Aeronautics. It had been built by Tulsa citizens, people with faith in aviation, such as Bill Skelly, J. Paul Getty and Waite Phillips, and was home base for such prominent fliers as Frank Hawks, Charles A. Lindbergh, Ira C. Eaker, Wiley Post and Will Rogers. The school was run by the beloved "Captain" Max Balfour.

While training in Hurricanes at Debden, Miner was allowed to take a test flight in a Spitfire. It was love at first flight: "The little Spit seemed to wrap itself around the pilot. A joy to fly. For the first time, I really fell in love with an airplane."

From there, Miner went to Eglinton, Northern Ireland, where transition training from Hurricanes to Spitfires took place. Among the duties of the trainees was provision of cover for convoys which were threatened by the Germans' big, four-engined Focke-Wulf Condors flying out of Bordeaux. Miner recalls, "Bill Wallace and I shared quarters, and had become a team, as had many of the others—the RAF encouraged this. We had finished up an uneventful patrol, and as our relief from Limavady arrived, I called Bill to follow me. We dove down to mast level, went screaming through the length of the convoy, pulled up, did a series of rolls into the sky, and left for home.

"We thought at the time that we were showing those sailors some smart flying. An hour after we landed, we were told that the Royal Navy wanted us in Belfast immediately. There could be no waiting for a train. We were sent there in an ambulance.

"On arrival, Wallace was taken aboard one trawler, the *Pirouette*, and I was placed on another of the small escort vessels, the *Hornpipe*. All the British trawlers were named for dances. We were to go with the ships all the way from Belfast around the top of England and down the east coast to a colliery on the Firth of Forth, about 20 miles north of Edinburgh. This, it was hoped, would break us of the habit of showing off.

"Aboard ship, I was assigned a gun post in case of an enemy raid. Aside from a few drills, I was left largely to myself. The lesson we learned from our cruise was that the life of men at sea is not an easy one, and that our stupid stunt flying could have resulted in our deaths, if some gun-happy sailor had taken us for the enemy."

Sergeant Pilot Chesley H. Robertson, of Fort Worth, Texas, had a close call on his first flight in a Spitfire, when the plane developed a glycol leak on takeoff and caught fire.

"In a Spit, you always took off with the canopy open. As I slowed down, the flames came into the cockpit. I passed out coming across the field at grass top height, and the plane turned over on its nose.

"Afterward, the Wing Commander sent me up for an intelligence test. I did not do too well on it. They asked questions like 'Who is the Minister of State?' and I had been in England only three weeks. One day, though, the Wingco [Wing Commander] called me in. He wouldn't look at me, but handed me a letter from the air marshal in charge of Training Command. It complimented me on my airmanship in landing the burning airplane. By the end of officers' training I was leading my class in air firing. But that first Spitfire landing destroyed my confidence."

On his second or third day in 133 Squadron, Robertson accompanied Richard Beaty on his first experience in convoy patrol.

"I had been told that nothing ever happened on that kind of a mission," Robertson said. "I was up there looking at the sights and finding it all very interesting, when the R/T said there were some hit-and-run plots coming, 'a couple of Me 109s are starting back out and will be in your area.'

"I had fallen too far behind Beaty, and started trying to catch up when the R/T operator said, 'You ought to be seeing them by now.' Then a German plane started shooting at me from 200 to 350 yards away. I didn't know what was going on until I saw strikes coming out of the plane. The Me 109's gun flashes made it look like its whole wing was on fire. I had cut my power to make a quick turn to get in formation, because I had been going too fast. This saved my life. The Me 109 went right across me, on top. Apparently, he thought he had got me.

"I began to think now that I, who had been number one in air firing, was about to get my first kill on my first day and become a big hero. I started a gentle turn, and pressed the button to fire my guns. Nothing happened. I had forgotten to turn them on.

"By this time, Jerry was out of range. I began trying to catch him, when I remembered that there had been *two* enemy planes around. There was no convoy in sight, no England. I didn't know which way was home. Luckily, I was headed in the right direction."

Nick Sintetos's baptisms by fire also took place in Spitfires. The calls were very close, but not always the welcomes home. "Just as I was climbing into Gunner Halsey's Spitty, he said, 'Don't get the damn thing shot up.' He said it because a couple of days earlier, I was shot up in my Spit.

"The mission was to be a mass Rhubarb with 71 from North Weald. We kept at wave tops all the way over. Just as we crossed the Belgian coast, I was hit by two machine gun bullets on the left aileron cable, jamming my aileron in the upward position. Immediately, the Spit went into a left bank. I was doing about 200 mph. Too low to bail out, I felt like a doomed man.

"I cut the throttle, and held the control column to the right. The banking of the Spitty put me back on the coastline, with the speed diminished to a point where I figured I could crash on the beach ahead of me. I nosed down for the crash landing, and at the same time started firing at a gun position on the beach—one last thing before crashing. Suddenly, at about 110 mph, the right aileron took over, and the Spitty began banking to the right. I was back over the Channel. I eased my throttle forward and just held it enough to keep me from banking. If there had been any enemy fighters near, they could have nailed me cold.

"I flew home at 110 mph. When I got back onto the field, I thanked Gunner for the kite. I told him that I had taxied it over to the maintenance hangar, where it was in dire need of repair. He was teed off."

Of another engagement, Sintetos recalls, "We were jumped by Fw 190s off the coast of Belgium. The CO told us to let them go, but I didn't hear him. I chased them over the coast, and then found I was alone with about nine 190s at treetop level. I fired all my ammunition at them, and the ground fire was fierce. I received hits all over the aircraft. My canopy was blown off. I climbed for a low layer of clouds. On the first attempt, I spun out. I got control again, and made it the second time—and force landed at Dover."

Harold Strickland's diary reports his first attempt to land his Spitfire amidst England's winter coastal fogs and low ceilings. He was aiming for Martlesham Heath after an hour and 40 minutes of minesweeper patrol.

> The other pilots had a lot of experience handling this type of weather problem. When they descended through these extra-low ceilings, they found their way by topnotch pilotage, an art form developed by fliers who rely on their instruments but

augment this reliance with something in themselves—a sort of homing pigeon instinct.

I pulled up into the thick clouds for better or for worse, in the hope of avoiding a collision. All visual references disappeared instantly. I went into an instrument climb; I watched and adjusted the turn indicator, bank indicator, air speed, rate of climb and compass direction, and performed a climbing square-search pattern.

Spitfire radios usually had four different channels. We had been briefed that if we were in real trouble, we were to punch button D-for-dog and yell for a homing. The radio earphones in the helmet and the speaker in the oxygen mask had a long electrical cord and a bayonet plug that fitted into a junction box on the lower right side of the seat. The bayonet plug was fitted into the box loosely enough that if a pilot bailed out the plug would easily disengage. In order to make sure that the connection was tight before I called, I gave the plug a good push. It would have been better to leave well enough alone. That hard push caused the junction box and its lightweight supporting structure to collapse. It also disconnected the bayonet plug. The junction box and its supporting attachments fell under the seat and out of reach.

This left me with no radio connection. D-for-dog might as well have been on the moon, as far as the two-way radio was concerned. I looked under the seat, and tried to reach the socket. It was too far down in the innards of the Spit's wires and controls.

Instrument flying with a low ceiling and lowering fuel supply is difficult enough without having to stand on your head, which is what I had to do in order to retrieve the junction box. I disconnected the seat belt, shoulder straps and parachute, levelled off, released the controls, and sort of dived head first two or three times, but I still could not reach the box. On each such dive, the out-of-control Spitfire started into a descending spiral from level flight, but I could pop up in time to straighten it out and climb another thousand feet, still in the soup.

With the fuel gauge needle approaching zero, I was preparing to bail out. On one climb, I unexpectedly entered a narrow area between cloud layers, where I continued trying to get hold of the junction box. Finally, after an extra-long head-down interval during which the Spitfire again was tightening its downward spiral, I touched the bracket with my finger tips, held onto it for dear life, popped up again, levelled off, climbed again, connected the plug into the socket, wrapped them both around my flying boots, punched D-for-dog and called "This is Brawler Blue Two—emergency homing, please!"

Immediately, a calm voice responded. "Brawler Blue Two, steer 10 degrees magnetic for Coltishall." It was a girl's voice, compounding the miracle.

I had never heard of radar, but without doubt, I had been under radar surveillance and IFF identification ever since I had pulled up into the clouds. I turned the Spitfire onto the magnetic course and descended into the thick cloud layers, made a slight adjustment for compass deviation, hooked up the parachute, fastened the seat belt and shoulder straps, checked the lowering fuel supply, and held the compass on the adjusted course for Coltishall.

Fighter Control called: "Brawler Blue Two, descend and reduce air speed." I did.

Then, "Brawler Blue Two, level off." I did that, too.

Fighter Control vectored me down through the clouds in stair steps as I watched my altimeter. They suggested I lower the wheels and flaps. Suddenly, despite the awful visibility, just over my nose I saw the most gorgeous, most beautiful flare path in the world.

All I had to do was reduce air speed, ease back on the stick, land, and roll down the long runway.

After his second mission with 71 Squadron, an uneventful six-plane fighter sweep at 24,000 feet, Strickland borrowed the Spitfire of his section leader, Chesley Peterson, to practice cloud formation flying with Newton Anderson. Pete's plane had been serviced and needed a flight check.

"As Newt and I glided in tight formation for a landing on the muddy field at North Weald, flaps down, Newt gave a hand signal to lower the landing gear," Strickland said. "I lowered the gear and checked the *down* signal.

"In a tight formation landing, the wingman had better concentrate on the leader's plane. Perhaps Newt was a little high, but not too high when he levelled off. My wheels touched the ground with unusual softness, even for a wet field. Then there was a series of loud kerplunks, kerplunks. Pete's recently overhauled Spitfire seemed to melt into the deep mud as the landing gear collapsed, while Newt's Spitfire seemed to be far, far above eye level and rolling away from me as I fought the rudder to keep the two planes separated.

"I cut the ignition switch because of the 86-Imperial-gallon gas tank just above the pilot's feet. One of the wheels had a flat tire. Both wheels had collapsed because of an extra-large and extra-deep mud puddle and because the wheel locking mechanism had failed.

"The Spitfire skidded for nearly a hundred yards across the mud and wet grass, as the crash-wagon sirens began to wail. When we finally halted, I hopped out and looked at the damaged flaps and undercarriage. I never felt worse in my life. This beauty was the first aircraft I had ever damaged in my entire flying career—and it had to be Pete's.

"In the winter of 1941 we'd be ordered out in rain and low ceiling to cover a convoy of our ships in the North Sea, and 15 minutes later, with the ceiling getting lower, be recalled to base and vectored in for landing.

"It was under marginal weather conditions such as this, where RAF airdromes could be closed but adequate ceiling and visibility were available at some Luftwaffe bases, that the convoys would be attacked by German fighters, bombers, or torpedo-carrying aircraft. Therefore, if the convoys had even barely enough ceiling and visibility, and even if near-minimum conditions existed at many RAF airdromes, it was the practice to protect the coastal convoys despite the weather hazards.

"The mere presence of Spitfires circling convoys frequently prevented attacks. Under such weather conditions, however, especially over the water, the horizon line becomes deceptive or non-existent. Low-flying RAF aircraft collided with the water from time to time. These are the types of very high risks that the RAF willingly assumed because of the tradeoffs that must be made by commanders in wartime. It was essential to keep the convoy lifelines open, especially in poor weather. Spitfire and Hurricane pilots were expendable as compared to the high priority cargo vessels and their crews."

A November 1, 1941 Ramrod fighter attack in wind and rain by 71 and 222 Spitfire Squadrons and the bomb-carrying 401 Hurricane Squadron against military barracks and a power station near Le Touquet was a baptism of another kind:

The rendezvous with the Hurricanes was at Manston, then to Dungeness where the Hurricanes set course across the Channel at "nought feet" altitude, as close to the breaking waves as possible to avoid radar detection.

We crossed the French coastline at Boulogne still on the deck, flying at high speed just above the fields and treetops. Spitfires and Hurricanes, when flying this close to the ground, cast no shadows. From higher altitudes, the squadrons of low-flying camouflaged planes racing across the surface sort of merge into the landscape and become very difficult to see except to the practiced eye of the combat-wise pilots who know how to look, when to look, and have the opportunity to look.

This was only my sixth sortie, and I was flying No. 4 position in Pete's Blue flight, in a finger-four flight formation. I suddenly learned something fast—and here again I emphasize that there is a deadly difference between flying fighters and fighting fighters. No matter how much one has flown previously, combat flying is so different that there is absolutely no comparison.

Much of my attention was focussed on Pete's Spitfire, while checking ahead for targets and obstacles. Then I noticed other aircraft to starboard, on the same parallel course, flying low at the same high speed. They were Hurricanes, but how did they get out there? I thought I knew where the Hurricane flights and the other Spitfire squadron should be.

After turning slightly toward them and gawking at these strangers for a few seconds, but too long, I looked for Pete's Brawler Blue flight. It had disappeared. Twenty-four friendly Spitfires had disappeared!

I looked in all directions, but there was no trace of Pete, Squadron Leader Meares or any one of the others. I was alone. The only thing I could see was that flight of Hurricanes. I closed in on them. They, too, were hell bent for their particular target areas, and when I joined them, they probably were asking one another on the R/T, "where the hell did *he* come from?"

I turned on my gunsight, because I didn't know what else to do. Hopping over the treetops, the Hurricanes increased their engine boost, and we were all flying wide out. From my position on the wide side, over the nose, I saw a cluster of poles with electrical transformers near the top. I opened fire with my machine guns and two 20-mm cannon. Some of the cannon shells hit home, because I could see all kinds of explosions and blue sparks, while I kept on going with the Hurricanes, all the time looking for 71 Squadron.

Then the Hurricanes disappeared over the treetops, and all hell broke loose. Somebody was shooting up targets, and there I was, alone again. Alone and lonesome, far from home, on my sixth mission and the natives trying to kill me. I had lost two squadrons of Spitfires and one squadron of Hurricanes—some sort of a record, I suppose. I knew right then why the bomber crews loved the fighters and referred to them as "little friends."

So I changed course while jinking to avoid flak, looked at my watch, set the compass on the preplanned withdrawal course, and poured on the coal with boost, hopping over fences and dusting off the open fields. Soon, but far ahead, I saw a lot of familiar objects flying the same course. After a few minutes that seemed like hours, traveling almost as fast as a Spit can fly at sea level, I closed in—closed in on the most beautiful mix of aircraft imaginable: Hurricanes and Spitfires including those with 71's own XR Squadron markings.

As we flew, Art Roscoe was hit and wounded by hit-and-run Me 109s diving from above, but he landed safely at the nearest RAF base with considerable loss of blood. Then Pete's Spitfire was hit. When they had a choice, enemy AA gunners tried to aim at squadron leaders and flight leaders. The Hurricanes probably had expended all of their ammunition on the ground targets. Our first priority was to protect those homebound Hurricanes.

Luftwaffe fighter controllers must have been in close touch with this type of penetration soon after we approached the coastline, and they could identify some RAF squadrons from the R/T chatter, which was always limited for security purposes, but nevertheless was revealing to Luftwaffe intelligence.

Our squadron code word was Brawler. Luftwaffe fighter controllers who studied German intelligence records would have been familiar with the record of long-departed Me 109s, Ju 88s, Heinkels and Fw 190s, plus airdrome fixtures, barracks, AA crews, radio stations and probably some chickens and cows on Luftwaffe premises, whose demise or departure was attributable to RAF squadrons such as Brawler.

I was watching for enemy fighters, but I didn't see any on our side of the Ramrod, although R/T chatter ahead included the warning "bandits." Later, it occurred to me that if German pilots did report a lone Spitfire, after receiving warning of 24 other Spitfires and 12 Hurricanes in the same general locality, they might have thought that I was the focal point of a 36-airplane booby trap. Certainly, no Brawler pilot would be so dumb as to separate himself that far from his squadron.

Another factor that hit me hard at that time was the great gulf between the aircraft recognition courses and actual combat recognition of enemy planes as well as friendly planes. A tiny dot far away in, or near, the sun, or another camouflaged dot far below, were unlike the clear and distinct silhouettes and models used for teaching aircraft recognition to green fighter pilots. More important is the reaction time factor. Recognition and identification of the tiny dot, and tactical maneuvering, must be achieved almost within microseconds.

John J. Lynch was destined to become a triple ace, but his teammate, Leo Nomis, recalls that the path of this Eagle was far from smooth. Sometimes, brilliant careers are baptised in . . . well:

"One of the first things John Lynch did after his arrival at 71 Squadron from 121 Squadron, in November of 1941, was to outmaneuver the intrepid and talented Humphrey Gilbert in a dogfight right over the field. At that stage, bad weather was common and the squadron became relegated to winter scrambles and the monotonous convoy patrols off the Estuary and as far north as Orfordness.

"After the first of the year, Lynch was appointed a section leader. I was usually paired with him during that period and by February 1942, Lynch had managed to achieve notoriety in a couple of categories. He participated in a Rhubarb in about the middle of that month, the result of which was published in the London *Times*. I forget who his flying companion was during the mission, but it was academic, in view of what happened to Lynch.

"Under low-hanging clouds, they had attacked a train in railway yards south of Boulogne. Lynch had started his run too low, and as the Spitfire rushed toward the locomotive, he had to keep lowering the nose to contain the cannon rounds on target.

"The train engine refused to blow up, and Lynch held his run too long. He almost collided with the locomotive, which was spouting jets of steam, and when he pulled up, he did collide with a telephone pole.

"The top of the pole entered the leading edge of the wing at the root and broke off at the main spar. Lynch headed back across the Channel and landed at Manston with two feet of a French telephone pole protruding from the skin of the VB Spitfire. 'I rocked a bit after the collision but didn't realize it was such a near thing until I came home and found what a bulky souvenir I had brought with me,' he said.

"The endurance of the aircraft structure in this case could certainly contrast drastically with the instances, one week in

October 1941, in which two other Eagles, Larry Chatterton and Roger Atkinson, were killed because of Spitfire wing collapse in level flight. In fact, the Lynch incident was widely heralded at the time by the people at Vickers as evidence of the sturdiness of the Spit.

"Shortly after this episode, Lynch, because he was the hero of the telephone pole affair, was sent up to the Supermarine factory to bring back a new Spit VB for 71 Squadron. After a gracious reception at the hands of the factory officials, Lynch started back to Martlesham Heath in the new kite. He made a beautiful approach and came in and landed on the snow-covered turf with the undercarriage retracted.

"This unforgiveable type of negligence called for punishment, and the voice raised the loudest in demand for retribution was that of the ill-tempered engineering officer of 71, Wayne Becker. Squadron Leader Peterson decided against a mere reprimand in the form of a logbook notation. Something else was needed.

"For two days, Pete said nothing. On the third day, it was suddenly announced that all 71 Squadron pilots were to stand parade at the B Flight dispersal hut. The day was bleak and cold, and at 2:30 P.M., darkness was beginning to fall. No one knew what to expect as we stood in formation beside the hut. There was ice on the ground, and when we had lined up, sleet began to slant across the perimeter.

"Peterson arrived with Becker, and they stood stone-faced in front of the pilots. We were all standing at attention. Peterson retrieved an over-sized Iron Cross from inside his greatcoat and ordered Lynch to step forward. The outlandish cross had been forged for the occasion by Becker's engineering section. Ceremoniously, the squadron commander hung it around Lynch's neck. Peterson displayed admirable control, staring sternly as he awarded the decoration. Lynch tried to suppress a weak smile. He saluted, and turned on his heel— and slipped flat on the ice. I was one of those admonished by Peterson for laughing in ranks.

"Spring rolled around, and we began to feel warm again. On a bright clear morning over the North Sea, Lynch and I intercepted a Ju 88 which was flying flush on the deck. We both sighted it at the same time, but we had to turn 180 degrees to come around astern of the Jerry kite. When we levelled off, Lynch was about a hundred yards ahead of me.

"The enemy rear gunner immediately started firing with alarming accuracy. The first salvo hit Lynch's Spit in the engine, and a single round ripped through one of my propeller blades. Lynch's aircraft began to throw out black oily smoke, and he had the presence of mind to turn instantly for the English coast. His only comment to me on the R/T was to inform me unnecessarily that his engine had been hit. The date was April 17, 1942.

"Lynch made it across the coast, but he was so low he could not bail out, and then the engine quit entirely. He headed for a field back of the beach near Felixstowe, but lost altitude so rapidly that he clipped some trees and catapulted into a bog. The aircraft ended up inverted, and Lynch was pinned in the cockpit for two hours before some army personnel rescued him. His face and upper body were badly lacerated, and some of his front teeth were knocked out, teeth for which he never bothered to get replacements.

"Lynch possessed a quiet, almost introverted personality, but he also had an authoritative quality about him which impressed everyone who knew him. He was the last one to wish me goodbye at Debden when I left for the Mediterranean in July. I never saw him again, but nine months later, in May, 1943, he would win a prize of 100 pounds for destroying an Italian Reggiane. It was the 1,000th enemy aircraft downed by the RAF at Malta."

The Eagles' association with the Spitfire was warm and long-lasting. Even after the pilots transferred to the United States Army Air Forces, many stayed with the Spit for months. Dixie Alexander recalls an incident of December 12, 1942, that "proved once again what a wonderful piece of flying machinery the Spitfire was."

"We were to take part in the escort of bombers attacking Abbeville. We had been on the deck to about mid-Channel, and then started climbing rapidly before rendezvous. We had reached 22,000 feet when, after a few violent surges, my engine quit completely.

"After making all cockpit checks and starting to fall behind, I called Red Leader, and said I was turning back. I also informed him I was dead stick.

"I will never know why I was not given my wingman or another escort of some kind back to base. It was customary. The squadron commander, Malta Stepp, simply told my wingman to get up into my slot. Whoever was leading the wing—Pete, I think—let it stand. Anyhow, I was on my own, and I elected to glide back at 132 mph, the best speed prescribed for Spitties.

"A Spitfire at 20,000 feet with no engine is a lonesome place. I knew my approximate position to be 10 miles at sea, and just south of Boulogne. I knew Lympne Airdrome, the closest field, well, and I also knew how small and tricky it was.

"With my maps I was able to set a good course for Lympne. I refrained from immediate conversation, even though Controller was calling me after my first transmission to Red One.

"I figured I had 35 miles at 132 mph and 20,000 feet. I had figured my rate of descent, and thought it adequate. I knew I had about 2½ miles a minute at 140, and the aircraft felt good there. If I had no trouble for 10 minutes I would be well on the way home.

"I figured that Controller would read my silence correctly, and he did. As I expected, he also had two aircraft airborne to intercept and give me protection. I called in after 10 minutes and asked for a homing on *M'aidez* (Mayday). I got it after the usual count, and my course was pretty well right on.

"My intercept aircraft never did find me until I hit Lympne at about 4,000 feet. I made two complete orbits while advising of my status, and went in to a successful wheels-down landing.

"After the squadron's return, Malta Stepp called to congratulate me on a successful handling of a situation, or something. I remember I was a bit testy, and said something to the effect that it was normal for me, but no thanks to him."

Baptism by new machines, by combat, by what was sometimes a hostile environment of miserable weather, by the strains of fear and loss as only war can create them—to survive that was a triumph in itself for the Yanks of the RAF. Yet there was also another kind of introduction, to a different society, to people who spoke their language but in different accents, the people to whose cause the young Eagles had committed their lives, their fortunes, and their honor.

4

FRIENDS AND ALLIES

The centerfold color photo of the January 1975 issue of *Town & Country* depicts an imposing mansion, bordered by a putting green and a magnificent swimming pool, as the new home of the former Governor of Bermuda and as one of the grandest villas in the Lyford Cay community of New Providence Island. It is *El Mirador*, the Bahamas winter retreat of Lord and Lady Martonmere, whose association as members of the Lyford Cay Club extends back to 1960. Lady Orr-Lewis, of London, had been hired to redecorate *El Mirador*, which stands on the highest point of the club grounds and overlooks 1,200 feet of sandy beach.

Eagle squadron veterans who chanced to read the article thought back to the two years when they were flying with the RAF and when they exchanged information and banter with Robbie Robinson, aka Jack, aka J. Roland, now more properly referred to as Lord Martonmere. In those days, for John Roland Robinson, the noble title and a host of distinguished posts in the service of his monarch lay in the future, but even then, in the early 1940s, he was a man of service and responsibility: Member of Parliament from Blackpool and

Intelligence Officer of 71 Eagle Squadron of the Royal Air Force.

Robinson was automatically exempt from combat duty, due to critical injuries he suffered, along with his American wife, Maysie, in the crash of a small plane near Le Touquet, France, in 1939. As an MP, he was not subject to compulsory military service, but like other MPs under 40, he volunteered.

Being rejected for military service, before the arrival in England of the first American volunteers, was "perhaps my good fortune," Robinson suggests. "My first contact with the Eagle Squadron then newly formed was when Pete Peterson and Gus Daymond visited the House of Commons and, as a member with many American connections and interests, I was asked to show them around.

"A lasting friendship began that morning, and though I did not know it then, within the next two weeks, I was to find myself in uniform as an RAF officer serving with 71 Eagle Squadron."

Robinson joined the Squadron at Kirton-in-Lindsey shortly after its establishment, and remained with the Eagles through all the subsequent changes of base—Martlesham Heath, North Weald and Debden. The Americans quickly took to their new IO (their term for Intelligence Officer) and found him to be friendly, informal, thoughtful and intelligent. It was an added benefit that he was a wealthy and generous man, and had a charming wife who knew and understood Americans.

"As my IO, Jack Robinson was largely responsible for 71 Squadron's high *esprit de corps*," said Pete Peterson years after having served as squadron commander.

"He was an intelligent man of the world who knew how to handle Americans, and he was a consummate politician. Such a perfect politician, in fact, that we Americans used to go to him and get advice. He also had a lot of money and a beautiful home, *The Elms*, where the Eagles often were dinner guests."

Vic Bono, a Californian who joined 71 one month after Robinson, adds, "Robbie was a wonderful guy. If he had his last shirt on his back he would give it to you. He even loaned me his car."

Asked in 1980 about the nature of his work with the Eagles four decades earlier, Lord Martonmere, the former Jack Robinson, wrote:

"It is a little difficult for me to recollect all of the exact details of the duty of a Squadron Intelligence Officer. In the early stages, it was important for me to teach them aircraft recognition so that they knew their enemy when they saw him. For this purpose I studied all available documents and took cuttings and drawings of enemy aircraft which I kept in a loose-leaf book available to all of the pilots.

"In addition, from time to time, I gave talks to them in Dispersal. This was important in the training stage, though once they were operational they all knew what the enemy aircraft looked like and what type it was.

"Once squadron was operational, briefing became more important. One had to see that the pilots had any information about the enemy which had been obtained through intelligence or other sources.

"Then, of course, there was the interrogation of the pilots after an operation and the preparation of reports, which had to be sent immediately to Group Headquarters. This would include the assessment of the pilot's claims and the picking up of any useful information. For instance, one of our pilots reported that on coming out of France, between Le Touquet and Boulogne, he turned near some electrical installations on a cliff. I knew that area very well from the times when we had a house at Le Touquet before the war. At that time there was no such electrical installation in the area to which he referred. I reported that our pilot had seen a possible radar station. The result was that Group dispatched a photo reconnaissance plane. The next day, the photographs showed that my surmise was correct. Two days later, the station was destroyed.

"In addition to normal interrogation duties, squadron intelligence officers on any station had to take turns in interrogating the crews of any bombers that might come in to the fighter base after a raid during the night. Primarily, they would be coming in because of damage or fuel shortage, and we then had to send the reports to Group for forwarding to Bomber Command.

"At busy times, this could be rather an onerous responsibility. I remember once when the other squadron intelligence officers were either on leave or sick, and I had a period of three days of continuous duty, day and night. I was really exhausted when it was all over.

"I should add to my list of duties the fact that I also had to keep an eye on the general welfare of our pilots."

When the United States came into the war, Robinson was enlisted to help with the preparations for the creation of the Eighth Air Force in Britain, about which, more later.

Robinson's successor as Intelligence Officer of the first Eagle Squadron was Paul Pablo (Joe) Salkeld, a colorful roamer of the world, who contended that he had held about 35 jobs before he was 30. Born in London in 1909, he sketched his pre-RAF and Eagle Squadron experience in these terms.

"Worked for a year with West India Oil Co. (Standard) in Buenos Aires. After a spell doing odd jobs with a variety company at various theaters in Buenos Aires and Montevideo, went to Paraguay. War with Bolivia broke out; cold feet after starting to volunteer.

"Back to Argentina, worked *estancias* [ranch work] for some years, then went on the tramp from Buenos Aires to Santiago, Chile, and after a year or so back to Buenos Aires. Also covered parts of Brazil and northern Argentina; rode two creole horses most of the time. Happy days.

"Then on an oil tanker to Dutch West Indies, and back to B.A. When war started, joined RAF. Slung out of flying, owing to deafness to high tones, so became IO. Deafness now acute; am afraid I'll lose my pilot's license. Ran a glass fiber factory for 20 years.

"It was a bit of a comedown for 71 Squadron to be landed with me after Robbie, who was wealthy, well-connected, and influential. But it was my good luck to join them. I got along well with everyone in the squadron. I have nothing but happy memories.

"There were the uproarious parties at Debden: Sam Mauriello treating himself to a bottle of red wine to celebrate his birthday; Pappy Lutz and Howard Hively, the insepara-bles, keeping us in fits with endless comedy acts such as 'The Absentminded Duck Hunter' and 'The Red Baron'; Lulu Hollander playing *Home on the Range* and, accompanied by all at the top of their voices, the lewd version of *1492*.

"There was a fenced off space near Dispersal with a rustic arch over which someone had written TIMES SQUARE. Crews relaxed, played chess, and waited here.

"On any operation, there was always that twin feeling of apprehension and guilt inside me. An hour or so of waiting for the squadrons to return, while I, safe even from air raids, just stood by and hoped that all would come back safely.

"There was the sudden warning of an overseas draft, to Murmansk, called Operation Invective. O.R.s issued with tropical kit. Officers told not to buy anything until instructed. So obvious, that we might as well have been advised to prepare for the cold. Luckily, the posting did not come off. There were a number of celebratory parties, in one of which Group Captain Isherwood rode a motorbike around the mess. A night out in London, a great meeting up at the Station— and I have memories of the Bevin Boys, with their helmets and gear, eyeing us all with sadness and envy. The manpower shortage had led Labor Minister Aneurin Bevin to draft them to the coal mines, poor devils."

Operation Invective was a project to bolster Soviet air forces in the far North. This was in the summer of 1942, when most of the Americans were expecting to transfer out of the RAF. It was announced that 71 and two other RAF squadrons would constitute the 153 Overseas Wing and would proceed to a Russian station in the Barents Sea area. New Spitfire IX fighters were already on the way to Murmansk, and air crews would head northward shortly.

"The impending move was not looked upon with great enthusiasm by every member of 71," James A. Gray recalls. "Squadron Leader Peterson suggested that those who chose not to go might be posted to Halifax, Nova Scotia, or some other such place. Bill Taylor—William Douglas Taylor—and I were rooming together at Debden at the time. In London, on a 48-hour leave, we surreptitiously purchased a copy of a Russian language book, keeping a watch out for Scotland Yard, MI5, or whatever. Back at Debden, we assiduously applied ourselves to the study of Russian grammar for a week or so.

"And then, on July 14, the whole thing was called off. All of our Spitfires went down with one of the ships in the Murmansk convoy. We went back and reclaimed our old Spits, to rejoin the tussle over the Channel."

Little more than a month later, all three Eagle Squadrons took part in Operation Jubilee, the Allied Dieppe-area beach landings, since described by historians as the bloodiest, most costly commando raid of the war. It was the only mission in which the RAF's American units flew together, and they were part of a force of 76 squadrons, including 48 squadrons of Spitfires. The air units covered a British naval force moving 7,000 commandos across the Channel, and helped clear 11 miles of the French coast near Dieppe for a daylight strike. First planned for July 1942, the landings finally took place on August 19.

Salkeld remembered the Jubilee exercise especially well.

"We flew down to Gravesend for the first, abortive attempt. People got bored, and four pilots took off one dawn, after a party, on an unauthorized Rhubarb. I went out to meet them and someone leaned out of the cockpit, holding thumb and little finger apart, and called, 'Joe, get me just a finger of whiskey.'

"A notice on the board prohibited flying below 500 feet. A humorist had rubbed out the last zero, and we were treated to a very interesting display of flying. Punishment, on that hot day, was to walk around the perimeter of the field in full flying gear. All taken in good part, happy grins, and back at the start, a pint for each."

In *Life* Magazine's account of the Dieppe operation, Harold Strickland was identified as having fired the first shot of the air battle. Strick's squadron had taken off in darkness at 0450 hours; he had damaged an Fw 190 10 miles west of Dieppe and was back on the ground, refueling for his second sortie, at 0600. "I never claimed to have fired the first shot in the battle of Dieppe," Strick said later, "but I thought I might have been the first in 71 Squadron to fire."

"It was a secret mission," Hubert "Stew" Stewart said about Jubilee. "We were briefed by the Wing Commander the night before, told of the squadron assignments, and then were advised we could make no telephone calls and should go to bed. We were confined to the base."

"And we were told that should we be shot down, the recovery situation would be ideal," said Barry Mahon. "Much of the French countryside around Dieppe was going to be vacated late in the afternoon the day before the raid. Early on August 19, we were scrambled into action as a squadron, and we approached the French coast at about 25,000. The boats were concentrated in and near the harbor of Dieppe, and the air above was thick with enemy and Allied aircraft. At times, more than 400 planes were in the air over the battle area."

In the furious daylong series of engagements, one Eagle, James Taylor, was killed, and five others—Squadron Leader Peterson, Mike McPharlin, Barry Mahon, Gene Fetrow and Julian Osborne—had to parachute into the Channel from their disabled planes. Mahon was captured by the Germans, but the other four were picked up by British rescue vessels. Peterson had pursued and shot down a Junkers 88 bomber even after being wounded himself, and later received from King George the Distinguished Service Order, the highest honor conferred upon any Eagle.

Strickland summed up the day's results as he saw them: "The German air, ground and naval forces had failed to prevent a landing on the mainland of Europe! Many valuable lessons were learned at Dieppe that saved lives later in Normandy. However, the casualties were high—404 officers and 3,890 men killed, wounded or captured, over 3,000 being Canadians. Fourteen German bombers and 16 fighters were sent splashing into the Channel. But 106 RAF aircraft were lost, mostly to ground fire. Reportedly, 88 were Spitfires."

Among other memories of life at 71 Squadron that Salkeld shared is the following.

"Gene Potter made friends with the officer in charge of defense and was allowed to drive a tank around the perimeter. I also had a go at it, as did one or two of the others. Bud "Ossie" Brite wrote a silly letter to a girl friend. The censor read it, and Ossie was for the jump. Ossie let me wobble around the sky in the Moth trainer, and once we tried to emulate a squadron leader who had taken a WAAF for a trip in a Spit. It was impossible, and taxiing back was painful enough, for Ossie was a big lad. That must have been a very small squadron leader and a smaller WAAF.

"Sometimes we went for walks, and it was on a pleasant evening that I first got to know Joe Helgason, whom I had always felt disapproved of me. We were talking about postwar activities; some wanted prohibition back, others reckoned that illegal immigrant smuggling was safer—and when I said something about the future of road haulage, Helgy opened up. He had great ideas about the years ahead, but, alas, he hit a treetop and was plastered over a field. It was a very nasty and extremely sad occasion."

Squadron Leader Peter Powell's combat record in 1940 included enemy aircraft kills in January and April—each shared with two other RAF pilots and thus yielding him a score of one-third on each occasion; another German plane shot down May 10; two more May 11; two damaged May 18; one destroyed June 2; two more June 7; one damaged July 25. The Briton took command of 121 Eagle Squadron in mid-May 1942, and shot down yet another enemy plane on August 18.

"Quite a guy," comments one of his American pilots, John Campbell. "A good squadron leader with an excellent grasp on his job. He had a pit bull terrier that became the squadron's mascot. A woman had given it to him after his first dog was killed. The bull terrier used to sleep on Powell's fur lined flying suit."

Powell had received the DFC after his victories in May 1940. Following his promotion in January 1943, to command the Hornchurch Wing, he received a Bar for his DFC. Before the war, he had been a member of an RAF demonstration team which performed aerobatics in Gloster Gladiators with their wings tied together by ribbons.

"Powell told Leroy Skinner, Jim Daley and me one time about the fancy maneuvers they used to perform with the Gladiators," Campbell recalls. "One stunt was called 'Prince of Wales Feathers.' Three aircraft in a vic formation would dive on the field, and as they pulled up, the two outside planes would roll out and the center one would roll straight up. Then they would come together and land. It was quite spectacular.

"Skinner, Daley and I decided to try it. I was leading the section, and we did it there at Kirton-in-Lindsey—a perfect *fleur-de-lis*. It must have looked good.

"Powell called me in and said, 'That was absolutely beautiful. But look—we did this with Gladiators. You just proved you could do it with Hurricanes. If you ever try to do it again and don't break your neck, I'll break it for you.' Powell followed this up with a lecture on the value of military aircraft. The RAF had had a rash of accidents, and a directive came through from Fighter Command that all squadron commanders call their squadrons in. Powell went through the whole thing. He said a Spitfire pilot had been sent to put on an aerobatics display for a town that had raised funds to donate a Spit to the RAF. 'That pilot killed himself doing low aerobatics, and destroyed more than the town could possibly have raised in defense funds,'"

Reade Tilley recalls that Powell had a fine sense of humor, and was a great story teller. "One of his favorites was of his wedding night," Tilley said. "He had gone to great lengths to select an inn in a quiet little village. He had on hand a supply of vintage champagne, soft music and the whole bit.

"Then, just as he was drawing the shades, there was a hell of a racket outside. 'Some bloody idiot had shot down a Heinkel 111, and it crashed and exploded in the courtyard of the inn,' he said. His description of the rest of the night, with sirens and firetrucks and ambulances, was heart-rending."

Each of the other English leaders of Eagle squadrons— Henry Woodhouse, Stanley Meares, Hugh Kennard, Dudley Williams, George Brown and Eric Hugh Thomas—quite readily won the respect and affection of their American charges. Typical was Reade Tilley's opinion of Hugh Kennard: "Nobody better symbolized the character, fighting spirit and piloting capability of the RAF. Kennard was an aristocrat— brave, the finest type of English officer and gentleman—a hell of a fine person."

Kennard says firmly that, contrary to some reports, the Eagles under his command were not problem pilots. "When they arrived at the Squadron they were already pretty well trained. They adjusted themselves to the RAF extremely quickly, and in air combat, in each squadron formation, they were bloody good. I never noticed them as being in special need of discipline. I saw no real difference between them and British pilots at all."

For the fledgling Eagles, the British pilots were deep wells of experience and towers of example, for they had fought through the dark days of the Battles of France and Britain.

Royce Wilkinson had gone to France "at five minutes' notice" in 1940 as a Sergeant Pilot with Hurricane equipped 3 Fighter Squadron, where Flight Lieutenant Walter Churchill was his flight commander:

"We lost our CO about May 15, and Walter assumed command of the squadron. Walter insisted that I was Flight Commander of A Flight, even though we had another flight lieutenant with us and I was only a sergeant pilot. I was credited with nine confirmed kills at the time.

"Around May 21 or 22, a German column reached Arras, just south of us at Merville, and it was time to evacuate. I took five Hurricanes with me, and we did low-level strafing on the German column, and managed to halt it for four hours. I was credited with blowing up two ammo lorries and setting a petrol tanker on fire.

"During this time a 22-seat Imperial Airways Scilla landed at Merville. After everything had been stripped out of it, the plane took off with the entire ground crew on board—more than 100 men. It was well overloaded, but it made it back to Kenley.

"The rest of us flew out in our aircraft. They were all badly shot up by then, but being Hurricanes, they still flew. Mine had a large hole in the starboard wing from a cannon shell.

"When we got back, Walter Churchill was promoted to squadron leader and carried on as CO. I was commissioned and made flight lieutenant as officer in charge of A flight. Walter got the DSC, and I got the DFM—Distinguished Flying Medal—and Bar.

"When 71 Squadron was formed with Walter as CO, he insisted on selecting his own flight commanders, and so George Brown and I were posted to Church Fenton to form the squadron. Mamedoff, Keough, Luke Allen, and Red Tobin were the first Eagles to arrive, and we were given some Brewster Buffaloes which were originally destined for Belgium. After a few flights in them, we decided they were useless as operational fighters, and following several rows with the Air Ministry, we were given some Hurricanes."

After more than six months with 71 Squadron and 10 with 121, Wilkinson departed from the Americans in 1942 to take command of a new squadron of Hurricane fighter-bombers at Manston. He was shot down, but escaped from France by way of Gibraltar. As with the other English Eagles, he remained in touch with his former flying companions. He took part in the 1976 reunion of the Eagle Squadron Association in London, was elected the Association's Vice President for Europe, and, with his wife Joan and with George Brown and his wife Eve journeyed to Orlando, Florida, for the 1980 reunion.

George Brown's successor as 133 Squadron Leader, Tommy Thomas, required his pilots to practice formation flying and fighter tactics constantly, in all types of weather. "Tommy was a bit reserved—stand-offish, we called it—but he was a good leader," says then Pilot Officer Jessie Taylor. "He would get brusque at times, but in general, he got along with everyone."

George Sperry concurs. "Thomas frowned on individual heroics unless the action was necessary to get another pilot out of a jam. It was largely his personal leadership that whipped our unit into a first class squadron."

Before joining the RAF, Thomas had been a bank clerk and a keen sportsman. Cricket, hockey, rugby, tennis and golf were his favorites. When he finished flight training in May 1937, at the age of 19, his instructor's assessment of him was, "Keen pilot of undoubted ability; shows promise as a fighter pilot."

Thomas became a Spitfire I pilot in the summer of 1940. He started flying Spit VBs when the RAF Fighter Command went over to the offensive, with daylight sweeps and bomber-escort missions over northern France. The day after he assumed command of 133 Eagle Squadron in mid November 1941, he received the DFC for having participated in 60 sorties over enemy territory and having destroyed at least three enemy aircraft. He was promoted to Wing Commander at Biggin Hill at the end of July 1942, and received a Bar to his DFC. The following February, he was awarded the Distinguished Service Order for "gallant leadership and unfailing devotion to duty." Said a colleague: "Tommy wasn't a high-scoring fighter pilot—not an ace in the sense of shooting down a large number of enemy aircraft—but he was an outstanding fighter leader."

Another popular English figure with the Eagles was Sir Michael Duff, 121 Squadron Intelligence Officer, godfather of the Earl of Snowdon, who was to marry Princess Margaret. The Earl, born Anthony Armstrong-Jones, took his title from Mike Duff's family estate, Snowdon.

Sir Michael always signed his reports at 121 Squadron M. Assheton-Smith. The Americans did not discover that "Smitty" was something special until they noted that the telephone contact number he left, when absent from the base, was that of Buckingham Palace. It turned out that Queen Mary was Mike's godmother. When the pilots of 121 complained to him that they had been too long in the backwaters of the war, the squadron quickly was moved from quiet Kirton-in-Lindsey to the key station of North Weald. The Eagles were quite sure they saw in this the influential hand of tall, quiet, elegant "Mike Smith."

"Mike was always immaculate in Saville Row tailored uniforms, and his precise command of the English language was something to marvel at," says Reade Tilley. "Often he must have been somewhat aghast at the casual sloppiness of most Eagles and the way they murdered the mother tongue, but he never showed it."

Sir Michael did show his high regard for the Eagles by remaining in touch with them and by taking part in their 1976 reunion in London. When Sir Michael died, in 1980, "we all felt a keen sense of loss," said ESA President Jessie Taylor.

The Eagles especially appreciated the work on their planes performed by the dedicated ground crews. Engineering Officer R. T. Wood, of Iver, Bucks, discussed these duties.

"The EO's job with 133 Squadron was to keep the aircraft serviceable by all means at our disposal. The aircraft we had on formation were early type Hurricanes, and had been well used. The enthusiasm of our Eagle pilots merited serviceability, and we, the ground crews, did our utmost to see that they got it. It meant working all hours, and this was greatly appreciated by them.

"My other, unofficial job was that of driver when the boys went out on 'stand down.' I'm not sure which job I liked the more.

"The moves from Coltishall to Fowlmere and then to Eglinton did not make life any easier, and it was difficult to keep sufficient aircraft serviceable. However, we survived. We were very pleased to arrive at Kirton-in-Lindsey, a stepping stone to 11 Group and to Biggin Hill. The Eagles were a grand bunch of boys, a pleasure to work with. Once one had learned that aircraft were "ships" to them, and that if a motor cut out it had "quit," then things were fine and one was proud to wear the Eagle shoulder flash."

R. C. Morris of Heath Meadow, Colwell, Freshwater, Isle of Wight, has this to say on "the part we as mechanics played with the Eagles, and how we coped with the Yanks."

"First, I was part of a team working on the flights keeping the Spitfires serviceable and ready for action at all times. We as fitters, the riggers, the R/T men, the armourers were responsible for the aircraft being airworthy, and had to sign a form to confirm this.

"Whilst the Spits were flying on sorties, Rhubarbs or bomber escort, we would be waiting to refuel and re-arm them, ready for almost nonstop action; ensuring a quick refueling; standing by our allotted aircraft when we were on readiness; nipping into the cockpit; starting the engine so that it would be ready for the pilot to take off as soon as the scramble horn was sounded. The whole squadron would be airborne in a matter of minutes. Knowing it was all really very serious, we got a kick out of the fact that we were part of a team of very brave and dedicated pilots.

"As for coping with the Yanks, I can honestly say we respected them in every way. Every pilot in 71 Squadron was like a friend to us, and this showed in the faces of all when someone was missing.

"We knew we had to have discipline in the RAF, but whenever the pilots of the Eagles met any of the ground crew in pubs or elsewhere when off duty, no distinction was shown. The friendship and courage shown by them made me feel very proud to have served with such a great lot of dedicated men.

"I was especially pleased to see in *The Eagle Squadrons* a picture of the pilot I worked with, Sam Mauriello. The rigger and I were his ground crew on the Spitfire X R (G) for George, and he would always give us a little handshake both on taking off and when we saw him safely back from whatever sortie they had been on."

In September, 1980, another fitter, Kenny John of Stradbroke, Diss, Norfolk, sent from England a set of squadron plaques, one for each of the three squadrons saying, "I would like to present these to the Eagle Squadron Association as a token of my deep regard and affection for you all, and for all that you did and suffered in the cause of freedom. There is indeed no substitute for experience. I know what you all accomplished, and I am most proud and honoured, and indeed most fortunate, to have been elected an Associate Member of the Association." Kenny John went on to explain that at an RAF Bomber Command dinner, "There were various nostalgic items for sale, including two sets of the Eagle Squadron plaques. I snapped them up, one set for the ESA and the other set for myself."

Another admired Englishman who flew with the Eagles in September and October 1941 was Flight Lieutenant Humphrey Trench Gilbert, immediately known as Gil. When another Gil entered the Squadron—Gilmore Daniel, an Oklahoma Indian—he became known as Danny, to avoid confusion. Gil Gilbert, a daring pilot with five enemy aircraft to his credit, was a very British gentleman with a pronounced British manner and an Oxonian accent so extreme that to some of the Americans it seemed almost that he was speaking a foreign tongue.

"Gil was really Sir Humphrey Gilbert, and he was my flight commander," recalls Danny Daniel. "He rode me real hard, and I liked him very much. Once, when I came too close in formation and didn't fly the way he thought I should, he made me go up and do aerobatics over the airdrome, where he could keep an eye on me, for an hour. We had some real good times at the Thatch, our favorite pub. In the War Museum in London, there is a life-size oil painting of Gil."

Daniel was shot down on a bomber escort mission October 13, 1941. Months later, in a German prison camp, he learned that Gilbert had been killed in an aircraft accident.

"Gil had a two-seater Jaguar with a trunk on the rear which some of us Eagles used to ride in. He also had a very good friend who was often with us. I can't recall his name, but I know he was flying with Gil when they were killed. We heard that they both were tanked up and made a bet that Gil could loop a Spitfire on takeoff with someone on his lap. They just missed doing it by two feet. Really a waste of two good men."

Although some of the Eagles assumed that Gilbert was titled, a colleague said he was not. He was the son of retired

Royal Navy Commander Walter Raleigh Gilbert of Compton Castle, Marldon, near Paignton, Devon. "As the great Elizabethan seafarers, Sir Walter Raleigh and Sir Humphrey Gilbert, were both Devonians and were half-brothers, I would think that Humphrey Trench Gilbert was a descendant of that heroic family, and cast in the same gallant mold," the friend said.

Gilbert was a squadron leader, commanding 65 East India Squadron, when his Spitfire crashed May 2, 1942, killing him and Flight Lieutenant D. G. Ross. A Court of Inquiry found that the Spitfire had pulled out of a dive, went into another dive, and apparently struck the ground while flying upside down, possibly after making a stall turn. The Inquiry Court report added: "Cause was that the aircraft had two occupants in cockpit, although a single-seater, resulting in loss of control, probably due to cramped cockpit (passenger was approximately 16 stone), so that there could be little room for control movement. No one had any foreknowledge of the flight. Decision to make this flight was partly due to drink taken earlier in the same day."

Peacetime often does to the gathering places of heroes what enemy action could not do—dissolves them. But memories can be of sterner stuff than time. Paul Pablo Salkeld wrote:

"The original Dispersal hut of 71 Squadron—TIMES SQUARE —was to have been given to the United States Air Force Museum, at Wright-Patterson Air Force Base, in Ohio, but it was demolished. A nearby hut was identical, so it was offered instead. I flew down to Debden to look it over, in mid-September 1973, and was just in time. The runways were lonely and bare. The station had been turned into a dog training center; the only remaining aircraft were a few gliders in the grass. Shades of the past came back vividly to pilots returning here in peacetime."

Salkeld received permission to land at Debden RAF Station "immediately before its closing in 1975. I claim to be the last Eagle to put a plane down there and to take off again—albeit only in a 150-hp Lycoming Beagle Pup."

Places, things, the echoes of people—memories.

"A Rhubarb July 24, 1942—Daymond, Taylor, Sprague, and Hopson. Sprague hit by flak but got home. . . . I have a pint pewter tankard engraved with the names of most of 71 Squadron, but no longer keep it at the local pub. Too many eyes on it, and someone tried to buy it.

"I hope it goes to a good home one day."

5

FORTUNES

"Accidents and air combat losses were constant reminders of death. A squadron commander tried to put it out of his mind, tried to say, 'Well, that's tough.' This didn't always work, because there were some to whom you felt a little closer," recalls ex-Squadron Leader Chesley Peterson.

The list of Eagles injured or killed in flying accidents, in weather, or simply failing to return from missions went on and on, documenting the painful, inescapable cost of military aviation. December 12, 1941—Ken Holder, Buena Park, California, failed to return from a convoy patrol. January 8, 1942—Jack Gilliland, of Pittsburg, Kansas, apparently mistaking ground fog for a cloud, flew into a street in Ipswich and was killed. April 27—Flight Sergeant Jack Wicker was heard over the radio telephone faintly saying he had been hit; two days later, his body was found washed ashore at Dover. May 4—Robert Brossmer and Ralph Freiberg failed to return from missions.

Jim Griffin remembers well some of the crises that plagued him and his comrades and their leaders.

"Accidents and crashes were almost part of the daily routine. Two weeks before I had gone to 71, Tootie Mason had been killed in a crash near Kirton-in-Lindsey; and four months later, Jimmy Daley and I would collide in the clouds over North Weald.

"Most of us soon fulfilled the qualification for the Iron Cross—responsibility for the destruction of an Allied plane. I was involved in two crashes—wiped out a Fleet Finch biplane during elementary training in Canada, and I ran out of petrol over the mountains in Scotland and tore the wings off a Hurricane—besides the Spit II wheels-up landing and the collision with Jim Daley in clouds over North Weald.

"The official reactions to these crashes were two terse comments in red ink in my log book—the group captain commanding North Weald when I landed the Spit II with undercarriage retracted simply wrote 'Faulty cockpit drill and lack of care.' The Hurricane brought an even briefer comment from the air officer commanding 81 group, 'Inexperience.'

"Undoubtedly, inexperience played a part in all the crashes, but the only one I ever felt guilty about was the one in the Fleet Finch, and that should have been labeled 'stupid lack of care.'

"I had taken off on a cold winter morning without waiting for the engine to warm, and at a thousand feet was sitting behind a dead prop. Fortunately, the field was surrounded by a wide expanse of snow covered fields, and it didn't take much skill to put the nose down and glide to a rather inglorious end in a snowbank. It wouldn't have been so embarrassing, but my tracks were plainly visible, and I had landed so fast that when I came to the first few fences I simply pulled back the stick and flew over them. When I finally lost speed, I ripped through fences, and ended up in the snowbank in a tangle of barbed wire.

"The second crash was a little more involved, and if writing off an Mk I Hurricane that had probably taken part in the Battle of Britain can be considered funny, a little more humorous.

"Because of the great differences in terrain and weather, navigation—map reading and homing by D/F (radio direction finding)—was stressed at operational training units in England.

"At 59 OTU, a few miles from the Scottish border, there were no restrictions, and usually, when you had to practice such maneuvers as aerobatics or low flying, you headed north into Scotland where the country was rougher and there were fewer villages.

"On the day I was fated to run out of gas, I headed north as usual, climbed to get above a layer of broken clouds, and began a series of slow rolls and loops; then, when I felt I was far enough away from traffic, stalled, put the Hurricane into a spin, recovered. I didn't pay any attention to where I was headed, and at the end of an hour's time, I didn't know whether I was over England or Scotland.

"Losing my bearings had been deliberate. I wanted to practice radio homing, and there was no danger of really getting lost, since I could always drop below the clouds and use visual navigation to get back to the field—famous last words!

"I called base, asked for a practice homing, and was instructed to circle so they could get a fix. That was normal. The controller would get a directional fix, subtract 180 degrees to get the reciprocal, and give me this figure as a heading. Unfortunately, the young aircraftsman I was in contact with had just started training as a controller and apparently hadn't learned that he was supposed to take a bearing on an aircraft and have the pilot fly the *reciprocal*; every heading I was told to fly during the next hour took me deeper into Scotland.

"The only thing that saved me from ending up in the highlands north of Glasgow was the fact that I began complaining that something was wrong. The patches of countryside I could see beneath the clouds were getting rougher, radio reception was getting weaker. I was constantly flying in circles to allow base to get another fix.

"Finally, what had started out as a practice homing turned into a real emergency. My main tanks were getting dangerously low, and my reserve tank would just about give me enough flying time to find a suitable place to make an emergency landing.

"I tried switching to an emergency channel, but except for my young friend at the training base, all I could get was static. I told him I didn't have time to do any more circling, as I was making an emergency landing. I turned off the radio, switched to the reserve tank, and headed for a hole in the clouds.

"Thankfully, there was about a 2,000-foot ceiling, and visibility was good under the clouds. I was surrounded by hills and most of the land was wooded, but a mile or so ahead lay a small valley that was a patchwork of green and brown fields. There wasn't much choice, so I throttled back and headed into the nearest field. When I got close, I could see that it was a pasture and was occupied by a herd of about 50 large cows.

"I had no idea what would happen if a Hurricane tried to plough through a herd of cows, and I wasn't particularly anxious to find out. I gunned the engine, and it quit. I don't know what made me reach over to the fuel selector and switch back to the main tanks. The engine caught again, lifted me over the cows, then died for good.

"The only choice left was two small fields that were separated by a harmless appearing hedge. There was an unbroken stretch of woods beyond, but if I could touch down at the edge of the first field, slice through the hedge . . .

"When I was over the edge of the first field I glanced down and saw that I was doing 120 mph. Again there was no choice. I shoved the stick forward, and the belly of the Hurricane bit hard into the dirt.

"Slice through a Scottish hedge! That was a laugh. What had appeared to be harmless bushes from the air turned out to be young oaks. Fortunately, the cockpit fit between two of these, but the wings didn't, and when I came out of shock a few moments later, I found myself sitting in a fuselage with no wings.

"I could smell gas, and there were clouds of glycol steam from the cooling system. It looked like smoke, and all I could think of was fire or an explosion. I fumbled with the safety harness, cursing the straps that a moment before had saved my life. Then I was free. I opened the hatch, climbed out of the cockpit and fell flat on my face.

"I wasn't injured, but at the moment, I couldn't stand, so I crawled away from the Hurricane like a damned sand crab. When I was a hundred feet away, I felt safe, but my troubles weren't over. I looked up and found myself staring at the tines of a pitchfork in the hands of a fierce looking Scottish farmer who was demanding to know whether I was German or English.

"It was too much. I was going to be impaled if I didn't convince him that I was English rather than German, and all I could do was point to the Canadian wings on my tunic and tell him that I was an American.

I started to laugh. The whole flight had been a bloody farce. I believe it was the RAF markings on the crippled old Hurricane that finally convinced him I must be some sort of ally.

"The collision with Jimmy Daley came about when he and I had been scrambled to intercept a bandit that had been detected crossing the channel. It was a miserable day for flying. Clouds down to 800 feet, patches of rain and ground fog.

"As soon as we were airborne, the controller instructed us to climb to Angels 12 (12,000 feet) and head for the coast. Jim levelled out for a few moments to allow me to get the wing of my Spit behind his, then he started to climb. Unfortunately, I hadn't had time to get tucked in properly, and as the clouds closed around us, I found myself slipping away.

"Actually, losing contact was of little consequence. Jim would simply alter his course 10 degrees to the left, I to the right, and we would meet above the clouds.

"I was busy for perhaps a minute, adjusting the air speed, turning to the proper heading, setting the rate of climb. I don't know why I looked up from the instrument panel. There shouldn't have been anything outside but clouds, but suddenly Jim's plane was directly ahead, not converging as might be expected, but coming in from 90 degrees so that I was about to hit him broadside.

"I reacted instinctively, slammed the control column forward and went under him, knocking off his tail wheel and part of his tail.

"For a moment, it appeared that my own situation was critical. The instruments were fluctuating wildly, and since two of the three steel blades on the prop had split and curled back a foot from the end, the plane was vibrating violently. I was sure the engine would tear itself out of its mounts. I opened the hatch and was preparing the jump when I noticed that the air speed was steady, and the gyro horizon, although rolling from side to side, was centered enough that I could keep the wings level, and climb.

"I would like to say that I decided not to bail out because of concern for what might happen when the plane hit the ground—there were farms and villages below, and only a short while before, two other 121 pilots had collided, bailed out, and their planes had killed three people. The truth is, I wasn't sure I still had enough altitude to jump safely, and the tail of the Spit had suddenly taken on gigantic proportions.

"I called Jim, but received no answer. I didn't know 'till later that his radio was not working properly. He could receive, but not transmit.

"I managed to climb, and when I broke through the clouds at 12,000 feet, I levelled out and throttled back as much as possible to reduce the vibration. Usually, the sun was a blind spot to be leary of, but this day, it was beautiful.

"However, the relief of being able to see more than a hundred feet didn't last long. I called Ops to report that Blue 1 had crashed and to ask for an emergency homing. They gave me a heading, and when I acknowledged, told me to start losing altitude.

"Letting down into that cloud band, I didn't know how much vibration the average engine mount could withstand, or whether or not there would be any warning of failure. Such questions became academic as I neared 1,000 feet; below that, you rode whatever you had left in the way of an aircraft into the ground.

"At 800 feet, I broke out of the clouds again and breathed a sigh of relief. Not only because there was a wide expanse of open fields under me, but North Weald lay directly ahead, and all I had to do was reduce speed, let down the gear, and make a straight-in approach.

"When I taxied up to the dispersal hut and cut the engine, Jim was waiting beside the Spit that had just lost its tail wheel and part of its tail. He walked over, inspected the curled prop, and grinned, 'Where you been, Griff? I've been back for half an hour.'

I never understood how Jim Daley and I had gotten broadside after climbing a thousand feet on roughly parallel courses, but stranger things had happened.

"A Canadian friend had been climbing through clouds a few weeks earlier, when suddenly he had the sensation that he was in a power dive. His instruments indicated that he was at 20,000 feet and gaining altitude, but the G forces were building, pressing him back against the seat. He blacked out.

"Of course, there could have been a reasonable explanation for everything that happened to him up to that point—a loss of oxygen would play strange tricks—but it's the rest of the story that was a little unbelievable.

"A constable standing in a small park in the center of a town below heard the scream of a diving plane. He looked up and saw a Hurricane break out of the clouds at 3,000 feet. As soon as it was clear of the clouds the plane exploded.

"My friend didn't remember a thing about what happened from the time he blacked out till he woke up in a hospital. His safety harness had somehow become unhooked, he had cleared the wreckage, the rip cord of his parachute had been pulled, and he had floated down to land beside the constable in the park.

"Probably the strangest thing that ever happened to me was the dream I had the morning 'Tootie'—Earl Mason—was killed.

"*Sept. 15, 1941: Tiger Patrol—Army Cooperation*, is the way the day is recorded in my log book. Ironically, it had been a day when 121 Squadron was 'non-operational,' no sweeps, no convoy patrols, just a day of mock strafing attacks on British Army units practicing maneuvers.

"Cliff Thorpe and I had drawn the dawn patrol, and were more than a little resentful that we had to crawl out of bed in the darkness, down a quick cup of tea, and play war with the army. We scoured the area between Kirton-in-Lindsey and the North Sea for an hour and a half, and whenever we spotted a lorry, or tank, or even suspected that a grove of trees might be hiding the 'enemy,' we dove down and roared over the tree tops, gunning the engines to disturb army breakfasts as much as possible.

"Of course, not all flying was interesting or exciting, and up to that day, I thought the most boring thing a pilot could do was practice touch-and-go landings, or circle endlessly around a convoy of ships plowing slowly through the North Sea. However, boredom at several hundred miles an hour is purely a state of mind, and before the day was over, it would become apparent that playing at war could be just as deadly as operational flying.

"Cliff and I were content to confine our mock attacks to power dives, but an hour or so later, Tootie Mason would roar down to within a few feet of a line of tanks, raise the nose of his Hurricane above the horizon and begin a series of slow rolls.

"When Cliff and I landed and taxied up to the dispersal area, I could see Tootie and Bert Stewart walking toward the Hurricanes they would fly on the next patrol.

"Tootie has been described as 'a feisty, aggressive little guy,' and in the air he was certainly that—a tough fighter pilot—but on the ground, he was friendly, gentle, considerate. When I shut down the engine and climbed out of the cockpit, I found that he had veered over to my plane and was standing by the wing tip. He grinned, and patted me on the shoulder, 'You look tired, Jim. Go get some sleep.'

"I *was* tired. Cliff and I had closed the local pub and had had about three hours sleep. When we reached our room, we were both too weary to pull aside the blackout curtains and open the windows. As a consequence it was hot and stuffy, and I spent a restless hour or so tossing fitfully.

"I usually don't remember dreams, but the one I had that morning was so vivid I can still close my eyes and see the trail of black smoke that was left by a Hurricane as it flew over a forest, pulled up into a loop, and came down and crashed.

"I woke up at that point. Cliff was sitting on the edge of his cot, and I guess I looked so strange that he asked what was wrong. I tried to describe the vividness of the dream, but he looked a little skeptical. I think that at that moment, he was equating dreams with warm beer hangovers.

"A short while later, we were on our way to the dining room when a pilot from one of the British squadrons stopped us. 'Did you hear about Tootie?'

"I never checked the time element. Cliff and I had washed and dressed after I told him about the dream. Tootie had patted me on the shoulder—I was certainly the last person he had ever touched—had taken off and crashed while doing a slow roll. Why I had pictured a loop, rather than a roll, if indeed there was some sort of strange connection between Tootie and myself those last few seconds, I don't know. I do know the dream could have occurred at the exact moment Tootie crashed."

Don Smith, of Paris, Texas, had a nerve-shattering experience on his first mission in an Eagle squadron, a sweep into France. "At about 27,000 feet, the first piece of flak I ever did see hit the coolant system of my plane. I pulled away from the squadron, and headed back to England. The engine overheated, and I shut it down and glided in for a landing in a wheatfield."

On another occasion that day, Smith's roommate had to bail out of his disabled plane and was missing. Then Smith returned from his third sortie of the day to find a draft board summons that had been forwarded from Texas.

"I tossed my draft notice into the wastebasket, and moved my friend's cigarettes to my own side of the room, I was very glad to return the cigarettes later that night when he showed up. And I had no qualms about leaving the draft notice where it was."

Then there's the hazardous mixture of well-meant passion and live ammo. Bert Stewart recalls that a Polish fighter squadron stationed with the Eagles at one time was considered a special hazard in poor visibility conditions. "We knew those Poles had guts and a willingness to fight, but sometimes their judgment was bad. One time, we took off on a mission in foul weather, and as we orbited around I saw one of the Poles split off. It looked like he was getting ready to make a gunnery pass—one Spit after another Spit—so I gave a good little roll, hoping he would take a look and see my markings.

"Instead, he came in firing at me, everything blazing. When he went screaming past me, I could hear his cannon going off. I landed, went to the Polish squadron, and grabbed the guy and picked him up. I told Wing Commander Duke-Woolley, 'Don't ever let him go up again.' The Pole was transferred out right after that."

Dixie Alexander remembers the Poles shooting down a Ju 88 bomber. The plane crash landed in a field, and the German crew attempted to scatter. "The Poles alerted their whole squadron," Alexander says. "For the next couple of hours, they played hare and hounds, strafing the running Germans and everything else in the area. If I'm not mistaken, they cracked up two aircraft in that incident."

Of course, the fortunes of war were often dictated by the nature of the enemy, by what sort of an opponent an Eagle may draw in a fight. Was the German an easy mark—green, dumb, slow—or would he turn out to be an *Experte*, as the good *fliers* in the Luftwaffe were called, or simply an accomplished killer who knew all the tricks and who was, like the Allied high scorer, a true tiger?

What was the appraisal of the German fighter pilot by his American adversary? Leo Nomis, of Sherman Oaks, California, comments: "Some of the related issues and factors that played a great part in the comedy-tragedy of that age are often ignored or passed over. One of these was the quality of the enemy during the key years of 1941–1942.

"It is a matter of record that there were then no terrifically high scoring individuals in any of the Eagle Squadrons. One reason, in my mind, was the extremely efficient quality of the Jerry pilots in north France at that time.

"Due to their commitment in Russia, the Germans had to leave the defense of the West to more widely distributed but elite units. As 71 Squadron did not get into real action until the summer of 1941, right after the German invasion of Russia, this situation prevailed during the whole period of the Eagle sweeps.

"It is probably to everyone's credit in the Eagles—a hodgepodge of pilots with varying experience and skills, some of whom, sadly, should never have been in the skies over the Western Front, and some of whom were extremely good— that the record stands as it does.

"I know I asked myself, when the initial impact of reality dawned on me, what the hell I was doing there. I felt in that early phase, and correctly so, that I was sadly lacking, and was, in effect, a ridiculous figure in a tragic situation.

"Schlageter JG-26, more familiarly known as the Abbeville Boys, was a real thorn to the Eagles—and to the entire RAF in that area. They had Me 109s in 1941, and became really menacing when they were issued Fw 190s for the "spring festival" of 1942. In five years, they claimed to have destroyed more than 2,700 Allied planes. One unit was known as the Squadron of Aces.

"Because of the geographical aspect of the battles, it was impossible to know the enemy closely or individually. They were vague and sinister shapes in aircraft that always seemed to be faster and higher than ours.

"Walter Nowotny was one in that group who eventually achieved super acedom, and eventually gave his life. I'm sure it was Nowotny, then an up and coming sergeant pilot, who picked off Ben Mays in the first 71 Squadron sweep of the 1942 season, on April 12.

"Research on certain individual tactics that Nowotny employed certainly points to this. In this case, it was simply a single Focke-Wulf gaining superior speed from above and way behind, dropping down, and then pulling up under an entire squadron of 12 aircraft of 71 Squadron, led by Peterson, and hanging briefly in a vertical position, pumping various rounds into a No. 4 man—in this case Mays—who never knew what hit him, and then half rolling out and away. I was a bit shaken, and felt a real sadness at Mays' departure. He was one of those Texas people who quietly had a somehow soothing philosophy for everything.

"The abundance of Allied combat films released *later* in the war invariably showed enemy aircraft patiently absorbing salvos of bullets with a minimum of evasive action. The pilots of those machines must have been inexperienced. It was a rare day, in 1942, when we ran into this type of German oaf, who flew along straight and level. I, for one, somehow never managed to engage such a type, and I am sure the Eagles would have run up much higher scores if the competition had not been so adept on the Western Front that year.

"Getting blasted without seeing the enemy happened more frequently than one might imagine, especially with pilots on initial combat runs or those with the inability to readjust the eye for various ranges. Then there were the he-who-hesitates-is-lost types, such as Forrest P. 'Pappy' Dowling, who was in the fantastic dogfight on a sweep in late 1941, wherein 71 and the two sister squadrons of the North Weald Wing were jumped by an eventual total of over 70 Me 109s.

"Pappy watched an aircraft approaching his rear very rapidly, but decided to delay evasive action until he ascertained whether the machine hurtling toward him had a single radiator under the wing as did the Spitfire, or one under each wing as did the Me. He saw that it had the two at approximately the same instant that his aircraft began to mildly disintegrate. He barely made it back to England, and crash landed in a field. His main injury was a broken collar bone, but as in so many cases where a traumatic experience accompanied one's initial combat, it destroyed his keenness. He didn't want to go on any more sweeps. He had also just gotten married, which added to this reluctance.

"I had roomed with Pappy in the early days at 71, and had known him at Glendale. He was an excellent pilot, having had considerable civilian experience around Dallas, and he was probably the best instrument pilot in the squadron. He continued on at 71 for a few more months after he recuperated, but nothing escaped Squadron Leader Peterson, and Dowling

was transferred to an OTU. It's just an example of the early
side effects of combat—of the coming face to face with destruction and of one's reactions."

On July 31, 1942, on a bomber escort mission, Hugh
Kennard, Bill Kelly, and Frank Boyles each shot down a
German plane and Barry Mahon and Sel Edner got two each,
for the largest single-mission score run up by 121 Squadron.

On the same day that 121 Squadron rolled up its highest
battle score, it lost its newest member, Norman Young. Also
on that day, 133 Squadron suffered its most grievous air
combat loss: three pilots—Grant Eugene "Ike" Eichar, Carter
Woodruff Harp and Coburn Clark King were killed, and
Jessie Taylor was very badly wounded. Squadron mate Dick
Alexander noted that Coby King was highly experienced as a
ferry pilot and RCAF flight instructor before joining the RAF,
and he called Harp "one of the finest pilots I ever flew with."

"Woody Harp had been a wing walker, and he enjoyed
surprising us with little feats of daredeviltry," Alexander said.
"Once he removed his shoes in front of the Administration
building on the base and proceeded to climb up the brick wall,
hanging on to the corners, and then walking about on the
cornice of the roof."

Eichar was a great-grandson of James O. Grant, a Civil
War veteran who was a second cousin of President Ulysses S.
Grant. On the squadron register, however, he always used the
name of Eldon Eichar. Eichar had been an Eagle Scout and
troop scoutmaster. In high school, in Elgin, Illinois, where he
won letters in football and basketball, he also won the
American Legion "Boy of the Year" award for courage, honor,
leadership, service, and scholarship. "Ike was my roommate,
and just a real fine person to live with," Alexander said. "He
was quiet, had an easy sense of humor, and was really not as
shy as he outwardly appeared to be. He was good fun."

Leo Nomis reminisces about yet another teammate and
a different mood.

"If ever there was a Gary Cooper type, Long John Flynn
fit it. His past seemed obscure. I think he was from Chicago
originally. He was one of the few married pilots. His wife was
a very fine English girl. Brought me some peanut butter when
I was in the hospital at Ipswich after a crash.

"Flynn was a fixture at 71 when I arrived there November 1, 1941. I flew in Red Section A Flight as his No. 2 man

during part of that winter. The conversation when he and I were together sometimes consisted of no words at all.

"Long John went out on a sweep on a real bright day when spring had rolled around, and like so many at that time, he just never came back. It was the same action in which little Oscar Coen and Mike McPharlin shot down three Fw's. I did not participate in it due to a nose broken in a recent crash.

"The day before, Flynn and I had gone pheasant hunting in the fields around Martlesham, he with a formidable shotgun, and I with an ancient .22 that wouldn't hit anything. The most vivid thing I remembered about the day was that he had killed a big pheasant on the fly, and when I walked over to him, he was gazing down at the dead bird with a sad, preoccupied expression on his face.

"That night, he bought a bottle of wine from the mess bar, and we had the service cook prepare the pheasant for us; and he and I—no one else, he and I—dined on it. The dinner itself, in the mess dining room after everyone else had gone, had a strange depression about it.

"We ate in silence, and then the next day he was gone, and it was such a delightful spring day that no one could believe it. That evening, I missed Flynn more than I could remember missing anyone, but it was the fashion in those days to keep such things to one's self."

In the April 27, 1942, engagement in which John Flynn was killed, Squadron Leader Peterson accounted for two of the five German planes shot down by Eagle pilots, and damaged a third. Other RAF squadrons accounted for five more enemy planes, and the British teams lost four pilots.

"We were bombing St. Omer heavily when the Focke-Wulfs tried to dive on our bombers, and Pete gave the order to dive on them," Art Roscoe told reporters.

"Pete fired a burst at one Hun. It rolled, and went straight into the ground. Then he saw five more below him. He attacked one, and it crashed. He went after another, and saw pieces falling from it.

"We got between the attackers and the bombers, and were able to keep the Huns away, but then 15 more Fw's dived on us. For about 10 minutes, the sky was absolutely filled with planes."

Roscoe and Robert Sprague, of San Diego, were credited with probably destroying two of the enemy aircraft. William

"Abie" O'Regan's plane was hit badly, but he nursed it gently back to England. That evening, back at the base, Pete Peterson and actress-dancer Audrey Boyes announced their engagement.

About the mood of the time, Leo Nomis again recalls, "Then there was 'Gentleman Jim' Crowley, with whom I flew most of that winter as No. 2. We called ourselves Twig Section. I don't know why—it was one of the childishly silly things that people did then. We even had a Twig Section theme song to the tune of *Old McDonald's Farm*. I remember we'd roar with laughter when we sang it in unison.

"We all seemed to laugh a lot that year. We made a joke out of everything, and it helped us face what was waiting for us. Jim was a bit older than most of us, an extremely clever pilot with a high I.Q. and also an obscure past. Upon hearing the Base CO's congratulations on the downing of three Fw's that day, Crowley offered to trade them back for Long John Flynn.

"Crowley got married to a WAAF officer that spring. He had been saving a bottle of rare Scotch for the occasion. We were rooming together at the time, and I had found the precious bottle's hiding place. I had consumed at least half the contents several days before the wedding. He discovered it the day before the ceremony and called me a son-of-a-bitch.

"Notwithstanding this little falling out, Crowley and I were quite close. I was sorry to see him transferred as a Flight Commander to 121, and I flew down to visit him at Southend a couple of weeks before Art Roscoe and I were posted to Malta that summer. We reminisced over the past as if it had been 10 years before. After I took off for Debden from Southend that day, I never saw Jim again."

Something puzzling: there were two Gentleman Jims in 71 Squadron. On paper, in the personnel files, they were enough alike to be twins—green eyed, brown haired, around 160 pounds in weight, about 5 feet 8 inches tall. Gentleman Jim Crowley, Gentleman Jim DuFour.

An entry of July 14, 1941, in the RAF Operations Record Book of 71 Squadron, says: "P/O Crowley and P/O Driver arrived on posting from 56 OTU." The entry for July 17 shows Pilot Officers W. R. Driver and W. R. Crowley taking part in their first mission, high altitude escort for bombers.

Not until July 28 does the Records Book correct the initials to identify Crowley as J. J., not W. R.—James J. Crowley.

On August 5, just 22 days after he joined the squadron, W. R. Driver was killed when his plane failed to come out of a dive. He had had time to take part in only eight missions. Crowley, meanwhile, went on 14 missions in August—bomber escort, convoy patrol, sweeps over enemy territory—an average of about one every other day. September and October were almost as busy, but with the approach of winter flying conditions, activity slackened. Crowley flew only 10 missions in the first two months of 1942, and nine in March. His last missions were two on April 24, one on April 27, and three on April 28, 1942. After that, his name never appeared in the Operations Record Book.

When a pilot dropped out of Squadron activity, the Record Book usually noted the reason: posted to another unit, missing, hospitalized, captured by the enemy—or dead. For Gentleman Jim Crowley, nothing; simply, no further mention. Some 34 years later, in 1974, the roster of the Eagle Squadron Association still carried his name on its list of 157 deceased Eagles.

Gentleman Jim DuFour, born in Oakland, California, in 1909, was commissioned in the RAF in November, 1940. He joined 71 Squadron at North Weald July 3, 1941, the same month as that shown for Jim Crowley. The first combat mission for him was noted in the Records Book as of April 29, 1942, the day after Crowley's name was listed for the last time. Furthermore, although DuFour, like Crowley, was known as Gentleman Jim, his first name was not Jim but John. His full name: John Guilbert DuFour.

By the end of the war, DuFour had flown in combat 1,500 hours—including 350 hours on 115 combat missions with the Eagles. He was credited with destroying two Messerschmitt 109s, probably destroying a third, and damaging two. He was awarded the Distinguished Flying Cross, the Air Medal with three Oak Leaf Clusters, and two Presidential Unit citations.

Along with most of the other Eagles, DuFour transferred from the RAF into the USAAF 4th Fighter Group. By March, 1943, he had risen to the command of 336 Squadron, which had been formed out of the old 133 Eagle Squadron. In

September, 1943, DuFour became Deputy Commander of Combat Operations at Headquarters, VIII Fighter Command.

In 1975, DuFour unraveled the puzzle of the twin Jims.

"You ask about the name Crowley. It goes like this.

"Shortly after war broke out in Europe, I went up to Canada and tried to join the RCAF. I was turned down because at that time, the Roosevelt neutrality pact was strictly adhered to, and I returned to the States. Unable to buy passage to Europe for love or money, I returned to Canada and enlisted in the Seaforth Highlanders. I did so under the name of Crowley and as a Canadian citizen, because they already had my name of DuFour from my earlier attempt to join the RCAF."

The Californian applied for fighter duty with the RAF, and when he was accepted, it seemed easier, and less likely to cause a lot of paperwork, to retain his false identity than to try to reestablish his real name and his United States citizenship. However, he fell in love with an Englishwoman, and decided to get married. He hired a lawyer to reclaim his real name and nationality.

"The Air Ministry stood the squadron down on my wedding day, May 9, 1942—no missions," DuFour recalls.

Scrapbooks and faded letters oft-time shine a revealing light on the too-brief lives of airmen who gave their lives in World War II. This letter from Miss Anne A. Hoxie to Mrs. Marguerite Anderson, Washington, D.C., postmarked Shannock, Rhode Island, February 2, 1944, is an example. In response to Miss Hoxie's query, the War Department had informed her that Mrs. Anderson was next of kin (mother) to red-haired, blue-eyed Captain Stanley M. M. Anderson, formerly of 71 Eagle Squadron. Miss Hoxie wrote:

Last June two letters which I had written to your son were returned to me marked "missing in action."

I knew almost nothing about Stanley except what pertained to his daily routine and was related to the service. It might have been two years ago that he received some cigarettes which my brother and myself had sent to the American Eagles in London. We both are intensely interested in our men who are doing the flying over across, and wanted to make some gesture to show it.

Your son acknowledged the cigarettes and in that way we have had several letters from him. The last one was to tell us of his DFC and his commission as captain, all of which we rejoiced in.

This letter was dated April 10th and was his last. It was my reply to it, congratulating him, that was returned to me in June, 1943.

I had a feeling when I answered his letter that he soon would be undertaking missions that would be dangerous. For the once, I became personal to the extent of asking if he had parents living, or possibly a wife or sweetheart. I knew that if he met with any accident, I would want to write.

We liked your son's letters for something which bespoke his integrity and quiet dignity, also his enthusiasm for his work. In writing to the War Department I hoped that if he were a prisoner of war, we might locate him and through the Red Cross do something for his comfort. We wanted him to know that we would not let him down, because he was so fine and we appreciated him.

I am not a young woman. My war work was done in the last war, and in this one my health has not permitted me to be too active. So I have given up my time to writing the boys in the service and cheering them on as far as is within my powers.

I know that you will accept my sincerity and believe that both my brother and myself are in full sympathy with you. Charles, my brother, will never for a moment admit there is a doubt about Stanley's coming back and his ability to take care of himself. He will never allow me to have any doubts or express any. That is why now I can write you and ask if you will be so kind as to advise me if any definite word comes to you. Until then, may you be given the strength and courage and hope to go on.

Army Air Force Headquarters in Washington sent Mrs. Anderson a letter March 7, 1944, enclosing photographs of the presentation to her by Gen. H. S. Hansell of the Distinguished Flying Cross and Air Medal with three Oak-leaf Clusters that had been awarded to First Lieutenant Anderson. The letter added, "The Army Air Forces join you in the pride you must feel in your son's distinguished record of meritorious achievement in aerial flight."

The DFC citation, dated March 20, 1943, was for exceptionally meritorious service in 10 fighter combat missions over enemy territory in Europe. The Air Medal was for shooting down a Focke-Wulf 190 with his Spitfire in combat over Europe October 2, 1942. The Oak-leaf Clusters were for action as a Spitfire pilot on 10 combat missions in the last four months of 1942, and for shooting down two German planes early in 1943.

Yet another letter was sent to Marguerite M. Anderson, dated May 8, 1945, from Captain Edgar H. Brohm, 4th Fighter Group Chaplain.

> Pursuant to request from the Commanding Officer, we desire to inform you of the information we have received with regard to the change of status of your son. He had been reported as missing in action. According to official information, his status has now been changed to determined dead, as of 15 April, 1944.
>
> We know that you have been awaiting further news of your son, and it grieves us to pass on this information as we deeply sympathize with you at your loss. . . . Our few words of consolation are small and seemingly inadequate, yet we assure you that you are in our prayers and thoughts.
>
> Your son gave up his life that freedom again may be born on this earth and that this world may live in peace. His sacrifice will live for long on the list of our gallant dead. He served his country well and now rests from his labors. May God grant you His blessing of grace and comfort in your sorrow.

As Pete Peterson said, "There were some to whom you felt a little closer." For some, the closeness and individual care expressed made the blows of the fortunes of war at least less harsh.

The Eagles entered the war with determination and the Hawker Hurricane. Above, the cowl of Wendell Pendleton's Hawker reflects the Eagles' spirit. At right, Robert G. Patterson with his Hurricane.

As 71 Squadron was being formed, left to right: Gus Daymond, Ed Bateman, Chesley Peterson, Dean Satterlee, Squadron CO William Taylor, Honorary CO Charles Sweeny, Richard "Jim" Moore, Byron Kennerly, Hillard Fenlaw, and Jim McGinnis.

Under the threat of Luftwaffe attack, "at readiness" meant being set to mount up and take off in five or thirty minutes. From left: Ben Mays, Mike Kelly, Harold Strickland and Tom Andrews on five-minute call.

At left (left to right): Eagles Eugene Tobin, Peter Provenzano, Sam Mauriello and Luke Allen enact a scramble to their Hurricanes for the press. The heavy suits worn by three of them are actually bomber crew gear and weren't used by the pilots "on ops."

Eagles wait for orders at the 71 Squadron Ops Building, North Weald, in early 1941. Left to right: Gus Daymond, John DuFour, Ross Scarborough, Art Roscoe, Chesley Peterson, Hubert L. Stewart, Charles Tribken, Thomas C. Wallace, Newton Anderson, and engineering officer W.A. Becker.

No. 71 Squadron pilot Jim Gray in his Spitfire. The fold-down side made for easy access. Another 71 pilot (below): Vic Bono.

Five 71 Squadron pilots during the tough early days (left to right): Nat Maranz, Andy Mamedoff, Gene Tobin, Luke Allen, Kenneth Taylor.

A pause for a royal visitor from the Netherlands. Left to right: Ed Bateman, Andy Mamedoff, Robert Sweeny, Prince Bernhardt, CO Bill Taylor, and J.R. "Robbie" Robinson, who was destined to become Lord Martonmere. Such visits and attendant publicity meant much to the Allies' propaganda and morale boosting campaigns.

Members of 71 Squadron pose in front of the officers' mess. Back row (from left): Stanley Kolendorski, Gregory Daymond, Vernon Keough, Andrew Mamedoff, Luke Allen, Byron Kennerly, Chesley Peterson, Ed Orbison, and Jim McGinnis. Front row (from left), British officers: Pilot Officer F.N.B. Bennett, Flight Lieutenant George Brown, Squadron Leader Walter Churchill, Flight Lieutenant R.C. Wilkinson, and Assistant Adjutant F.H. Tann.

Gene B. Fetrow   Denver "Lucky" Miner   Leon Blanding

The Spitfire, which seized air superiority in the critical days. These are Mark VCs of the 126th Squadron at Luqua Airfield, Malta. No. "E" is Eagle Pilot Officer Reade Tilley's.

Pilot Officer William Robert Dunn, first U.S. WW II ace, who began his war career as a mortar man in the Seaforth Islanders.

No. 133 Squadron Leader Carroll "Red" McColpin and Flight Sergeant Richard "Dixie" Alexander at Great Samford Airdrome after a sweep into France. The year was 1942.

Right: Clarence "Whitey" Martin, 121 Squadron, in his Hurricane at Kirton-in-Lindsey, July 1941. Far right: George B. Sperry.

The Messerschmitt 109E was Germany's air-superiority fighter in the worst days of the Battle of Britain. (*U.S. Air Force photo*)

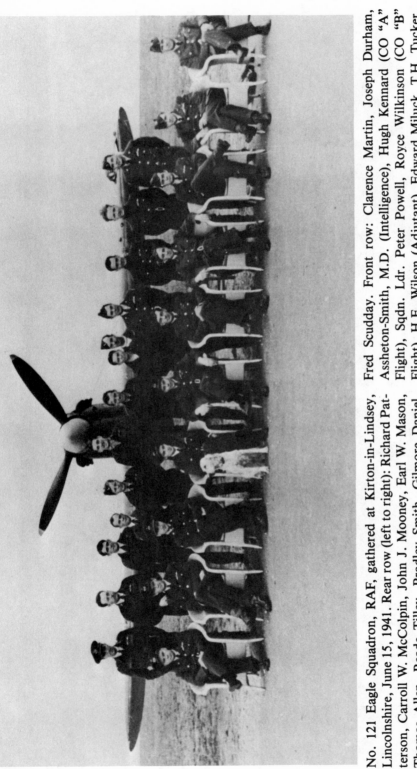

No. 121 Eagle Squadron, RAF, gathered at Kirton-in-Lindsey, Lincolnshire, June 15, 1941. Rear row (left to right): Richard Patterson, Carroll W. McColpin, John J. Mooney, Earl W. Mason, Thomas Allen, Reade Tilley, Bradley Smith, Gilmore Daniel, Hubert Stewart, Donald Geffene, William Jones, Warren Shenk, Fred Scudday. Front row: Clarence Martin, Joseph Durham, Assheton-Smith, M.D. (Intelligence), Hugh Kennard (CO "A" Flight), Sqdn. Ldr. Peter Powell, Royce Wilkinson (CO "B" Flight), H.E. Wilson (Adjutant), Edward Miluck, T.H. Tucker, Vivian Watkins.

No. 133 Eagle Squadron, RAF, gathered at Biggin Hill, Kent, June 10, 1942. Rear row (left to right): Leonard T. Ryerson, George H. Middleton, Richard N. Beaty, Ervin L. Miller, Dick D. Gudmundsen, Donald Lambert, Donald S. Gentile, J.M. Emerson, (Intelli- William A. Arends, Gilbert Omens, Edwin D. Taylor, Coburn C. King, Sqdn. Ldr. Eric Hugh Thomas, Donald Blakeslee, George B. Sperry, Eric Doorly, K.K. Kimbro, William H. Baker. Missing from the picture due to injuries or leave are Carroll McColpin, M.E.

Those on a "show," fight it out; those who wait, sweat it out. Watching at Biggin Hill for returning flights after a 133 sweep are (from left): J.M. Emerson (Intelligence), Pilot Officer Bill Slade, Flying Officers George Sperry, Coburn King, Eric Doorly, "Jack" Jackson, Bill Baker, Edwin D. Taylor, and Bill Arends, P/O Fletcher Hancock, and F/O Carl Miley.

The first three Eagles to receive the RAF's DFC (from left): Carroll W. McColpin, Chesley G. Peterson and Gregory Daymond, posing with Sholto Douglas and Charles Sweeny.

His Majesty honors his American pilots. King George VI visited the Eagles at Bournemouth in October 1941. Left to right (foreground): Queen Elizabeth, F/L Penguin, P/O Carl Bodding, P/O Jack Evans (profile behind King George), King George, P/O Gilbert Omens, P/O William Baker, and P/O Barry Mahon.

6

MALTA, ALAMEIN AND BEYOND

Malta was often called Britain's unsinkable aircraft carrier. It was also one of those points, critically targeted by the Axis, which suffered deep wounds, endured great agonies and *held*, marking turning points in the fateful year of 1942. Other such points were Midway, Stalingrad and, in North Africa, El Alamein. At Malta and in North Africa, Eagles from America helped turn the war around.

Located to the south of Sicily and east of Tunisia, Malta was a constantly galling factor among the Axis' pressing logistical problems. Mussolini had hoped to make the Mediterranean his domain. But the presence of the British Navy and unconquered Malta put one more great stamp of vanity on Il Duce's affectations.

If Malta could not be sunk or conquered, perhaps it could be laid waste. In June, 1940, the day after Italy entered the war, Mussolini's air force began the campaign. Before long, the Luftwaffe joined in, subjecting the island to such severe punishment for so long a time, that in 1942, Britain awarded the entire population the George Cross for heroism.

The aerial siege of Malta was as killing as the Battle of Britain, and the RAF acquitted itself there as splendidly. The

British did have one advantage—as they had had over England —for they had secretly installed on Malta the first experimental radar station to be shipped out of the United Kingdom. The device gave the island 15 minutes' invaluable warning against the approach of enemy bombers. Outnumbered, weary, short on equipment and supplies, the RAF needed all the breaks it could find or make, including the infusion of new talent and blood in the form of Yank pilots.

In May, 1942, the British Air Ministry disclosed for the first time that Eagles were taking part in the defense of Malta. A typical London dateline story resulting from that announcement stated:

> Sweeping over the French coast was much too tame for 20-odd American pilots fighting with the Royal Air Force, so they volunteered for transfer to the hot spot of oft-bombed Malta.
>
> The Air Ministry disclosed how the Americans asked for the Malta assignment today while simultaneously revealing a few of the exploits of the pilots.
>
> In a recent air duel over Malta, which lasted only 60 seconds, Pilot Officers Donald William McLeod, of Norwich, Connecticut, and James Elvidge Peck, Berkeley, California, former members of the RAF Eagle Squadrons, each downed a German bomber. Then one nonchalantly radioed the other, "Okay—that's today's. Let's go home."

An insight into how Malta preoccupied the British command and affected the thinking of many Eagles is provided by Harold Strickland. "Art Roscoe, Leo Nomis, Reade Tilley and other Eagles from all three squadrons—Doug Booth, Fred Scudday and Hiram Putnam, from Bobville, Texas—got together in London and found that a Spitfire pilot from any squadron would be welcome to volunteer for besieged Malta. If any Spitfire pilot in any squadron almost anywhere volunteered, RAF Fighter Command could rush him off to Malta almost immediately.

"Normally, transfers were coordinated with the respective squadron and wing commanders, at least for courtesy purposes, but they had no veto over a transfer to Malta, the unsinkable aircraft carrier, where warm incoming bodies were most welcome.

"I decided that for me, with only one inconclusive dog-fight under my belt, it would be preferable to commit suicide later in my fighter pilot career than earlier."

Reflecting on the nightmarish battle conditions there, Malta ace Reade Tilley takes issue with the idea that almost any pilot would be accepted for Malta duty. "This is simply conjecture and not true. Sending inexperienced pilots to Malta was bitterly contested. The Air Officer Commanding sent ranking envoys to England to beg Air Ministry not to do this, because often, that could be a death warrant for the novice. In the desperate fight for the survival of Malta, the cost in Spitfires, food, petrol, etc., would be irreplaceable."

Although several American pilots lost their lives while flying missions out of Malta, the records indicate that only one of those victims had come there from an Eagle Squadron. Hiram Aldine Putnam, of 133 Squadron, was killed in action April 21, 1942. However, Group Captain Walter Myers Churchill, the British pilot who commanded the first Eagle Squadron, 71, when it was established, also was killed, on an operation from Malta to Sicily August 27, 1942. Of approximately a dozen other Eagles in the Malta campaigns, many escaped death or serious injury by what they called sheer luck, pure chance.

Nick Sintetos was among several Eagles aboard four aircraft carriers delivering pilots and planes to Malta. The convoy, about 20 miles off Algiers, included the *Furious*, the *Eagle*, the *Victorious* and the *Indomitable*; plus 2 battleships —the *Rodney* and *Nelson*—2 heavy cruisers, about 20 destroyers, 13 merchant vessels and the tanker *Ohio*.

Sintetos recalls that "One carrier—the *Eagle*—was torpedoed just as we were taking off from the *Furious*. The *Eagle* carried a load of Hurricane fighters intended for Malta, and she sank in four minutes.

"I took off in the first group of four Spitfires. We had small blocks of wood wedged in our flaps to give as added lift. They were to be dropped after takeoff, by our lowering the flaps.

"Taking off from a carrier, especially in a land plane, makes for a tense feeling. All those other Spitties are in back of you awaiting their turn, and you hope your kite starts up all right and you don't pull a stupid thing to mess up an important operation. It all happens fast, once you start up.

"The *Furious* had a rise in the flight deck about two-thirds of the way down. When I hit this rise during takeoff, I kind of bounced into the air and never even got a chance to use full throttle.

"The *Furious*' call sign, by the way, was PYFFO, meaning 'pull your fat finger out.'"

Leo Nomis recalled one particular Malta engagement because its outcome was so unexpected.

"Eight of us in the tropical Spits—we flew without cockpit canopies out there—were bounced by six extremely clever Kesselring 109s. There was an exceptionally high wind blowing, which carried everyone in the ensuing dogfight miles downwind of the island.

"It was one of those brilliantly clear mornings that somehow stay in one's memory. The wind had been blowing hard during the night, and was continuing this day, with tremendous gusts causing long streamers of spray across the sea surface.

"At the time, I was still suffering the after effects of sand fly fever, and found myself to be quite weak when we got into the air. This fact, together with the turbulence, made it necessary for me to use both hands on the control column.

"We climbed to about 15,000 before we got bounced. I remember the moment before, retaining mentally the picture of the sky—a pale blue in the east, darker in the west, the whole air with an aura of brilliance, and the sea a dark blue below. Every detail of the island under us was absolutely clear.

"Then there wasn't time for anything but the 109s which we had observed above us. They hesitated not at all before they were on top of us.

"As usual in these circumstances, things became confused. I suddenly found myself with no wingman and no leader. I remember trying a ridiculously long-range deflection shot at one of the 109s. This proved to be prophetic, because I found out instantly that the system was jammed. Neither the cannons nor the machine guns would fire.

"As I was contemplating what to do next, I racked the Spit upward to port and in one of those strange occurrences found myself practically in formation with a Yellow-nose who evidently had been coming up quite rapidly from below. We found ourselves almost locked together on a parallel course at the same speed and curving to the left in a climb.

"My first impulse was to turn away, but I had an instant realization that this would be fatal. The 109 pilot had evidently resolved this also, because I could see him fanning his rudder in an attempt to slow down more quickly and drop behind or under me.

"Even then, at the verge of panic, I remember registering the extreme clarity and beauty of the scene, incongruous as it was—the enemy plane, the yellow nose etched perfectly against the dark blue of the sea below. I remember staring fascinated for a second at the number 24 on the 109 fuselage.

"I was slowing the Spit down to keep pace with him, and at the same time fighting the urge to panic. It was at this point, when our wingtips were literally together, that the brilliant idea struck me. I could make an appeal to chivalry.

"Our gazes at each other had never faltered since the beginning of the predicament. We could see only each other's eyes; he wore a mask, and I did too. So, in a motion which I considered should explain everything—remember, he had a cockpit canopy but mine was open, so every movement must have been perfectly clear—I pointed dramatically down at the port wing cannon with a gloved finger, then raised the finger and drew it across my throat. This, I figured, would indicate that my guns were jammed and therefore mercy could be accorded me.

"Panic promotes foolish actions. Where in hell I got the idea of chivalry, especially at Malta and especially from a Yellow-nose, I do not know. The gesture, however, did have an effect.

"The 109 pilot stared, it seemed almost incredulously, at me and then, in one lightning movement, went onto his back and did the most rapid split-S I ever saw. He was a miniature against the seascape by the time I could follow him with my eyes.

"I looked around, and found myself absolutely alone. The whole thing seemed like a dream. It was only when I was almost back to Takali that the truth of the farce hit me. I became weaker as I started to laugh, because I could suddenly picture the 109 pilot after he got home—telling the experience and saying that those Spitfire pilots must either be crazy or tougher than hell—they indicate by gestures what they are going to do to you before they shoot you down."

After service in Malta, Leo Nomis went to El Alamein with No. 92 RAF Squadron, and all the way across Cyrenaica, in Libya, during the great German retreat to Tunisia. His two years with the Royal Air Force ended in the late spring of 1943 with his transfer to the USAAF in Egypt. Nomis describes this portion of his fighter pilot career.

"The theory at Malta was that if a pilot survived three months there, he was shipped back to the UK for a rest and a soft assignment. There were exceptions to this rule, and the live pilots shipped back to the United Kingdom usually fell into one of two categories: those with a splendid record of victories and heroism, and those who got along extremely well with the brass.

"Since I decidedly did not fall into either category, and, on the contrary, had even incurred the special ire of the brass, I was, at the end of my memorable Malta tour, ordered stern-eyed to a punishment squadron. But I'll say this—as disastrous as many events seemed at the time, I value the memory of those days in Malta and the Middle East very highly. I would not have had it any other way. The harsh life and hard days are mellowed in retrospect, but even so . . .

_"An assignment to a Western Desert squadron was considered by RAF pilots to be a punishment assignment. Many pilots substituted the name for the official designation when referring to the desert units.

"There was only one Spitfire wing in the Middle East, 92 being one of its four squadrons. They enjoyed the reputation of being a suicide unit, mainly because of the Wing Commander, one 'Pissy' Darwin. Our No. 92 (East India) Squadron had a distinguished history. It was a regular RAF squadron with a brilliant record in the Battle of Britain, and consequently, it was one of the highest scoring squadrons at that time.

"On my first mission with 92, a couple of days after I had arrived at the squadron and just before the breakthrough at El Alamein, I was flying a No. 2 position. Regardless of experience, this was the procedure on entering a squadron in a strange theater of operations.

"We had taken off at about 8 a.m., and it was already hot—one of those clear, bright, orange mornings typical of the Middle East and the Mediterranean. I had little knowledge of the area at that time, so I was content to follow my section leader, a South African chap, closely.

"There were eight of us in two flights of four. The mission was a general roving one, with the specific objective of strafing motor transport on any course to or from Alamein. We had gotten as far up as Mersa Matruh in Egypt (where Cleopatra had taken a bath some time previously), when the leader of the first flight, a perfect little bastard of an Australian, Rose, decided to test out some Jerry armored vehicles which had been maneuvering below.

"We had been droning along at no more than 3,000 feet, and had been the object of a certain amount of varied flak since we crossed the line, and I was feeling very uncomfortable already. That flak, it turned out, was nothing compared to what awaited us as we began a dive on the armored targets. They threw up a veritable curtain of fire, forcing all of us to turn off before we could get into effective range.

"As a newcomer I was following dutifully behind the allotted section leader—No. 4 in a line-astern flight. I assumed the leaders knew what the hell they were doing. I imagine they assumed the same of me, although it was generally conceded in the Middle East Command that a pilot out from Malta was already a mental case. At any rate, the armored vehicles being denied us, we swung down on a line of truck transports on an inland road between Mersa Matruh and Halfaya Pass.

"This time, we all opened fire on the now stationary trucks, from which the occupants had already sprinted for the sidelines. As we came over them—one flight after the other in line astern—we were again greeted with an absolute shower of flak from both sides of the road. Where it came from I don't know, because I never saw the guns, just the tracers. Again, miraculously, no one was hit.

"Two 109s suddenly appeared above us. As I looked up and glimpsed the pale blue under sides with the black crosses, I was reminded for all the world of two sharks coming in among a school of tuna. It was one of these perfectly clear Middle Eastern mornings, the sun already climbing bright and hot, the air balmy. The canopies of the Spits were removed there as in Malta, because they were impossible to keep clean and free of dust. Since the 109s were always faster than the Spits, the increased drag of flying with an open cockpit made little difference in combat ability, and vision was improved.

"The two 109s bounced the eight of us, and the altitude varied between 1,000 and 3,000 feet above the flat terrain as they began what proved to be a series of individual attacks. The words *clueful*, for clever, and *clueless*, for stupid, were in overuse with the RAF out there at that time. Clueful would be the one to describe these 109s, particularly the leader. The two German pilots provided a classic example of deflection shooting, and of how a 109 should be effectively used against a Spitfire.

"They kept their advantage of speed and altitude at all times; they never allowed themselves to become a target; they attacked individually and yet in unison; and it wasn't more than a minute before they had us all over the sky and split up into sections of two. My first vivid recollection after being split up was of being in a climbing turn right on the tail of the South African and observing two Spitfires about a mile off rolling over and hitting the ground, one after another, leaving great towers of black smoke in the blue air. These proved to be another South African and an English sergeant pilot, victims of a lightning inverted overhead pass by the 109 leader, who seemed a positive wizard at this.

"The instant tragedy caused everyone to start yelling at once on the R/T, and an insane garble was the result. Meanwhile, the 109s were far from breaking off the attack. In retrospect, it seemed as if we had been catapulted into a nightmare, with the two 109s the central supernatural characters. It seemed unreal that two 109s could possibly achieve the systematic destruction of eight Spitfires.

"The battle had come down to offense and defense, with the six of us who remained trying to defend ourselves against the varied and unpredictable single attacks of the two 109s. It was impossible to take the initiative from them. They kept their altitude and speed superiority with admirable consistency. If they saw that they could be in danger of a deflection shot themselves, they broke off and went above to plan something else.

"The only counter tactic we had under these circumstances was the ability to turn inside of them. Since we could not get behind them with equal speed, this was a defensive move only.

I had discovered somewhere along the line that I was somehow above average in defensive flying. I had little offensive ability, and this was absolutely imperative if one was to achieve anything more than scattered chance victories.

"But the magic charm of being able to spot enemy planes quickly, to sense their intentions, and to counter accordingly came to me as the months rolled into years. I cannot really remember just when—the ability was simply there one day, and its main purpose was to permit one to survive longer than those who didn't have it.

"Now, on this morning, it was really put to the test. I had tried to keep both 109s in sight, and it wasn't easy. I was hanging right on the tail of the South African, Charlie Hewitson, as RAF discipline required to the death. It was unpardonable for a No. 2 man to forsake his leader.

"The next event in the drama also shook us to the teeth. Rose, the Australian, was gibbering wildly on the R/T that our petrol was getting low, a fact of which we were all acutely aware. He and his No. 2 had cut across above Hewitson and me and were about 500 feet above and 1,000 yards ahead when they received a 90-degree deflection burst from one of the 109s. Nothing seemed to happen for a moment, and then the No. 2, a Canadian sergeant pilot, began to stream a thin but very visible vapor of petrol.

"I was watching this as though it were a film unfolding before me in a cinema. From previous experiences I knew that petrol vapor usually signalled an impending explosion. Just as I was thinking this the Spitfire did explode. Pieces of various sizes fell back toward us, and the engine plummeted straight down.

"We were in another climbing turn, and I remember a large piece of wing spinning by, and then the horror of seeing the pilot's body falling down and away past our wingtips. The clearest memory I have of that moment is that the body seemed to be leaving a trail of papers in its wake as it fell away and became smaller and smaller. Probably, these were maps and charts that had been tucked into the man's boots. I watched fascinated for a second more and saw no parachute open.

"This grisly scene had no sooner unfolded than the South African and I were the chosen ones. As we came around in our turn, here was the 109 leader boring from the port side with so much speed that he had obviously just pulled up from a dive. The 109s in Africa all were the same color—tan on top, blue underneath, with white wingtips and a white spinner. I could not see the other 109, but the spinner on this one was getting larger and larger as he began racking back on us.

"*Hewitson was not turning into him*! I began to yell to him on the R/T (the Australian had mysteriously ceased nattering when he lost his No. 2) to turn into the 109 quickly, but he just continued in a gentle turn. This seemed suicidal, so I said to hell with it, the devil-take-the-hindmost. As soon as I saw the nose cannon on the 109 begin to flash, I turned into him vertically as hard as I could.

"Hewitson faded out and away to my right, and the 109 almost immediately broke off his attack and pulled up to regain his height. I was nearly out of ammunition, (even if I had been allowed a shot at him), so the only thing gained by this maneuver was that I saved my life. And probably Hewitson's, as he had lost a good chunk out of his rudder in the attack.

"As suddenly as it began, the shambles ended. We had been trying to circle back to the British lines. Not only were we low on petrol, but everyone had little ammunition remaining. Then the 109s were gone, almost as if they had been phantoms. They also must have run short of petrol, or God knows how it would have ended. The five of us remaining made our way back to base, saturated with perspiration.

"For a week after, there was much speculation in our squadron as to the identities of the 109 pilots. Hans Marseille, the German Star of Africa and a phenomenal air fighter with a long victory list, had been killed in an accident a month earlier, or else we would have assumed he was the 109 leader. The leader's wingman had certainly proved that morning to be an able protegé. We eventually learned from sources at Middle East Headquarters that the Jerry leader was Major Eric Rudorffer, then the leading Luftwaffe ace and destined to go even higher. We did not know then that Rudorffer was generally conceded among his contemporaries to be the best deflection marksman in the Luftwaffe, as well as a natural pilot. It was and still is my theory that his wingman was Joachim Muencheberg, another top German ace said to have arrived in the Middle East from the Malta sector, where he had accumulated 19 additional victories."

*   *   *

War has a way of turning what it touches into symbols, as the journalists and historians who report about it work to make order out of it's chaos. What happens to people, to armies, navies and air forces, to nations and to alliances inevitably seems to be translated first into numbers and lines on maps and broad accounts of massive movements, and then into blocks of triumph or defeat. When personalities emerge from the symbolism of Us *versus* Them, of Allies and Enemies, of Heroes and Victims, they tend to be scrubbed and highlighted as if they were characters on a stage, contrived to make this point or that for home consumption.

Certainly, the Eagles have had their share of scrubbing and highlighting. Yet to read and hear their own accounts of their day-to-day experiences is to realize that beneath the contrivances that wartime symbolism sometimes invents, are people made far more interesting and certainly undiminished by naked truth.

Many Eagles, keenly aware that they were taking part in an historic adventure in leaving home for a foreign war, faithfully recorded their day-to-day experiences. This book and its predecessor, *The Eagle Squadrons*, owe their being to that willingness to share such narratives. Sometimes the accounts prove to be windows into the person behind the helmet, goggles and oxygen mask of the fighter pilot; sometimes they provide a sense of the ebb and flow of war's fortunes that the campaign accounts of military historians can not capture as vividly.

In the accounts of Eagles Harold F. Marting and Michael Miluck, we have such self-portraits. In their diaries, these pilots do not, of course, speak *for* the Eagles, but in relating their part in the Eagles' war, they shed light on a picture greater than the individual events they relate.

When Harold Marting enlisted in the Royal Canadian Air Force, at Vancouver, British Columbia, in October 1940, his sister, Lennie, gave him a diary and wrote on the flyleaf: "Buddy, you'll be glad later that you wrote it down, so please do. And some day, I want to have my share in telling it." She would do that, more than 20 years later, in making the diary and other information available for this book.

Marting took flight training in Canada, at Brandon, Manitoba, Regina, Saskatchewan, and Windsor and Dunnville, Ontario. In December 1940, he went home to Farmland, Indiana, for a visit of one day. He observed in his diary that this was quite a shock for his family—"they hadn't heard from me in about four years." He also said he did not have a chance to see his small daughter, Marilyn.

After receiving his wings on March 29, 1941, standing third in his class of 38 pilots, Marting went home again, for seven days leave. This time, he planned to see his former wife, Frances, as well as their child.

> March 30. My mind was occupied with apprehensions of meeting Marilyn for the first real time. We arrived home in the very early hours. Marilyn was asleep, but waked up long enough to say hello. Later this morning when we all got up, Marilyn came into the room and to me immediately. Our meeting was the most natural thing I have ever seen. A wonderful thing.

> April 1. Fran and Marilyn went back to Indianapolis this morning. I took them back on the bus. We had a wonderful time in Farmland, and I wish we could have stayed there until I have to go back. It is practically settled that Fran and I will be remarried soon.

> April 7. Reported in at Central Flying School, Trenton, Ont., for training to become an instructor. Am very disappointed; it was the last thing I wanted to be. However, being on this side of the Atlantic will be better in some ways as Fran and I want to get married again. I know that Fran and all of my family are very happy over it.

Marting was notified on May 9 that he was to report at Halifax May 21 for shipment overseas. He wrote. "Much to do in the meantime. We plan to get married again as soon as possible. Fran probably will go back to Canada with me to stay until I sail. Marilyn has the measles."

> May 14, Indianapolis. This is the day. Fran and I were married in the Broadway M.E. church. It was a very nice wedding. Fran and I went to Peru afterward.

> May 15, Peru, Ind. Played 27 holes of golf with Forrest and the pro, Jesse Watkins. Had a lot of fun but Forrest won the money. Leaving tonight.

Three rounds of golf, without his bride, on the day after the wedding?

The newlyweds found accommodations in Halifax scarce and expensive. Shopping was difficult. Marting wrote on May 22, "Have looked and looked for something to send Marilyn, but it's very hard to find nice things. Finally settled on a little gold locket. Got rather irritated at Fran because she got such a laugh out of me trying to find something. Impossible to get rooms or apartments here, so I guess Fran will have to go home."

Frances Marting left Halifax the following day. "Rather hard saying goodbye after such a short married life, and I wish we could have found a place so that she could have stayed longer," the bridegroom wrote. In effect, these were his last diary references to his bride.

Marting sailed from Halifax for England May 30, 1941. Upon being assigned to 121 Eagle Squadron, he wrote: "Am not too keen on that as the Eagles don't have a very good reputation over here yet and also because they are still flying Hurricanes."

The following day, he had arrived at a more favorable frame of mind: "Very agreeably surprised at the station as it seems very nice. The mess and quarters are good. Three old friends are here: W. L. C. Jones, Sgt., who was in my class in Canada, and also Sgt. Shenk, and P/O Patterson, who was an instructor at Dunnville. Seems like a very good crowd, and they made me feel right at home."

In mid-August, Marting went to London on leave and met "a very nice WAAF, 'Jimmy' Grinson—she works in Air Ministry." Within one week he took her to dinner and night-clubbing four times—to expensive places such as Maxime's, the Piccadilly, the Normandy Club, the Albany Club, the Hollywood Club and Chez Auguste—and to luncheon three times. He managed the final luncheon only after going to the bank and borrowing five pounds. The night before he went back to the base he wrote, "To bed early again as I can't afford to do much now."

Marting had one more dinner and nightclub party and two luncheon dates with Jimmy in October. Thereafter, there were no more diary references to meetings with her.

The late autumn blahs set in:

> November 7, Kirton. Have had some trouble in regard to my bar chits this last month. There apparently is some mix-

up in names. Have asked very emphatically to be transferred out of this squadron and am sure I'll get it this time. Wasted the whole day trying to see the Group Captain about a transfer. Am damn well fed up with this squadron and this station.

November 17, Kirton. Found out I am going to 71 Squadron tomorrow.

November 18, North Weald. Reported to the CO of 71 Squadron, S/L Peterson. Seems to be a nice bunch of fellows here now. All but two or three of the original Eagles are prisoners or dead.

November 20, North Weald. Weather is terrible here. Am missing the bridge at Kirton as there is nothing to do here in the evenings and I'm too broke to go to London.

November 28, North Weald. No flying today, thick fog. Am fed up. There is no prospect of anything doing until spring. Thinking of handing in my resignation tomorrow.

December 16, Martlesham Heath. Had another talk with S/L Peterson about going East. Would still like to get out of the Eagle Squadron. Don't like waiting for someone to die to get a promotion.

December 29, Martlesham. Am going on four days leave. Can't really afford it but it is New Year's Eve coming up.

December 30, London. Was stopped on the street at noon by a girl that recognized me from a picture Patterson had shown her. She asked about him, and so we discussed it over lunch. Her name is Margaret Coates, and she is very nice. Met her after work, and we had dinner and several drinks afterwards.

Marting took his new friend to luncheon December 31, to a New Year's Eve party at the Strand Palace that night, and to dinner on New Year's Day. She visited him at Martlesham Heath one weekend. They had four more dinner dates in London in the last week of January, 1942. These were the last references to her in his diary.

At the end of February 1942, with a week's leave, Marting went into London to "stay as long as what little money I have lasts." He checked in at the Eagles Club, went to movies, traveled out to Uxbridge to inquire at 11 Group about a posting to the East. "Was told I can go," he wrote. "Am beginning to dislike London more every time I come here."

Bud Marting finally won his transfer to the Middle East and said a happy goodbye to England. He arrived in Durban, South Africa, May 18, 1942. "Certainly a lovely place," he wrote in his diary. "Just like most any American city, and the weather is just like southern California. Swimming in the salt water pool on the beach; water 70 degrees, just right."

Two weeks later he discovered the recreational facilities—golf and horse racing—that were open to officers waiting for new combat assignments. He played his first game of South African golf June 4 at the Durban Country Club—"one of the most beautiful courses I have ever seen"—and the next day bought golf shoes and played the more difficult but less sporty Royal Durban Club. He could play 18 holes in the morning there and watch the races in the afternoon.

From June 4 through June 26, Marting was on the golf course every day. On June 24 he wrote, "Getting tired playing around and am out of money. Have played 25½ rounds of golf in the last 20 days—460 holes, to be exact."

"Marting was a gambling golfer," his friend Eddie Miluck said. "He had his clubs with him in England and Cairo and also on our flight back to the States in a Liberator that stopped at Khartoum, Accra, Ascension Island, Belem and Miami."

On June 27, Marting and three other former Eagles—Miluck, Mike Kelly and Wally Tribken, all of whom had volunteered to serve in the Far East in the China-Burma-India war theater in hopes of joining the Flying Tigers—boarded the *New Amsterdam*.

"This ship is a beauty," Marting wrote. "Kelly and I have a cabin with private bath. We are all wondering where we are going.

"The news from Egypt looks bad. If we are going to Cairo we wonder if we will be there in time for the evacuation."

"Will we be there on time?" all four of the onetime Eagles were asking themselves. "Or will it be too late? Will Rommel be in Cairo and in control of the Suez Canal before we know it?"

The war had been seesawing across the Cyrenaica sector of Libya since Italian forces first surged from Libya across the border and 60 miles into Egypt to Sidi Barrani, in September 1940. In December, the British forces defending Egypt launched an offensive, captured the important Libyan ports of Tobruk and Benghazi, and moved on to El Agheila in the Gulf of Sirte, almost half the way to Tripoli.

Late in March 1941, the Germans forced the British back out of El Agheila, shortly afterward recaptured Benghazi, and drove the British in retreat into Egypt. The Allied forces at Tobruk withstood the Axis assault, however, and after eight months of siege, were rescued by another British advance. By the end of 1941, the enemy had been pushed back once more to El Agheila.

In an offensive in the spring of 1942, the forces of German General Erwin Rommel recaptured Tobruk and then pushed the British yet again into Egypt, first to the border town of Es Sollum, then to Mersa Matruh. Now, at the end of June 1942, the British were holding steady, for the present at least, at El Alamein, only 60 miles short of Alexandria.

In Egypt, the four Americans were assigned first to Kas Farite, a camp 80 miles south of Cairo. They spent as much time as they could in Cairo, and Marting played several rounds of golf at Club Gezeri. Kelly, Tribken and Miluck were posted July 13 to a camp midway between Cairo and Alexandria. Marting, wondering why he was not sent with them, called at the American legation in Cairo to inquire about a transfer into the U.S. Army.

"I am pretty well fed up with this red tape and the stupidity of the English," he wrote. "The colonel in the Air Corps was promising. I applied for a transfer, but it may be some time."

A week later Marting applied for a transfer to the U.S. Navy air force, but did not think it would do any good. In Cairo, he kept bumping into former Eagles, such as Bob Mannix, formerly of 71 Eagle Squadron and now of 127 Hurricane Squadron, and Fred Almos, formerly of 121 and just returned from Malta.

Marting was reunited with Kelly, Miluck and Tribken briefly at a desert camp near Cairo, training in the Curtiss P-40E Kittyhawk, and then was assigned to No. 450, an Australian squadron, "supposed to be the best in the 239th Wing." After flying the Kittyhawk for an hour he reported, "No trouble at all—I like the plane pretty well. It isn't nearly as good as the Spitfire, but it's better than the Hurricane."

Marting had his first taste of desert operations on August 2, 1942, dropping 500-pound bombs on a concentration of German tanks and trucks at Wadi, near Qatton Springs, and then going back twice to strafe. His diary report for September 14 reads: "We were scrambled with No. 3 squadron, and over the central front, we ran into 20-plus 109s. There were 18 of us, and they came down in one big bunch to attack. During the ensuing dogfight, we were joined by 250 and 112 squadrons, so there were at least 50 planes in this fight.

"They came at us out of the sun, and in a couple of seconds there was no formation left—just one big mass of planes milling around the sky. I saw a 109 on the tail of a Kitty and went for him. He was turning away from me, and when I opened fire, my shots hit him in the belly.

"I was forced to break off then as another was attacking me head-on. Had a couple more long-range shots which missed, and then I saw a Kitty diving in front of me with another 109 on his tail. The 109 opened fire about the same time I did, and I saw his shots hit the Kitty, which turned out to be Sergeant O'Neil.

"My first squirt made the 109 pull up, and I followed, firing all the time in quick bursts. When he reached the top of his climb, he rolled onto his back, and as he rolled my shots hit him in the belly of the plane from about 100 yards. He fell on his back for a second and nosed down, me right after him. As he dived he rolled back right side up. I followed down to about 4,000 feet and saw him go straight into the ground and explode in one great big sheet of flame.

"There were three other planes burning on the ground already. I climbed back up to the scrap and saw two parachutes coming down right in the middle of it, and the third chute already on the ground.

"The Jerries decided about then they had had enough and left. Two planes collided in the melee, but I didn't see it. Sgt. Ewing is missing from our squadron. No. 3 lost two fellows."

Marting learned the following day that six pilots were missing, but that Army troops at the front saw 13 planes crash. "That puts us ahead 7 to 6," he remarked, keeping score as usual.

Marting went to take a good look at a captured Me 109. "It had been shot down with very little damage and is now in flying condition," he said.

"It is the most compact machine I have ever seen, and is so small it looks like a toy. It is beautifully built. The only thing I don't like about it is the poor visibility from the cockpit."

An excerpt from Marting's diary dated a week later, September 22, Cairo, notes:

> Ran into P/O Nomis, who was in 71 Squadron with us. He had been to Malta and was sent here for transfer to U.S. Army. He got the French Croix de Guerre in Malta for something that the RAF tried to court martial him for. He took a Spit off at night from Malta without permission, flew to Sicily, and shot down a Heinkel 111, wrecked a train, shot up some houses, and came back all right.

Marting's flying and golfing colleague Michael (Eddie) Miluck, a wisecracking cowboy-like character from North Dakota, provided from his own diary another graphic version of the heat, dust and desolation of the Egyptian desert area around El Alamein, and of the dangers of combat with the air forces of Field Marshal Albert von Kesselring, Axis Mediterranean commander.

> October 1. "Stukas at 9 o'clock," the radio sputtered, and I began to sweat. They were coming straight out of the west— 18 of them, with a dazzling sunset behind them. Our leader was so excited that none of us could understand him, but we climbed instinctively to get in position for attack. The most amazing thing was the ugliness of the Stukas, with their wheels hanging down . . . big, clumsy birds of prey, heavy with unlaid eggs.
> "Messerschmitts coming down!" The sweat really began to pour. Half our flight started out for them. Soon it was a shambles up there and a massacre below—so many planes buzzing about I kept wishing my .50 calibers were shotguns.
> The Stukas began jettisoning their bombs, a delightful sight. They were directly over their own lines. I think I damaged a Me 109 as he overshot me and climbed past my nose. I also managed to make a head-on attack into a Stuka. The bullets sparked against the motor, but I had to turn away before I saw what happened, as tracers were streaking past my wings from behind.
> Returning, I overtook a Stuka diving for the ground and helped him on his way with all I had left. It must have been enough; he hit with a hell of a thump. When I looked around again, five or six Jerries were burning in the air and the rest were limping off. The score: six Stukas destroyed, six probably destroyed, many more aircraft damaged. We had forced them to bomb their own troops. The 12 kites of 250 Squadron, RAF,

by some miracle were intact, without a single bullet hole in a fuselage.

The strange behavior of two Me 109s that overtook me on my way home puzzled me. Passing over 500 feet above, the leader did a half roll and took a good look before rolling out and stooging on. The second did exactly the same thing. As I was out of ammunition, I could only stick the nose down and weave like hell, keeping them always in sight in case they decided to play; but they ignored me and climbed back toward their own lines.

October 7. After admiring another brilliant moon and the tranquil peace of the desert, retired to bed at midnight. Then it began. That familiar drone of Jerry engines—how well I remembered it from England.

I had not bothered to dig a slit trench, so I decided to ignore them. Not Wally Tribken. He started to dress and was already leaving when it dawned on me that it was *our* airdrome they were after. Stark naked, with only my tin helmet, I flew out of the tent at his heels. We had reached the halfway mark to the nearest slit trench when down they came, and we fell flat on our faces.

I noticed then that my torch was still shining. I tried to turn it off, but my fingers were too shaky. Wally kept yelling, "Put that goddam light out." Finally I had to lie on top of it, feeling as if I were trying to cover a powerful searchlight, with every damned Jerry in the sky watching me.

Two of our planes were destroyed and three damaged. The bullets of one were still popping at breakfast time when we went out to view the dozen-odd craters in the middle of the field.

Midnight, October 9. Due to recent heavy rains and the resulting sticky mud, Kesselring got caught with all of his Me 109s concentrated in a small area on several 'dromes. The entire RAF went into high gear at dawn and hasn't let up yet. Where the fighters and day medium bombers left off, the night bombers took over. Every field in El Daba area has been bombed, dive-bombed and strafed.

On our first show, we just bombed. On the other three, we bombed and then strafed. On the second, we were attacked by several 109s and I squirted at one for a hell of a long time. When the next one came by, I remembered to turn on my gun switch and did much better.

F/Sgt. Rodney forgot to come back, and an Englishman bought it this morning, making the score two to one, not in our favor. Wally Tribken tangled with a dozen Macchi 202s

and Me 109s, but escaped with four cannon slugs in his
cockpit and minor holes in fuselage and wing. When he crash
landed on the field, the poor kite just sighed and collapsed. So
did Wally.

Returning now to Marting's diary:

> October 14. Air Vice Marshal Cunningham, the A.O.C.,
> called on us to tell about the coming push. We are to push the
> enemy right out of Africa. We are numerically superior by
> about four to one in troops and five to three in fighting planes,
> so they think it will be a cinch this time. This wing and two
> others—12 or 13 squadrons—will be the main striking force in
> the air. I think the U.S. Navy is going to have to wait for me.

> October 20. We were top cover and the bombing was
> beautiful, the best I've ever seen. On the way home we were
> attacked by six or seven 109s and Macchi 202s. The first one
> seen came up behind P/O Winn and I turned into him and
> fired from about 600 yards, closing down to 400. My No. 2,
> Prowse, saw my shots hit and the Macchi went into the
> ground. It was a lucky shot as three of my guns stopped, and I
> only used 100 rounds altogether.

> October 21. Went up for an hour to test the guns. Have
> been having too much gun trouble. Had five stoppages again
> today.

> October 22. Tested my guns again, and again there were
> five stoppages. Have taken the plane off operations on that
> account. Our new squadron leader, Williams, told us the push
> starts tomorrow night. There will be no rest for us for some
> time now. This coming battle is intended to be the turning
> point of the war, so I am proud to be in the main striking
> force.

Harold Marting was amazingly correct when he wrote on
October 22, 1942, that "this coming battle"—the push starting
"tomorrow night"—was meant to be "the turning point of the
war." He erred greatly, however, in his plans to be part of the
main striking force.

The action on the night of October 22–23, which has
since been referred to as the Battle of El Alamein, indeed
proved to be a crucial development in the Middle East conflict. British guns, tanks, ships and planes maimed the attacking German and Italian forces at El Alamein so severely that
night and over the following days, that Rommel was compelled to order a general retreat back into Libya. The surprise

landing of American and British forces at Casablanca in Morocco, and at Oran and Algiers in Algeria, November 8, 1942, and the surrender of the Vichy French units there within three days, further darkened Axis' prospects.

The victors at El Alamein fought their way across Libya, taking Tobruk, Benghazi, El Agheila, Sirte and Tripoli in succession, and by the end of January 1943, had moved on into Tunisia. Winston Churchill said later that before El Alamein, the Allies had never had a victory, "but after Alamein we never had a defeat."

The morning after writing his appraisal of the action in which he was so proud to be taking part, Hal Marting led a flight of six Kittyhawks in the much anticipated big push. This time, all his guns stopped firing. Enemy antiaircraft gunners shot him down, and Italian troops made him a prisoner.

Miluck's diary carried the action past the point at which Marting's narrative ended. Miluck wrote:

October 23. Warned this morning that the big push begins at 10 p.m. tonight. Starting today, six Spitfires are doing patrols over Daba to keep the Luftwaffe in the air. Marting missing this morning from a wing bombing of Daba. They say he must have chased a 109.

October 25. We went on a long-range sweep, looking for trouble, but nothing happened until we started home. Then one of the new pilots became separated. Suddenly the radio crackled and a voice yelled, "Help! Help! I'm being attacked by 109s. Help!"

Since we were at 8,000 and he was away behind and below on the deck, it was useless to try to locate him, so we continued home. A few seconds later, "For Christ's sake, help me! The bastards are on my tail!" We stooged on. Finally someone drawled, "Have you bought it yet?"

He got back—boiling mad, but very willing to keep in formation in the future.

Starlight time—another sand storm. Impossible to see my tent, 50 yards from the mess, but I fixed that by tying a guide rope between them. Just like the snow blizzards you read about. Sand in your eyes and ears and mouth, gritting every time you take a bite.

Most of us keep handkerchiefs tied around our faces and the only time we have our hats off is when we sleep. I drank a lime juice, keeping my hand cupped over the glass, but a quarter inch of sand soon settled in the bottom anyway. The powdery stuff floats through the air, settling on everything, sifting into the cockpits of the kites and covering the floor. Wally did a slow roll and claimed he had to come out on instruments.

October 26. We damaged 120 aircraft in the Daba-Fuka bombings. Falconer-Taylor walked casually into the mess today after crash landing in enemy territory and walking more than 90 miles in three days with a broken hand.

October 27. Up again in the middle of the night for another dawn show. At four shows a day, our ground crews have to work damned hard, so I bought mine several beers each to show my appreciation. Since we are rationed to three cans a day, at 35 cents a can, I couldn't do more. Mine is one of the best and most experienced crews in the desert. What I do reflects on them; if I shoot down a kite, they also have shot it down.

November 1. Twelve of us were on the deck, strafing motor transport, when a standing patrol of Macchi 202s jumped us; nor did anyone see them until Sergeant Martin was shot down. There were clouds of smoke from the bombed transport below, which I thought came from Martin's plane. Thank God, somebody saw him belly-land okay.

What an unusual sight—12 Kittys and four Macchi 202s turning and dodging, skimming the deck, no one ever getting over 500 feet into the air. Now and then one kite would leap above the others like a fish jumping out of water, then fall back and disappear, only to have another kite leap. In complete chaos, the Kittys were squirting at each other more than at the 202s, when the leader told us to turn about.

Seeing a Kitty quite a distance behind and hearing the radio screech, "Come back, you bastards, come back! Christ, what a bunch of bastards!" we made a circle to allow him to catch up. The next thing we saw was a blurred streak as he shot by, nor did we see him again until we landed.

November 2. Bombed the front lines today. When we landed, we were pleased to learn that 200 prisoners had walked in, hands up, immediately after the bombing.

November 3. Another dawn escort of Baltimores and B-25s. Ack-ack amazingly accurate, and a B-25 was hit. It limped home on one engine, and three of us stayed behind to protect it.

Hurried off to Alexandria for the rest of the day. Had a relaxing hot water shower, followed by a rub with a clean towel, then the usual lunch of prawns-mayonnaise, fried onions and sweet potatoes. Felt homesick after seeing the movie, *They Died with Their Boots On*, which had many scenes of North Dakota, especially around Mandan. [The film was about General George C. Custer, and The Little Big Horn.]

Returned to the hotel and chatted with Miss O., a shy but charming and intelligent young woman who was watched like a hawk by her mother. A quiet, sober manner . . . straight black hair parted in the middle and knotted at the nape of the neck, framing a very lovely face . . . definitely appealing. But she does not leave the hotel without a chaperone, especially after mother gets a good look at the gleam in my eye. To take her out means mother's permission, then buying dinner for one or maybe two chaperones. So I sighed, and strolled down to have my hair trimmed around the ears.

November 4. Wally shot down a Macchi 202, one of five that attacked the squadron. He was later attacked by two more and had to do aileron rolls down to the deck before he could shake them. What shook him was to find himself on his back at 400 feet, going down like a bomb. He dusted the deck pulling out.

The army has increased the bulge, and big results are expected. We are on one-hour notice; in case of an advance, half the squadron must be on the road in an hour's time, the rest flying to join them as soon as a base is located.

Our wallets now contain no personal papers; just a minimum of Italian money and a chit written in Arabic, if we are forced down. It offers a liberal reward for our safe treatment and return. The only trouble is that none of the desert Wogs can read.

November 5. Awakened at 6 A.M. with the news, "We're moving. They're on the run past Fuka!" Breakfasted on a lime juice and a handful of peanuts, packed my kit and took down our tent. There's still time to do a scheduled patrol, but we're out of petrol. The army is said to have armored cars beyond Mersa Matruh, doing great damage. Daba is cleared and we captured nine shiny new Me 109s at Ghezal Station. There are 109s everywhere, crashed or otherwise damaged.

Now comes the word that we must wait till dawn for departure. Everyone has to unpack. How we hate this waiting. Dinner tonight will strangely resemble breakfast and lunch— peanuts and beer. But really very filling.

We hear that 4,000 prisoners have been taken. The Greeks sent a pathetic message, "We have more prisoners than troops. What will we do?" Yesterday the Aussies refused to take the Italians who surrendered until barbed wire cages could be provided for them. They told the Italians to "come back tomorrow." And they did.

November 6. On a reconnaissance flight over enemy airdromes, saw burned transports and tanks making charred black patches on the ground. At least 1,000 prisoners were in a close cluster. Huge collections of motor transport and tanks were pushing toward Fuka. No enemy aircraft in the air, but plenty crashed and abandoned on the ground. Exhilarating flight.

6 P.M. Arrived at our new landing ground and almost wrote myself off twice, due to the rush of pilots trying to get in before dark. No flare paths in this area.

Our new mess tent has a large red banner with a swastika on a white circle in the center and a large picture of General Field Marshal Rommel. Looting is well under way. Luger pistols and Leica cameras have already been found, and quantities of rifles, ammunition, water containers and personal articles—proof that Jerry pulled out in a hell of a hurry. The quantity and range of personal issue equipment astounds us. All of it is far superior to ours; Jerry lacked for nothing. The bloody flies are everywhere. We ignore them.

November 7. Scared myself to death on a two and one half hour long-range strafe west of Sidi Barrani. On the third strafe, my instruments all went to cock, so I dove for the deck, expecting the engine to stop at any minute. The motor kept running. I flew on the deck all the way home and landed on my emergency undercart. "A few slugs here and there, nothing to worry about," the mechanic said casually.

The others shot down three Ju 52s loaded with petrol, but got separated in the excitement. P/O Calver and F/Sgt. Norm Chap formed up with Troke, but had hardly turned for home when they ran into a Stuka party of 20, escorted by 30 109s. Calver either didn't hear or ignored Troke's advice not to attack against such odds, and was last seen busting into a Stuka with guns blazing. Later, Chap chased a Macchi 202 off Troke's tail, but received some cannon slugs in his cockpit and crashed in flames. Troke got the bastard.

November 8. "A" flight has lost four pilots within 48 hours, leaving only five. "B" flight has seven pilots. Only 10 kites are serviceable. The commanding officer is down with malaria. As a final blow, "A" flight commander and two senior pilots, looting in a nearby field, overran a Jerry mine-field. Up went the mine, off went a wheel and over went the Jeep. One pilot has broken teeth and a severe concussion. Another has a broken arm. Of course, the one who got the idea of looting in the first place escaped minus patches of skin.

We have no beer left and no water to make soft drinks. S/Ldr. Barbar visited us with the news of U.S. troops landing in North Africa. Tunis, here they come! Everyone is afraid they'll beat us to Tripoli, which would be a dirty trick after all our stooging.

November 9. Arrived at our new base southeast of Matruh. They say we are here for only 48 hours, then off for a new base south of Sidi Barrani. This coastal area is very damp and abundant—for the desert—with green camel thorn. It gives off a pleasant sage odor that is soothing when one dozes off.

November 11. On the move again. Landed on a cracked-road runway in a region so barren that it consists of nothing but flat horizon dotted with a few trucks. Impossible to drive tent stakes into the rock base, so we are living under a big canvas cover held in place by guide ropes tied to barrels filled with rock. . . . We still receive only two pints of water per day—hardly enough to drink. No washee, no shavee. Back at Alamein, we lived like kings. I even remember giving some water away.

November 13. Moved to Gambut. . . . This is the worst 'drome for dust to be found in the desert, they say, and I believe it. Tobruk fell today. The army gives us a new advance bomb line every few hours.

November 14. Refreshed after 12 hours' sleep. Wonder if a normal bed will ever feel the same again. I do not sleep as well either in Cairo or in Alexandria as in the desert.

November 15. Left Gambut at 8 A.M. and unpacked at Gazala at noon, which shows what paved roads will do. Our drive was pleasant until we approached Tobruk. . . . Pitiful Tobruk is nothing but a crumpled pile of rubble and shattered buildings, surrounding a harbor full of half-submerged derelict ships. For all its war fame, it is still a mere Wog village, cowering under the drone of planes. . . . This place is beyond description in filth and dust. Any resemblance to an airdrome is purely coincidental.

November 20. Led top cover on a dawn armed reconnaissance of the St. Meus, Antelet and Agedabia areas. The army said yesterday that we had taken these points and would somebody please fly over to make sure. Over we went at 5,000 and got everything thrown at us but the kitchen sink. We pulled out in a hell of a hurry and were still cussing the army when we landed. . . . A Stuka is used to bring mail and beer from Alexandria. Surprising how much beer a Stuka will carry.

November 27. A visiting Hurricane pilot says that Bob Mannix bought it while ground strafing. I hope he is wrong. Bob came with us from the Eagle squadron and only a few weeks ago became Squadron Leader of 33 Hurricane fighter squadron, which is damned good for a Yank in the RAF.

Hurricanes saved England, but are so outmoded that we call them suicide squadrons. Bob used to say you could always tell where a Hurricane squadron had taken off because of the furrows in the sand where the pilots' heels had dragged. After a pilot was tied into the cockpit, with one hand chained to the throttle and one to the stick, the ground crew fixed the ignition so it couldn't be switched off and used a slingshot to get him into the air. When enemy aircraft were spotted, all the pilots began milling around in circles, shooting as fast as they could; then all would come on the radio at once: "Ammunition exhausted. Going home."

I wonder if Wally knew about Bob.

December 6. En route from Almaza airport, Cairo, to return to the squadron at Martuba, stopped at Mersa Matruh long enough to see the boys in 127 Squadron, but they were mostly on leave and I couldn't find out any more about Bob Mannix. Looks kind of bad, and that has taken a lot out of us.

December 11. Arrived at our new camp at Belandah. Again we are in the middle of nowhere, surrounded by nothing. This is one of the smallest, dustiest and rockiest fields we have yet been on. Water is so scarce that I hate to waste it even by sweating. Four of us share a tent, each one getting two pints of water daily. To stretch it we use our rotation-ration system, which involves a four-day period.

Being first today, I took a cup of water and thoroughly washed my hands and face. When I had finished, Wally used the same cup of water to wash himself, then the other two had their turns. Mike Kelly was the last on washing, so he was first on shaving, still using the same cup of water; and as I was first on washing, I was last on shaving.

Our toilet completed, the cup of water was strained and put into another canteen kept for that purpose. When the canteen is full—two pints—it is my turn to take a bath, which means that we get a bath once every 10 days. When I'm through bathing, the water is still mine to wash my clothes. After that, to hell with it. It's probably dirty, anyway.

December 16. Marble Arch, Mussolini's gateway to the Italian resort land, is just a marble arch and nothing more. Our entire personnel and equipment arrived on schedule by plane—a remarkable feat and a triumph for modern air warfare. As Jerry had mined the landing grounds and ploughed the runways—a sure sign he doesn't intend to return—the army made us a landing field in half a day's time with a couple of road scrapers. Since this is the most advanced base, it has more traffic than LaGuardia.

December 17. They really pasted us last night. Never have so few been bombed by so many, with so much, for so long a time.

December 23. Tonight the drinks are on the commanding officer, Wally and me. We have done better than 200 combat hours, and have been recalled to Cairo for reassignment to a non-combat area for a few months.

December 28. Cairo. Glad to see Lance Wade in the Continental Savoy, just returned from the States after six weeks leave.

New Year's Eve. Yippee! Harold Marting walked in this evening, very casually, as if he had just been out for a drink when, in truth, he had just escaped from the Germans in Greece.

More good news. Wally Tribken and I are transferred to the U.S. Army Air Corps and are being sent to the States immediately.

Home! We're still alive. We're going HOME.

Part II

USAAF

7

FOURTH BUT FIRST

From Harold Strickland's diary:

7 December 1941. Three North Sea minesweeper patrols with Newt Anderson for a total of four hours and 40 minutes, which used up most of the short daylight hours. . . . After the final mission and dinner, I turned in early and was reading in bed when the batman pounded on the door, entered and shouted, "Pearl Harbor has been attacked by the Japanese!" He told me that the BBC had just announced the news, and added that most of our battleships had been destroyed.

I jumped into my clothes and headed for the bar. Pandemonium was in progress. We knew that it was now only a matter of time until thousands of American warplanes would arrive in Europe, with hundreds of thousands—millions—of fighting men and the equipment to back them up. Now there was no question in our minds that we had been fighting for the United States as well as Britain.

Strickland's prediction would indeed come true. Furthermore, Washington was only too eager to transfer the invaluably experienced American fighter pilots already in place in Britain to the United States Army Air Force. The Eagles themselves had immediately determined upon the move, had dispatched representatives to London on the night of December 7 to volunteer for them personally at the United States Embassy and had been assured of their welcome by President Roosevelt on the telephone. The machinery was soon set in motion.

The first need was for information.

A few months after the United States entered the war, a team of senior USAAF officers went to England to initiate the Eighth Air Force. One of their first actions was to visit 71 Squadron, and they arrived with almost no advance notice. Intelligence Officer Robbie Robinson happened to be away on a 48-hour pass, attending to his duties at the House of Commons. All members of Parliament retained their seats while on active service with the forces, and returned to the House of Commons when on leave from the military.

"In my absence, the boys from the squadron must have shot a very good line about what I had done for them," Robinson, later to become Lord Martonmere, says, "because I was asked the following weekend to go to London to meet these people and discuss their plans for setting up operations in the United Kingdom. At the end of the meeting, I was asked if I would join them and assist in this work. Naturally, I agreed, and they asked the Air Ministry to post me on detachment to the Eighth Air Force."

Robinson was amazed, 10 days later, to receive a notice of posting to the RAF at Takoradi in West Africa:

"I told the squadron adjutant that it must be a mistake and that I had been confused with some other Robinson. The adjutant told me that orders had to be obeyed, and that action could be taken against me for disobedience."

Upon Robinson's insistence, the adjutant sent a signal to group headquarters that the Member of Parliament understood he was to be posted to the Eighth Air Force and felt that, under the circumstances, it would be an unnecessary waste of effort in war time to send him to West Africa and back for a week. The diplomacy worked, the correct posting came through, and Robinson found himself at Eighth Air Force Headquarters at 20 Grosvenor Square, London. The headquarters at that time consisted of five officers and three enlisted men. It was to grow, under the command, first of General Carl Spaatz and later of General Ira Eaker, to a force capable of staging an attack with 2,000 bombers and 2,000 fighters. Robinson's role would also deepen as the force evolved.

At the Eighth's Headquarters, Robinson briefed the air staff daily on operations. When it became necessary for a team to visit Washington to brief General Arnold and the air staff on operations in Europe, Robinson was chosen as one who had studied the operational use of air power in Europe and had the whole situation at his fingertips.

After briefing the air staff, cabinet members, and Congressmen, Robinson made a three-week tour of the United States to lecture at all of the American staff colleges and to speak to more than 25,000 officers and air crew members in training.

Robinson was recalled to the United States twice for further briefing duties. On the third trip, he accompanied General Curtis E. LeMay on a tour of major bases. Upon returning to England early in 1944, he received an invitation from General Ira Eaker, who had just become Commander-in-Chief of the Mediterranean Allied Air Forces, to join his staff in Italy.

Robinson spent the next year at MAAF Headquarters, at Caserta. During that time, he took part in the liberation of Rome, became the first Air Force officer into Athens, and on three occasions was put into Yugoslavia on short missions with the Tito Partisans. At the end of the war, he received from the Americans the decoration of Officer of the Legion of Honor.

The USAAF decided that the three Eagle Squadrons it would receive from the Royal Air Force would be formed into a new, single unit of the Eighth Air Force, the 4th Fighter Group. Pilots who preferred not to make that change would have the option of remaining with the RAF or of joining other parts of the AAF. Most of the Eagles did elect to join the 4th, but some stayed on with the RAF for brief periods.

One such was Bill Dunn, who remained with the British because they had promised him his own squadron. For six months, he served as commander of No. 130 RAF Fighter Squadron, with the rank of acting squadron leader, the equivalent of a U.S. major. In June, 1943, the AAF told him to transfer, period. Dunn embarked on a long career with the USAAF and later the USAF.

In preparation for the transfer, the Eighth Air Force Fighter Command summoned the Eagle with the greatest amount of command experience, Squadron Leader Chesley Peterson, to help line up the new organization. General "Tooey" Spaatz, chief of the U.S. air forces in Great Britain, had let it be known that he planned to break up the old Eagle squadrons and redistribute the pilots among other USAAF units. That was not a popular idea among the Eagles. Peterson describes the confrontation over the issue.

"When we got ready to transfer out of the RAF, we had a difficult time with the USAAF. I had a conference with Spaatz, and he commented that the Eagles were unique as pilots because they had been in combat for two or three years. Especially, he wanted those highly experienced Eagles who were flight commanders and who now held the RAF rank of flight lieutenant sent not into the 4th Group but into new American units that would be coming over. 'They will come into the USAAF not as captains but as majors, and they will be commanding squadrons,' Spaatz said.

"'General, I don't think that will work,' I told him. Our pilots have been flying British equipment, and in many respects they lack the experience and background in U.S. aircraft and in U.S. Army organization that they will need. Many of them are quite new to the Eagles, and some may not be capable of handling that much rank. I don't think they are ready for it.

"'Furthermore, the new outfits coming over from the States have flown together and trained together. They have their own squadron commanders and know them and like them and have confidence in them. Even though they lack combat experience, it does not seem to me that relieving their squadron commanders, and replacing them with men from the Eagle squadrons, would be a good idea at all. It would be bad for morale.'

"I did not add that I had selfish reasons also for opposing the plan. I wanted to keep all our experienced people in our own organization, the 4th. But Tooey Spaatz was determined. 'That's the way I want it,' he said, 'and that's the way it is going to be.'

"I stood my ground, and told Spaatz I was sorry, but if that was the situation, the Eagles would remain with the RAF. After several conferences, we reached a compromise. Our three squadrons did transfer totally as a unit. We formed the new 4th Fighter Group and put it all together.

"Spaatz warned me that once the Eagles were under his control, he would be pulling some of them away from the 4th Group. My one request to the General was that when he did take away experienced Eagle pilots, he do it in an orderly fashion so that the group would not lose its most highly qualified officers in one fell swoop. I was perfectly willing to let loose of a lot of my experienced pilots whom I felt deserved promotion and commands of their own.

"Spaatz agreed with this position. After two or three months, other American units did come over and get into combat, and some personnel transfer did take place. We did lose some flight commanders, who were promoted to major and sent to other units as squadron commanders. But the normal personnel actions took place. It all worked quite well."

Peterson's initial resistance was representative. Joseph E. Durham recalls the letdown at the news of the arrangement:

"I am confident that most of the Eagles shared my disappointment that the squadrons were broken up, and we were dispersed wholesale into various U.S. fighter squadrons, after the transfer from the Royal Air Force to our own U.S. Air Corps. We had hoped to keep the squadrons intact and to carry on as usual after the change-over, but the U.S. High Command apparently felt that our combat experience would be more valuable if spread out as much as possible into the still battle inexperienced American fighter units."

How well Spaatz' policy did work was reflected by Major General Frank O'D. "Monk" Hunter, Chief of VIII Fighter Command, speaking at a ceremony in February 1943, in which he awarded the Eagles with RAF medals in the form of miniature lions:

"Five months ago I came here when the first group of you were transferred to this command. You will never know what it meant to us to receive a group of fully trained operations pilots.

"You have formed a nucleus around which we have built our fighting machine. We have been able to select men from among you to send to other units to train and lead them. All this, and everything the RAF taught you in three years of fighting the Huns, has been of invaluable aid."

The United States Army Air Forces ordered the 4th Fighter Group into being on August 22, 1942, and activated it less than a month later, on September 12, at Bushey Hall, Herts, England, Headquarters of VIII Fighter Command, Eighth Air Force. The Fighting Fourth, they called it, and rightfully so. All of its pilots were combat hardened with the Royal Air Force; they had been the personnel of the three Eagle squadrons, each of which in turn had led RAF monthly totals of enemy planes destroyed. The group took as its motto "Fourth but First" and never ceased to deserve it. The veterans and the younger pilots joining them were to make the 4th the top scoring fighter group of the USAAF in World War II. Later, in Korea, the 4th would be the highest scoring Wing in that combat theater.

Colonel Edward Wharton Anderson, of St. Petersburg, Florida, a former Stanford University athletic star who had been a pilot since 1928, was appointed Commanding Officer of the Fourth 11 days before his 39th birthday. Major Chesley Peterson, at 22, was made the group's executive officer with a promotion to lieutenant colonel.

The Eagles went onto the USAAF payroll, though they remained on detached service with the RAF through September 1942. In the RAF, as pilot officers, they had been paid $76 per month. As first lieutenants in the USAAF, the Eagles received $276. When the Eagles came to don their new AAF uniforms, they retained their special identity. They now wore U.S. wings on the left side, but wore their RAF wings on the right.

As the official transfer neared, RAF business went on. With the departure of Peterson, the RAF promptly replaced him with Gus Daymond as 71 squadron leader. Daymond had come into the squadron the same day as Peterson, constantly had flown the toughest combat missions without injury, and had matched Peterson plane for plane with battle scores that made both men aces. He had even upstaged Peterson's DFC with his own DFC and Bar.

Three days before the formal ceremonies marking the transfer, what was supposed to be business as usual turned grim. In newly delivered Spitfire IXs, 12 pilots of 133 Squadron set out on what at first appeared to be another routine bomber escort mission. This time, they were to accompany American crewed Boeing B-17s on an attack against Morlaix, a Channel port 40 miles east of Brest.

The result was sheer disaster—"a mission that should never have been flown," the surviving Eagles called it. Not one of 133 Squadron's new Spitfires returned. This was the only Mark IX mission to be flown by any Eagle squadron. The effect was traumatic. Harold Strickland put it starkly in his diary: "133 Eagle Squadron missing."

The September 26 tally:

All twelve planes lost. Four pilots—William H. Baker, Gene Neville, Leonard Ryerson and Dennis David Smith—shot down and killed. Two—Acting Squadron Leader Gordon Brettell, the only Englishman in the group, and M. E. Jackson—seriously wounded and taken prisoner along with four others who bailed out or crash landed unhurt or with minor injuries—Charles A. Cook, Jr., George Middleton, George Sperry and Gil Wright. One pilot, Robert E. Smith, managed to evade capture after bailing out and, with the help of the French underground, escaped to Spain. The twelfth participant, Richard N. Beaty, force landed out of fuel in England, and survived injuries.

Brettell, the British leader of the mission, was to meet an especially sad end. He took part in an historic mass escape from prison camp, was recaptured, and was among 50 participants executed by the Germans.

Four young men from Visalia, California—Dave Logan, William Allen Arends, George Middleton, and Donald "Mick" Lambert—had joined the RAF together, styled themselves The Four Horsemen from Visalia, and declared they would have that caption stencilled on their Spitfires. Logan was killed soon after their arrival in England, in a training accident. Arends tangled with Fw 190s during a bomber escort mission to Hardelot and St. Omer, France, June 20, 1942, and his plane was last seen diving earthward. Now there were only two Visalia horsemen.

Then came Morlaix.

Among the missing: George Middleton of the Visalia Four. Mick Lambert wrote despairingly to a friend: "I'm the only one left. I can't stand that *Four Horsemen* label on my plane any longer. I'm having it painted off. The new one will be *Lone Ranger*."

After the transfer of the Eagles into the 4th Fighter Group, the loss of his three closest friends began to prey on Lambert's mind. The four had attended the same schools, taken part in the same sports, dreamed that they might form a championship team some day. Finally, the troubled survivor went to his squadron commander and said, "I guess I'm yellow."

"You are not yellow, Mick," the CO replied. "But you need a change." Assignment with two of his fellow Eagles, as instructors, to an operational training unit in England followed.

The change-of-command ceremony at Debden on September 29 was simple and stirring. The Squadron Leaders of 71 and 133 Squadrons RAF became Majors Daymond and McColpin of the United States 334th and 336th Fighter Squadrons, respectively. British Squadron Leader Dudley Williams, of 121, transferred his charge to Flight Lieutenant William James Daley, now Major Daley, of the 335th. Air Chief Marshal Sir Sholto Douglas, chief of Fighter Command, awarded each Eagle the RAF Medallion, and told the Americans that in shooting down at least 73 enemy planes and, over several months, leading the scores for all RAF squadrons, "You have proved yourselves grand fighters and good companions."

A guard of honor, a parade and review, the hoisting of the Stars and Stripes, a band playing *The Star Spangled Banner*, and an Eagle era had ended.

The 4th was carrying on.

The new group, which until December represented the entire fighter strength of the Eighth Air Force, proudly displayed its origins not only in its motto, "Fourth but First," but in a shield showing a spear garnished with three Eagle feathers, and in a crest displaying a wreath of colors on the face of a lion, the symbol of Great Britain. The transplanted pilots were delighted with the USAAF's selection of Colonel Edward Anderson as their new Commanding Officer.

"Of all the personnel actions I have seen in thirty or more years in service, most of them wrong, that one was absolutely right—putting a colonel's hat on Anderson to form and lead the 4th Fighter Group," Pete Peterson said almost four decades later. "Andy arrived before we had transferred. Our transfer was held up while we took part in the Dieppe commando operation, so Andy was there for two weeks, observing RAF operations. He stayed with the 4th almost a year. He was terrific. He taught me everything I know of the Air Force."

Peterson succeeded Anderson as 4th Group Commander in August 1943, when Anderson was made a brigadier general and given command of the 66th Fighter Wing. The step up in rank, when he was 23, made Peterson the youngest full colonel in the U.S. Air Forces.

At the outset, the 4th was an Anglo-American hybrid. "On paper, we were an Army Air Force unit, but the only Americans in the group at the time of the transfer were the pilots," Mac McColpin recalls. "The aircraft mechanics, ground crews and even my squadron adjutant were English. We flew the same planes we had as Eagles.

"It wasn't until March, 1943, that the 4th started resembling an American organization. By that time, most of our men and officers were from the States. For the first time since the war started, we were flying an American Fighter, the P-47.

"Besides the change of uniform, unit designation, and ground personnel, the difference that gave me the greatest pleasure was the pay. As an RAF squadron leader my pay was equal to that of an Army buck sergeant. As an American major, my salary went up considerably. The most unpleasant change was the paperwork. Everywhere we turned, there was some correspondence or form to sign, write, or file. With the RAF it was much simpler. You didn't have paperwork, period!"

For the transition of the Eagle Squadrons from the RAF to the USAAF, with its temporary overlapping of commands, Debden Wing Commander Raymond Myles Beecham Duke-Woolley retained control of 4th Group flying. Duke-Woolley had been one of the first RAF pilots to destroy a night-raiding German airplane, in 1940, and he was also the first British pilot to be awarded an American DFC. Before his eventual posting to nonoperational duties, he was credited with shooting down 11 enemy planes.

While still in the RAF, the Eagles had heard that for the USAAF they would fly the new, still secret Republic P-47 Thunderbolt. Anderson confirmed the rumor, but added that until the P-47s were shipped to England, the 4th would continue flying Spitfires.

Thus it was that the first combat mission of the new American unit, a fighter sweep into France on October 2, 1942, was led by a British Wing Commander and flown in British aircraft. German Fw 190s intercepted the Spitfires over the Calais area. Oscar Coen, Gene Fetrow and S. M. Anderson each shot down an enemy plane, and Duke-Woolley and James A. Clark, Jr. shared in the destruction of another plane.

The first Eagle to lose his life after the transfer was A. J. "Tony" Seaman. His Spitfire crashed into the North Sea after an apparent engine failure on October 20, 1942. A month later former Eagles Bob Sprague of San Diego and James Harrington of Buffalo, New York, collided, and Sprague was killed. Harrington, who bailed out successfully, after the war became pilot and maintenance engineer for a Spit IX and three DeHavilland Tiger Moths owned by actor Cliff Robertson. Harrington died in the crash of a Twin Beechcraft near Abha, Saudi Arabia, September 3, 1967. Killed with him was his passenger, Sheik Bin Ladin.

Before the end of 1942 Frank Smolinsky, Roy Evans and Fetrow each had shot down an enemy plane. Evans had to bail out but was promptly rescued from the English Channel. Soon afterward Stan Anderson and Robert Boock each destroyed an Fw 190.

While they were waiting for the Thunderbolt and other American equipment that had been promised them, the three squadrons had started repainting their Spitfires with American insignia. Peterson recalls that Jimmy Clark was making a test flight in one of the newly painted Spits when a small British Miles Hawker transport cut through his flight path:

"As any good fighter pilot would, Jimmy promptly made several 'attacks' on the small plane, and gave it a rough time. Then he landed back at the base in Debden.

"Jack Robinson, my intelligence officer at that time, came running and said, 'My God, who was it that just landed?' Then he rushed out to Jimmy. 'Harold Balfour just phoned,'

Robinson said. 'He wants to see you immediately. You are to get back in your plane and fly up to Duxford. He is waiting for you.'

"Balfour was the Undersecretary for Air, a very great friend of ours. Robinson said Balfour told him he had been terribly frightened by some wild American pilot beating him up in the air.

"When Jimmy got back, he told me that as he taxied up to the ramp at Duxford, the wind was blowing strongly, and this tall figure in full morning dress—striped pants and tail coat—came out of Base Operations. 'He headed into the wind, and looked just like old Beelzebub himself coming down the ramp,' Clark said. 'He wanted to know if I was the pilot who beat him up. Then he gave me the worst chewing out I have ever had in my life.'

"Jimmy's eyes were big and blue. He was really a frightened young man. I shall never forget his description of the Undersecretary for Air striding up the tarmac, tailcoat blowing in the breeze, looking exactly like old Satan personified."

The American Ambassador to Great Britain, John Winant, himself a former pilot, was an occasional visitor to the base. Jimmy Clark was the Ambassador's nephew, and Winant would come out to see him. When he was feeling low about diplomatic matters, it cheered him up to talk with the American fighter pilots."

"After the transfer," says Lee Gover, "we were still flying Spits and doing a lot of convoy escort work in the English channel. One day, Mick Lambert and I went out on patrol. The tail wheel on a Spitfire did not retract, and on takeoff, Lambert picked up a telephone line on his tail wheel.

"It was a very poor day for flying—low ceiling, and visibility only about a tenth of a mile. I was busy flying vectors to find the convoy and hadn't paid much attention to Mick except to notice that he was there. We finally located the convoy, and then I saw the 150 or 200 feet of telephone wire on Mick's wheel. The Spitfire radios were poor at best, so when I called Lambert and said he had wire on his tail, all he heard was 'on your tail.'

"Well, you never saw a more beautiful instant aerobatic show in your life. After he had settled down and we were about to leave the convoy, I called again and said, 'Red Two, you have a couple hundred feet of cable on your tail.' Once again, he only heard 'You have a couple ———— on your tail.' The air show was on once again.

"When we landed back at base—and his landing roll was very short—he now knew what it was all about. He came up to me and said he had wondered why in hell I hadn't come to help him fight off the Luftwaffe instead of flying along straight and level watching him."

Eleanor Roosevelt visited Debden and the 4th Group on November 4, 1942. Three days later, American forces landed in Africa. In England, authorities announced that church bells would be rung on Sunday, November 15, for the first time since the fall of France. Such festivities inspired Dixie Alexander to resolve that it was time for special activities.

"I decided that a good publicity stunt for the USAAF, and a good way for me to get an early DFC, would be to foreshadow the inevitable landing of U.S. troops in France by dropping an American flag at the Arc de Triomphe on November 11, Armistice Day.

"I went through channels from Squadron to Pete to Anderson and through the British on the base up to and including Duke-Woolley. I even practiced dropping a flag wrapped around a small brick, and it worked. All was in order.

"On the 11th, I would fly into France well before first light, to hit the target at about daybreak. I would make landfall west of Dieppe, fly south on the deck, pick up the Seine near Rouen, and follow the river, using the Eiffel Tower as a landmark. I would slow down, pull back the canopy, and heave out the flag at about 200 feet. Then I would run for the Coast. If there were clouds, as was to be expected, I would head for them; if not, I would come back on the deck.

"I had a souped-up Spit IX with long range tanks, and felt reasonably sure I could outrun or outmaneuver any opposition that would be lucky enough to find me. The Wing would be airborne at dawn and, after setting up a good diversion or two, would meet me at the coast and give me top cover.

"All was approved and readied. Somehow, the plan went through Group Command in good shape.

"On the night of the tenth, the whole plan collapsed. Someone at Fighter Command remembered that they had rejected a similar request by the French on Bastille Day. With this last minute discovery, Air Ministry barely got into the matter, and an incident possibly offensive to an ally was narrowly avoided. The plan had to be turned down. At Group Headquarters there were a few unhappy moments for several persons of importance."

As the time for adoption of the new P-47s approached, the Spitfire operations began to wind down, but certainly not entirely.

On January 22, 1943, the 335 and 336 Spitfire Squadrons escorted RAF Bostons to bomb St. Omer. Oscar Coen, Stan Anderson and Bob Boock each shot down an Fw 190. Chet Grimm bailed out off the French coast, and was not found.

On February 25, the weather was bad and Bill Kelly organized a shipping recco. Six Eagles took off in Spitfires to look for shipping along the Belgian and Dutch coast. Near Oostvoorne, they ran into a 12-ship convoy which was heavily armed. Bill Kelly was hit in the radiator and Don Willis was hit in the wing. Kelly headed for home, but his engine soon overheated and caught on fire. He was attempting to bail out when he crashed into the sea. Willis, who had flown for Finland and Norway before joining the RAF, made it back to the base safely.

"My last mission in the Spitfire was a Rhubarb to the Dunkirk area," recalls Leroy Gover.

"I took Ken Peterson and Bob Mirsch along. We flew at zero feet, crossed the French coast above Le Treport, swooped inland, and turned right. All the time, we were down on the deck, hopping over houses and trees. I spotted a train, and shot hell out of it. The other pilots were off to my left, and doing the same. I turned to start for home, and found myself flying right down the main part of Dunkirk, with the ground defenses shooting like mad.

"A gun on top of a three-story building was shooting at us. I poured a long burst, and he quit firing. I reached the harbor and was firing at a boat dead ahead when I was hit from behind. The shell went through the tail, and blew the radio behind the seat all to pieces. Another shell hit me, and passed through the cowl and propeller blade. I started skidding to evade the enemy, and saw their tracers going by.

"As soon as I was out of range I set a course for England, but with no radio. Mirsch and Peterson had become separated. Ken had his right wheel shot up and a big hole through his wing. He crash landed in England, at Bradwe Bay. Mirsch also crashed on landing.

"Fog had closed over England and I couldn't see a thing. Almost out of fuel, I was about to hit the silk when I spotted North Weald through the mist. I landed with five gallons of petrol. I had been airborne for two hours and 10 minutes, a long time for a Spitfire with no external tank. I received the Air Medal for this mission.

"On January 16, 1943, 24 of the 4th Group pilots were picked to start training in the new P-47 fighter. I kissed my Spitfire *Sondra Lee* goodbye and went over to 334 Squadron, where we were to train."

Gover served in three different RAF squadrons, and always had his own plane.

"When you first came to a squadron, you flew as spare until someone was shot down, then moved into what I guess you'd call First String. The only time anyone flew any of my planes would be when I'd be off to London on a 24-hour pass and a mission came up. *Sondra Lee* was named after my little niece."

Not long after the transfer, three of the veteran Eagles— Dixie Alexander, Bert Stewart and Don Lambert—made their way as instructors into the first American operational training unit. It had been set up near Shrewsbury, a Western England city which was noted for its Gaelic, Norman, and Roman ruins. The OTU took the name of the plain on which it had been erected, Atcham. Alexander became deputy flight commander of the 109th Observation Squadron.

"Atcham was a mudhole when I arrived and when I left," Alexander says. "We flew off a couple of metal strips, and the surrounding area was mud wherever you walked, with temporary buildings serving for everything. We were supposed to instruct pilots arriving from the States on operations and tactics—both low level and high altitude. Atcham was bedlam! We instructed colonels, majors, lieutenants, bomber pilots, fighter pilots—all types. What it really amounted to was a big holding area; there was nowhere else in England for the new men to go."

At Atcham, pilots were trained first in the Miles Master, and then in the Spitfire A and, finally, the American P-39 Airacobra.

"The Miles Masters always presented a problem," Alexander says.

"Due to shortages, they were equipped with three different types of engines—the Griffon, the Hercules, and the Rolls-Royce. The Hercules ran counterclockwise, making it necessary to trim the aircraft opposite to that of the other two, to compensate for torque, which in the Master was extreme. It was a common sight to see a student pour the coal to a Master and go screaming across the base in a big circle, hoping to mire in the mud before running into a building."

The commanding officer at Atcham was a reserve lieutenant colonel, newly arrived in England and fresh from his job as a postmaster in Kansas. He was said to be a personal friend of Harry S. Truman, who was then a prominent U.S. Senator, and to have been a flight instructor in World War I.

"He did fly the L-5 a couple of times when I first arrived," Alexander recalls, "but when we checked him out in the Master, he somehow grabbed the undercarriage lever instead of the brake release, gave the throttle a burst, and settled to earth, grinding his way into the runway. He never flew again, at least at Atcham, and was relieved of his command when promoted to the rank of full colonel and given a program of acquiring land close to all of the new American bases being set up. It became his job to supervise the development of base vegetable gardens, with the help of the Home Guard."

One group of pilots arrived from the States on a Thursday, and by Friday had been given weekend passes to get them out from under foot. The Germans picked that weekend to make their last raid on London, and by Sunday afternoon most of the pilots were back on base. Alexander reflects on that irritating period.

"It was discouraging to see all of these people, with their rank and many decorations, strutting about, while we slogged in the mud after a year of operations with the British and nary a decoration of any kind.

"We solved this by going to the local stores. The British had always issued suspenders rather than belts for airmen, and they came in many beautiful color assortments. By snipping off about an inch from each pair and folding them over with the help of a seamstress, we found that they made beautiful ribbons. From then on, Lambert and I wore about 16 each, which no one could identify.

"We also developed fearful twitches and nervous wild habits in the mess, on the flight line, and in the air, to shatter the calm of the new pilots.

"Britain's crack train, the Flying Scot, came close by Atcham on the run between London and Edinburgh, at more than 100 miles an hour. Knowing its schedule, it was easy to take a new student for a ride in an L-5 or Master and fly alongside the train, waving to the engineer and ducking under high tension wires. With the twitch and other erratic habits, we gave the new pupil much to think about."

The matter of scores and records and the notoriety that could accompany high numbers began to take on more importance for the American pilots, especially as new units became rivals of the veterans.

In July 1943, Captain E. V. "Eddie" Rickenbacker, the leading American air ace of World War I, visited the 4th, and told the assembled pilots that he would give a case of Scotch to the first man to break his record, then considered to be 26 enemy planes and balloons destroyed. The offer from the aging war hero, who was at the time head of Eastern Air Lines, poured fuel on the developing rivalry between the 4th, headed by Peterson, and the "Wolf Pack" 56th Fighter Group, then commanded by Peterson's classmate and fellow ace, Dave Schilling.

Unit pride ran high, according to Peterson: "The 56th never would recognize the fact that the 4th was the better outfit. At one point, they finally had a higher total score, but just toward the end of the war, we got into a lot of stuff, and the 4th Group wound up with 23 more kills than the 56th. They objected, because we counted 180 enemy aircraft that we had shot down while flying with the RAF.

"I never paid much attention to the individual scores. The numbers didn't really mean a damn thing. Bob Johnson in the 56th began to get the high scores and Hub Zemke, the Group commander, would put three guys around him on a mission, just to make sure that Johnson would be the one who would shoot. It didn't work though. Dick Bong, out in the Pacific, shot down 40 enemy planes, and became the leading American ace of the war."

Some of the American fighter pilots in the Royal Air

Force, flying in units other than the three Eagle Squadrons, had received a considerable amount of publicity, even though the RAF discouraged this singling out for attention. Peterson mentions Billy Fiske, Art Donahue and Lance Wade:

"The effect was not good. I remember in particular, too, the unhealthy competition that developed between Paddy Finucane, the Irish ace, and Bluey Truscott—Keith Truscott—the Australian ace. They were in separate RAF squadrons, and the rivalry got so bad it really started some exaggerated claims.

"In the Eagles, we were terribly strict about our scores. An enemy plane practically had to break into a thousand pieces, come down in flames, and be seen by the whole squadron, in order to be recorded as destroyed. But then the gun camera came along. It gave a bit of leeway to those who liked to fudge on their scores a little."

Among the Eagles, too, there were stars, the aces with their exciting tales of combat, their pictures and publicity. And there were the run of the mill pilots, risking their necks just about as often, fighting equally as hard, yet when asked to list their aircraft destroyed, ships sunk or trains blasted, were obliged simply to jot down "none."

Reade Tilley, a Malta-based ace, puts it this way: "Some flew to beat hell, shot at a lot of people, and never hit anybody. Some flew their tails off on routine convoy patrol missions much of the time, unglamorous chores to insure that coals from Newcastle got to the factories of London. These men always hung in there and were the biggest part of the fighting force. They were vital to the conduct of the war, but compared to the star performers, their story was no big thing.

"Then there were still others who barely crossed the stage, without a speaking part. Many were killed in training without having fired a shot in anger. A few returned home for one reason or another. Some were clobbered on their early missions.

"In the RAF, the DFC and DFM were normally awarded automatically with the fifth kill; a second medal, or Bar, at the tenth kill; and the DSC or DSO—I forget which—at the fifteenth. There were exceptions for special so-called acts of valor or performance. Mauriello had one at three, the lowest I know of. Mine came at four. Peterson received the DSC with less than 15. One or two Britishers won the DSC at around 10 victories, but they were completely mad—fighting on after severe wounds, taking on squadrons singlehanded, and the like.

"In the British military those who won awards were credited with them after their names, in all military records and correspondence, and were otherwise entitled to such use. Awards such as the DFM, to enlisted men, included a small cash bonus."

The title of ace came into use early in World War I. Initially it applied to a pilot who had destroyed 10 or more enemy aircraft. When the United States entered that war, the standard was lowered to five enemy planes, in order to offer recognition to American pilots.

A 1920 policy statement by the director of the U.S. Army's Air Service said:

> The U.S. Air Service does not use the title "ace" in referring to those who are credited officially with five or more aerial victories over enemy aircraft. It is not the policy of the Air Service to glorify one particular branch of aeronautics, aviation or aerostation at the expense of another. . . . The work of observation and bombardment is considered equally as hazardous as that of pursuit.

The U.S. Air Force's Albert F. Simpson Historical Research Center, Maxwell Air Force Base, Alabama, said in a 1975 paper that the Air Service policy of 1920 had been retained by the U.S. Air Corps, the USAAF and the USAF, and was in effect during World War II and the Korean War.

"In other words, so far as the Air Force is concerned, there are no aces," the study said.

"These men have been applauded and feted, and acclaimed by the public as heroes; but from the Air Force they have no special reward, not even a medal, a ribbon or a badge to signify that they are aces. Nevertheless, people persist in using the title. The Air Force never has prohibited, or even discouraged, the informal and unofficial use of the title within its own organization.

"The word 'ace' appears frequently in official documents. . . . The use of the title actually has been encouraged by the practice of awarding official credit to individuals for the destruction of enemy aircraft."

Official adoption of the title has been avoided in part because of the difficulty of defining an ace—of deciding whether to broaden the term beyond fighter pilot to extend to bomber pilots and gunners, or to include remotely controlled airplanes, helicopters, gliders, spacecraft, or aircraft destroyed on the ground, in the scoring.

On one spectacular mission in northern France, Jessie Taylor shot down an Fw 190 and an Me 109, in the Coutances area of Normandy, and shared a third kill with Second Lieutenant Robert R. Meyer. Another member of the flight destroyed one Me 109 and probably shot down another.

The keeping of combat scores necessarily was haphazard and uncertain, Taylor said. "I know 20 to 25 of our people were not properly credited. I didn't have more than five or six enemy planes confirmed on paper, along with six or seven probably destroyed.

"I know I shot the wing off of one plane—I saw four feet of wing fall away—but I only was credited with a damage. I know damn well what happened. Some ground personnel looked at the pictures and made the decision. Another time, I was strafing shipping on a canal in Holland and looked back and saw an oil barge on fire. But the gun camera's picture was fogged, and not a damn thing showed on the film."

Dixie Alexander says that the granting of credit for enemy aircraft destroyed was relatively severe early in the war, and often lax in the latter stages of the air offensive.

"The RAF was tough. You either had good pictures—and just strikes were not enough—or you had to have confirmation by a couple of persons. Later in the war, claims became a laugh.

"I broke in several of the later real big aces, and without mentioning names, they never showed me too much. They were not good shots and were not the best in the thought department—two very necessary items. Some of these huge scores were run up on confirmation such as A confirming two for B, and B confirming three for A. This went on and on, with the same people working together.

"After 168 sorties of various types in combined operations in the two armies, I finally wound up with six destroyed and one probably. Don Blakeslee, who was just about the best, had 12 in about 450 missions. There were many more of the same.

"It seems unlikely that some of the other fellows could get over 20 kills in 100 missions or less. There just weren't that many German aircraft around, and the sky was too big. The records bear this out. However, we needed our glamor boys— our Gentiles, our Gabreskis, our Gables and our Lyndons. It helped morale, and served well for recruiting purposes. In our own world, we were too busy to worry about these things, and, of course, we knew the truth.

"I remember a show on August 1, 1942, when gunners on the bombers were credited with 17 German aircraft destroyed. The truth was that we were bounced on the way out from the target by three 190s. They came down from about 30,000 feet, and were going full bore when they made their pass. They went over on their backs, belching diesel fuel, and on to Germany. We couldn't have caught them with anything less than a jet.

"I saw no hits, and we didn't even bother with them. Anyhow, the bomber boys all fired, and claimed 17. There were 17 Air Medals handed out for this one."

Bill Dunn, himself an ace, concurs.

"We used to get a kick out of the bomber combat reports, especially the air gunner reports. These air gunners would claim they had shot down more Me 109s and Fw 190s than there were in the sky.

"A 190 would come diving through the bomber formation, making about a three-quarter stern attack, fire, and then roll over on its back and split-S away. The minute it rolled over, a puff of black smoke would stream out behind, caused by the fuel injection system. No problem. But those gunners would all take a squirt in that general direction, and each one would claim he had shot down an enemy aircraft. And the glory hungry Eighth Air Force would approve all these claims. It was unbelievable.

"Sometimes the fighter escort wouldn't see more than 10 or 12 enemy aircraft on the whole mission, but the bomber gunners would claim they had shot down at least 30 or 40. It got to be a big joke, even with the German air force, who would report their own losses accurately."

Alexander makes some critical points about unit effectiveness in terms of the so-called kill ratio.

"The British kill ratio in the war was about three and one half enemy aircraft destroyed to one lost. The record of the

4th Fighter Group, Blakeslee's outfit, showed a ratio of four and one half to one. This was the oldest, most experienced fighter group in the ETO, studded with experienced and accomplished leaders. It doesn't make good sense to believe that the 56th Group, a younger, less experienced outfit flying in the same skies with the same type of aircraft, could achieve a record of eight to one.

"All the other outfits are somewhere in between in the scoring. The figure given by the 56th, to bring up its ratio, has got to be fictitious, and no doubt has a great deal to do with the fact that they harbored such aces as Francis Gabreski, Dave Schilling and Hub Zemke within their group."

The Air Force Simpson Historical Research Center completed in 1979 an exhaustive study of American claims for the destruction of enemy aircraft in World War II. There were numerous fractional scores, since many kills were shared by two or more pilots. The Center's final listing recognized 16,591 full and partial credits.

From this compilation, *Air Force* Magazine identified 51 pilots as having destroyed 15 or more enemy planes in combat. Only three of these—Don Gentile, with a score of 19.88, Duane Beeson, with 17.33, and Don Blakeslee, with 15—had flown with Eagle Squadrons before entering U.S. service, and only Blakeslee had been credited with victories while with the Eagles (three wins as an Eagle in addition to the 15 U.S. credits.)

A list compiled by the American Fighter Aces Association, also published in 1979, in *The American Fighter Aces Album*:

Don Gentile, 21.84; Duane Beeson, 17.33; (Blakeslee unlisted here;) George Carpenter, 13.33; Howard Hively, 12; Carroll McColpin, 11; James A. Clark, 10½; Chesley Peterson, Reade Tilley, 7 each; R. L. Alexander, Raymond Care, Gregory Daymond, William R. Dunn, 6 each; Selden Edner, James Peck, 5 each.

A listing by Raymond Toliver and Trevor Constable in *Fighter Aces of the U.S.A.*, published in 1979:

Gentile, 19.83; Beeson, 19.33; Blakeslee, RAF 4, USAF 11½; Carpenter, 13.33; John J. Lynch, RAF 13; Hively, 12; Clark, 11½; McColpin, RAF 3, USAF 5 [RAF figure at variance with narratives in this book;] Daymond, USAF-RAF, 7; Tilley,

RAF, 7; Peterson, RAF 6, USAF 1; Care, Roy Evans and Henry L. Mills, 6 each, USAF; Dunn, RAF 5, USAF 1; Peck, RAF 5, USAF 1; Oscar Coen, RAF 3, USAF 2½; John A. Campbell, Edner and Jackson B. Mahon, 5 each, all in the RAF; Richard Alexander, RAF 2, USAF 3; Kenneth G. Smith, USAF 5.

Although the Eagles, by virtue of their record and experience, were an elite group within the Air Corps, they did not carry their sense of identity too far. Donald H. Ross, of Huntington Park, California, was an Eagle for only a few hours. He had arrived in England as a sergeant pilot in April, 1942, but joined 121 Squadron only on the very day it changed into the 335th Squadron of the USAAF. The closely knit clan of Eagles happily recognized him as a full-fledged member of the exclusive Eagle Squadron Association formed after the war.

Ross readily distinguished himself as a fighter pilot, but in December, 1943, he had to bail out of his P-51 Mustang after shooting down an Me 109. He was captured near Leipzig and was interned in Stalag Luft I. His subsequent Air Force career saw him flying F-86 jets in Korea and, with Carroll McColpin and Chesley Peterson, becoming one of three Eagles to make Major General.

In the way of honors, to put things into perspective, Ernie Beatie, of 121 Squadron, may have been the only Eagle to receive the Legion of Merit. "I didn't even know what that award was when I received the 'letter from the President,'" he says.

"We were socked in for about two weeks at one period during the winter of 1943. At the time, I had some kind of Mickey Mouse duty as 'Group Gunnery Officer', the principal duty and advantage being that I could spend hours looking at the combat films after they were developed. Interesting; and I couldn't help noticing what lousy shots we all were.

"An idea evolved in my head that perhaps I could design a crude form of trainer that might help us all. I didn't discuss this with anyone except a sergeant down at the hangars, who volunteered to manufacture the trainer if I would give him the plans. I've forgotten his name entirely, bless him!

"My biggest problem was that of basic supplies, until I confiscated an unattended bicycle. That solved my metals requirement. Then a peanut can solved more of the supplies problem, and I 'found' a gun sight that had been 'abandoned'. I figured out the mathematics of the thing, and the sergeant did the rest. We tested it, and the damned thing worked. I got permission to put it in the Link Trainer room. I don't know whether any of the fellows even remember it.

"One day, I was in dispersal waiting to take off, when I got a call to report to the Link Trainer room. I was scrubbed from the mission, and wondered, 'What in hell have I done wrong now?' When I arrived, General Devers greeted me. I went into shock. He was playing with my machine—and having a ball. Naturally, I felt proud.

"At his questioning, I replied, 'Yes sir, I designed it. No sir, I didn't make it. Sarge actually made it. Yes sir, I scrabbled the material from all over the place. Yes sir, those are bicycle spokes. Yes sir, some of the bicycles on the base are missing one or two spokes. Won't hurt them, though. Yes sir, that is a peanut tin as the lamp holder.'

"I thought no more about it when the general left, but I remember being annoyed at having to miss the mission. Then, about two weeks later, I was called again to the Link Trainer room. This time, a sergeant from headquarters was there. General Devers had sent him to 'professionalize' my plans, supposedly to put the thing into production. I had no plans, of course. I merely gave him what drawings I had.

"About a year later, when I was stationed in Baton Rouge, Louisiana, I received the letter announcing the award of the Legion of Merit. I went to the base office to ask what the Legion of Merit was, and was surprised to learn that it is the fourth highest award in the Armed Forces. I'm proud of it, but why in hell I received it I still don't know. They must have had one left over somewhere."

Squadron mates and correspondents gather around Harold Strickland's Spitfire on Strick's return from a dawn sortie over France during the Dieppe raid. He has tackled four Fw 190s, the first Allied pilot to fire in anger during the fateful Operation Jubilee.

Jim Daley (left), Joe Durham (above), Hank Ayres (below), and Tommy Allen (lower left). The emblem on Durham's Spit is a charging razorback, symbol of the University of Arkansas.

P/O Reade Tilley, an Eagle who transferred to Malta, waits in his plane at Luqua Airfield during a fast between-missions turnaround. His fitter is pulling the prop through prior to start, while an airman, sailor, and soldier reload the Spitfire V's 20 mm. Oerlikon cannon. To increase the Spit's rate of climb, the two outboard guns have been removed from each wing, under the principle that "if you can shoot, you don's need six guns." *(Imperial War Museum photo)*

Leo Nomis and his Spitfire, February 1942. Ahead lay successes leading to victory in the Middle East.

A formation of Spitfires returning from a mission.

George Carpenter, of 121 Squadron, in his Spitfire. Note the rearview mirror, essential for the fighter pilot.

P/O James E. Griffin in Alexandria, Egypt, December 1942. The course of the war was now turning.

A Spitfire of the 335th still carrying its RAF letter designators but now sporting an American star insignia. This was in late September 1942, when newly transferred Eagles were awaiting their Republic P-47 Thunderbolts.

The Focke-Wulf 190 was an improvement over the Messerschmitt 109. Sometimes mistaken for the P-47 because of its radial engine, the 190 was powerful in the climb.

Enormous when compared to the Spitfire, the Republic P-47 Thunderbolt was at first disliked by many American pilots and generally not favored over the P-51, but many Eagles came to respect and score high in the fighter. The pilot shown here is Steve Pisanos.

Aubrey Stanhope Steve Pisanos Grant Eichar

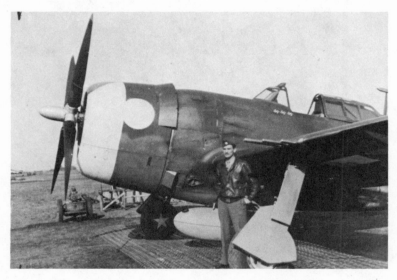

P-47 with extra range insurance—a fuel tank mounted on the belly and jettisoned in combat. The pilot is Don Young.

Above, left to right: the 335th CO, Major Roy Evans; Bob Mannix; and Michael Miluck home on leave June 1943.

The lethal P-51—the masterpiece that was almost dumped. Ace Don Blakeslee leads other D models of the 334th, 335th and 336th in a tight formation over France.

Howard Hively, "The Deacon," in his P-51.

Winners of the Distinguished Flying Cross (from left): Lee Gover, Bud Care, Duane Beeson, Aubrey Stanhope, Gil Halsey and Spike Miley. Note their new U.S. wings worn on the left side and their RAF wings on the right.

A welcome sight to U.S. bomber crews: A P-47 pilot—in this case, Don Young—tucks his Thunderbolt in for close escort.

Malta Stepp

Above, left: Brig. General Frank "Monk" Hunter awards George Carpenter the DFC. In left background is Don Blakeslee. Above, right: Sel Edner.

By all expectations, this battered P-47 on the emergency strip at Sainte Mère-Église, France, shouldn't have made it home after one of Edwin D. "Jessie" Taylor's bombing-strafing missions shortly after D-Day, while attacking a truck convoy. After hitting some trees and bouncing off the ground, the plane was nursed back with a runaway prop and seizing engine 70 miles to base. The engine cowling was badly damaged, two bottom cylinders of a 360-degree circle were shattered. A 10-inch segment of the cowling was

lost. The four .50 caliber machine guns in each wing were broken from their mounts, the right wing was set back four inches and the bomb racks were dislodged. Large chunks were gouged from the bases of the prop blades, yet the outer portion of the blades, which had been turning at high RPM, were not scratched.

Top: Taylor is debriefing his unit's intelligence officer. Right: Major Taylor is awarded the DFC for guiding a blinded comrade to a safe landing during one of four D-Day missions.

8

ENTER
JUGS AND
MUSTANGS

Three Republic P-47D Thunderbolts, among the first to arrive in England, joined the Atcham forces. Called the "Jug" by its pilots, the P-47D was a comparative monster of 14,000 pounds gross weight, with the enormous Pratt & Whitney R-2800-21 engine providing 2,300 horsepower. The squadron flight commanders at Atcham were given the honor of being the first in their sector to fly the Jugs, and Dixie Alexander was nominated to lead off. He still shudders at the memory of the flight he made on April 10, 1943.

"I had been up late the night before, listening to Pierce McKennon—later a great squadron leader in the 4th—play the piano and Buck Weaver blow a borrowed horn. Buck had been third trumpet for Louis Armstrong. Liquor had flowed, and I had a hangover.

"Sitting in a P-47 after having flown Spitfires was like coming out of a small office at the end of a gymnasium and walking into the playing area. It was awfully big.

"Checkout consisted of reading a tech order and a little familiarization in the cockpit. I cranked up, went to the end of the runway, got cleared, and roared off. Everything seemed to handle well. I was about three fourths of the way down the runway, when I checked my air speed and found that I had no instrument indication.

"The airplane was already trying to fly. I added a little more coal, and proceeded to become airborne, still with no air speed indicated. I climbed to nearly 10,000 feet, feeling the aircraft out and liking most of what I felt, before I called the control tower to tell them of my difficulty. No answer. I tried several times, while orbiting the field. I felt that I was transmitting but not receiving, and asked them to verify this with an Aldis light. They complied immediately. In this way we established communication to the point of their being able to answer yes or no. They agreed that I should fly around a bit and try to bring the plane in hot.

"Then the warning light on the wheels refused to go out. I slowed to what I thought was a safe speed, dropped down to about 5,000 feet, and flew by the tower asking for an opinion on the undercarriage. They could not be sure; so I put down the undercarriage, jerked the plane around a bit, and decided to make my pass at the field. I came in hot, the undercarriage stayed down, and I stopped before the end of the runway after burning off the rubber from my tires.

"I got out of the aircraft, nodded to the ground personnel and the blood wagon, which had arrived on the scene, and walked to the dispersal hut. It was just another of those rides a pilot likes to have behind him."

The pilots in transition training flew often to build up proficiency in the P-47. Leroy Gover reported "nothing but trouble" on one of his early Thunderbolt flights.

"I was flying at 21,000 feet when an oil plug came out," he said. "Oil sprayed on the engine and set it on fire. I started to bail out, then decided to try and put the fire out. I cut all switches, turned off the fuel, side-slipped the plane for about 2,000 feet, and the fire blew out. I was above cloud and called for a homing and to clear the field. Radar brought me over the field, and I broke through the overcast. With no engine, I came down rapidly but made a deadstick landing. I received the Army Commendation Medal for saving the aircraft."

Don Nee recalls that in mid-January 1943, when the Thunderbolt pilots were chosen from among the Eagles, "we had not even seen a P-47. At a lecture we were told that if a Thunderbolt was going straight down at 500 mph, it would take 17,000 feet to level off. This was not true, but it had us worried.

"One day in February, Spike Miley, John Mitchellweis and I went up to spin the '47s. Being from the old school, we wanted to know all its flying characteristics. John got his into a spin first and never recovered. We watched his plane go into the ground. He got out on the way down, but the terrific speed tore the chute from his body. He was found about a mile from where his plane went in, our first P-47 pilot loss. I still haven't spun a P-47. I guess from that day on, I never completely trusted them, until a long time later, back in the States."

Lee Gover says that he had just landed his P-47, *Sondra Lee the Tenth*, after a test flight to 36,000 feet, when Mitchellweis asked to take the plane up for the spin exercises. "All we know is that the P-47 buried itself and he was found two miles from the ship, and his chute was two miles farther on," Gover said. "When they recovered the body all he had on was socks and necktie. He must have been going so fast when he tried to get out that as he popped the parachute he was torn out of it."

On February 23, 1943, Gover's P-47 was painted white on its nose and tail for identification. Four P-47s had been shot at by Spitfires, Typhoons and ground defenses because they resembled Fw 190s.

On March 10, 1943, when most of the pioneers had accumulated about 50 hours in the Thunderbolt, they flew the first P-47 combat mission. The 11 pilots taking part in this initial operational mission of its kind in the European Theater were Group Leader Lieutenant Colonel Chesley Peterson, Colonel E. W. Anderson, Major Oscar Coen, Captains Leroy Gover and Spike Miley, First Lieutenants Abie O'Regan, George Carpenter and Don Young, and Second Lieutenants Kenneth "Blacksnake" Peterson, Jim Goodson and Don Nee.

They went into Holland at Flushing, flew inland, and came out at Dunkirk, through threatening flak, but no fighter opposition. The drinks were on Republic Aviation that night. They now had their aircraft operational.

Don Nee states that "on that first P-47 mission, the Group was not yet operational in the plane. We just wanted to find out whether it was any good. A lot of Germans were up there, but they just stood off and looked at us. They hadn't seen Thunderbolts before, and were wary. The P-47 proved to be a lot better than we had been led to believe."

Lee Gover resumes his narrative.

"Someone suggested that the P-47 might be good for dive bombing. At this point, we thought the plane wasn't good for anything. It was a matter of jumping out of a nimble 6,000 or 7,000 pound aircraft like the Spitfire into a 14,000-pound sled. Later, though, after a tough dogfight at altitude, I decided it was a pretty good mount.

"After the first mission, I was picked to start doing dive-bombing training. Between regular missions, I would take a four-plane formation with 100-pound practice bombs up to The Wash, a sort of tideland on the English northeast coast, and try to hit something. After a lot of experimenting, the Eighth Air Force decided that we should run over to Holland and blow up a gas refinery.

"We found that 14,000 feet was about the best altitude for accuracy, but of course, that was where the German flak was heavy and accurate. One day, eight of us strapped big, mean 500-pound bombs on the P-47 bellies, and the whole Group escorted us on a mission. It was good that they did, because we were helpless as hell with that thing underneath.

"I had sense enough to pass the target, then roll over, and drop the bomb on an outgoing heading. Everyone was to release when I released mine. On the way down, I thought I'd take it a little closer to the target. I did this about three times, thinking I'd really like to do a good job so they wouldn't send us back.

"We were getting up so much speed by now that the controls were becoming real, real heavy. I pulled the release—and never saw such a commotion in all my life. There were bombs passing me, P-47s passing me, and the ground coming up awfully fast. We had to trim the aircraft out of the dive, because the stick was now impossible to move. We came out across what land was left on the coast, at terminal velocity and right on the deck.

"When we finally slowed and formed up, I looked back and saw that our escort was having a real knock-down-and-drag-out battle with the German fighters. Seven Jerry aircraft were shot down.

"Ken Carlson, my no. 2, pulled up and said, 'Christ, Lee, I thought my bomb got you. It didn't miss you by six inches.' I said, 'Yes, thanks a lot. I saw it go by.'

"We never flew another dive bombing mission while I was with the Group."

Accidents plagued the P-47 program. Frank Smolinsky's plane caught fire in flight on April 3, and he was killed attempting an emergency landing at Sawbridgeworth. Oscar Coen bailed out of his burning aircraft. The P-47s at this time were being flown out of 334 Squadron. It was the pilots' bitter joke to call the 334th the Suicide Squadron.

The first P-47 mission to destroy enemy aircraft was flown on April 15, 1943, with Chesley Peterson, Don Blakeslee and Douglas Booth credited with shooting down Fw 190s. Two former Eagle pilots, Stan Anderson and Dick McMinn, were killed. Peterson had to bail out. Later he said that from the standpoint of pure terror, this was his worst day of flying.

"It was our first tangle with the Fw 190. I knew the P-47 could out-turn and out-dive the 190, and I knew it could not out-climb it. When we mixed it up, the 190 made the mistake of trying to dive away. It was really duck soup for me, and this became the first 190 to be shot down by a P-47.

"Unfortunately, it happened just inside the Belgian coast, near Ostend. As I shot the 190 down and pulled away to get back up to altitude, the engine blew up. A couple or three cylinders in front just let go.

"I did my best to glide back across the Channel to England, but the engine finally froze up. I was determined not to be taken prisoner; that would have to be the last thing that would happen to me. I got about five miles off the coast and was at very low altitude. I thought about coming down in the water but knew the P-47 probably would not ditch sucessfully. I made up my mind to bail out.

"The altimeter registered 500 feet when I rolled the plane over on its back, with my straps undone and the canopy open, still losing altitude. I fell out at around 300 feet and pulled the rip cord. The chute just streamed; it never did open.

"I made a beautiful swan dive into the Channel—a dive so absolutely perfect that the impact did not knock me out. I went down in the water 35 or 40 feet. The silk kept me from going too deep. I can remember trying to keep my eyes open and seeing it get darker and darker. When I came to the surface my eyes were swollen shut. I felt like I had swallowed half the English Channel.

"Somehow I managed to get into my dinghy, and I sat in the water for a couple or three hours. Finally a wonderful old Walrus airplane from the RAF Air-Sea Rescue practically flew into the Ostend harbor and picked me up. The Walrus was an amphibian built in the early '30s. It flew at 90 miles an hour, landed at 90, climbed at 90, did everything at 90 mph—a marvelous old airplane.

"The Walrus landed at Martlesham Heath, and they started to put me in an ambulance. 'No, I don't want to go to the hospital,' I said. 'Take me to Base Operations. I'll wait there for a plane to come from Debden and pick me up.' I was shivering from the cold and exposure. A pretty little RAF nurse said, 'You're freezing.' She took my hands and started rubbing them and my arms. Somehow, as she massaged, she shot me with a needle and put me to sleep.

"I bailed out on a Friday. On Monday I was back flying. That Friday could have been my worst day and my best day, all in one. I was terribly pleased to know that the P-47 was a great airplane, that I could shoot a 190 down with .50 caliber machine guns without any problem, and that 10 minutes later, having jumped out with a malfunctioning chute, I could have a happy ending.

"I had a difficult time, to a certain extent, because I had to tell my Group that I had been shot down. The P-47 was not a very popular aircraft in the 4th Group at that time, and I could not possibly let them know that the engine had failed. Officially I had been shot down. It was several years before I finally told people that the trouble really had been engine failure."

The Eagles came to respect the Jug. Bill Dunn's pilot report reflects his strong feelings:

"The Repulsive Scatterbolt, we called it. It had a lot of nicknames, most of them nasty.

"They were big mothers. The first time I saw one of them, I asked, 'Where in hell is the other engine?' This klunk weighed almost twice as much as the Spitfire. It was a great big hunk of iron—13,800 pounds, which was bloody heavy for a fighter in those days. But it really flew quite well, sort of like a big AT-6.

"Like the Spit, it didn't have too many bad habits, except compressibility. Its weight didn't make too much difference. It had good maneuverability; it dived like mad; it wouldn't climb worth a damn, but carried a big load of armament.

"We had eight .50 caliber machine guns and could carry eight 5-inch HVAR rockets, a couple of 500-pound RDX bombs, and belly or wing tanks. Really, it was quite a good airplane. It could take a lot of punishment."

Chesley Peterson agrees in general with Dunn's appraisal.

"I was not really very impressed with the P-47. It did turn out to be an exceptionally fine airplane, but not necessarily as a high-altitude escort fighter, which was my business. It ended up as an extremely fine dive bomber. Even as a high-altitude escort fighter, it could, if used properly, do a very creditable job against any of the German fighters. We did learn how to use it, and we used it very effectively.

"Men who had been flying smaller planes like the Spitfire, or even the P-40, found the P-47 to be a great big chunk of metal that wasn't exactly what they thought of as a fighter. Therefore, it wasn't really impressive from the standpoint of the pure joy of flying.

"Of course, being a comparatively new airplane, it had an awful lot of maintenance bugs and problems. The engine would quit at odd times. The supercharger wouldn't work here and there. The whole engine had to be rebonded to make the radio work. Normal bugs, but they destroyed pilot confidence in the airplane they had to have to fight with."

Peterson became commander of the 4th Fighter Group on August 20, 1943, after almost a year as second-in-command under Colonel Anderson. Just after his transfer from the RAF to the USAAF, Peterson was sent to Wright-Patterson Field, in Ohio, to fly all of the U.S. fighter aircraft and select the finest one for the Eighth Air Force. This meant test-flying not only the P-47 but the P-40, in its various versions, the P-39, the P-38 and many other available aircraft. It did not mean, he was to discover later, the plane he was most interested in.

Before leaving for the United States on the assignment, Peterson received a telephone call from Tommy Hitchcock, Assistant Air Attaché at the U.S. Embassy in London. Hitchcock, a polo-playing Yale socialite who had served voluntarily in Britain's Royal Flying Corps in World War I, was back in uniform as a reserve officer.

"I hear you are heading for the States to pick out a fighter for the Eighth Air Force," Hitchcock said to Peterson. "I'd like to talk to you about the P-51."

North American Aviation had developed the P-51 Mustang in 1940 under a British contract for a single-seat fighter to escort bombers on long-range missions. They had built the first prototype in a record-breaking 120 days. Production for the United States also had started immediately.

Hitchcock told Peterson he had flown the P-51 with its Allison engine. He described it as "a nice plane for low altitudes, but not worth a damn for us as a fighter—it can't get above 15,000 feet."

Hitchcock added that at Farnborough, Britain's center of aeronautical development just outside London, a couple of enterprising young British engineers had been tinkering around—largely in their spare time—and with a minimum amount of effort and engineering had replaced the Allison with Britain's Rolls-Royce Merlin engine.

"I saw it one day and asked if I could fly it. I was terribly impressed," Hitchcock said. "With the Merlin engine, the P-51 would have the Spit IX beat. It would be a dream airplane. I want you to come down to Farnborough and try it."

Peterson accepted the invitation. "The P-51 was a beautifully handling airplane," he said later. "The Merlin engine gave it a bit more power, a little more soup. The main thing was that the Merlin was turbo-supercharged, which immediately gave the P-51 the altitude it needed. No engineering had been done on the installation.

"At 25,000 feet, with the plane going as fast as it could, the tail empennage was slightly too small for the power, and the Mustang started slipping sideways—rather a peculiar feeling. Things like that are easily fixed. With a slightly larger tail surface, a little bit of fairing, the P-51 could be what it ended up being—just about the finest fighter that was built during the war."

At Wright-Patterson, Peterson and the Operations Officer flew all of the types of fighters that were on hand. " I asked for the P-51 with a Merlin engine to try out alongside the others. General Bertrandias, head of testing at Wright-

Patterson, turned me down, saying 'The P-51 is not in the inventory. It is not in the terms of reference.'

"This was the position also of General Saville, Director of Operations, and of General Stratemeyer, Deputy Chief of Staff. Every time I brought up the matter they would pull out this letter setting forth the 'terms of reference.' The letter said we must consider only USAAF fighters that were in the inventory. The generals said that with the British engine, the P-51 would not be a U.S. plane.

"Larry Kuter was the one general who would let us talk about the P-51. He was very interested, and he sort of greased the way for me to see General Hap Arnold. I told Arnold that while the P-47 was not a bad airplane, the best would be the P-51 with the Rolls engine.

"'The P-51 is finished,' Arnold said. 'The production line has ended. The last one coming off the line will be a dive bomber—and then, no more P-51s. You go back to England. You are getting the first group of P-47s.'

"I had dinner in Washington with Tommy Hitchcock, on my way back to England. 'They didn't listen to me,' I told him. 'They wouldn't let me tell the story.'

"Tommy was upset. He got in to see FDR. Two days later, President Roosevelt announced that a new version of the Mustang, with the Rolls-Royce Merlin engine, would be built.

"It proved to be the greatest airplane of the war. It was great not only because of its performance but because it was American built and thus could be produced rapidly in large volume. Hitchcock was 45 when General Pete Quesada gave him a fighter group in 1943. Perhaps he was a bit too old for that kind of flying. He went on a P-51 practice dive bombing mission and was killed."

The first USAAF unit in England to get the P-51 was the 354th Fighter Group of the Ninth Air Force. On a short-term loan from the 4th, Don Blakeslee led the 354th on the first Mustang sweep of the French coast. That was on December 1, 1943. Former Eagles Don Nee and Bob Priser also were sent from the 4th Group to the 354th, which was newly arrived from the States. Nee relates:

"General Pete Quesada, Chief of IX Fighter Command, had requested some experienced pilots, and Colonel Peterson sent us down there. After a 15-minute cockpit check, we went with them on their first mission, with Blakeslee leading. We flew several missions with them.

"Bob Priser got shot down, and I was sent up to the 85th Fighter Wing, to plan missions. Bobby Jones, the golf champion, was Wing Intelligence Officer. One of the Groups in our wing, the 404th, was commanded by Colonel McColpin, my old Eagle Squadron commander.

"Carroll McColpin, I believe, was far and away the best American fighter pilot I ever flew with. Not only in skill, as I know of no one who ever got the better of him in a practice dogfight, but he was cool and aggressive. On a test flight, he, alone, attacked nine German fighters. Before his retirement, he was combat qualified with every type of fighter in his command.

"Peterson, Blakeslee, Daley, Daymond—all were outstanding leaders who would have been tops in any air force. There were several who, once they reached the squadrons, wanted to go no further. They were perfectly willing to go back to training and tow targets. There were others who were willing, but lacked the required ability. These should have been weeded out somewhere along the way. Most of them were killed.

"The majority of pilots, I believe, were above average. This was proven by their records. They were there, I am sure, for many reasons, the primary one being their love of flying. Some were washouts from flying cadet training. Some were there for pure adventure. All were restless."

Blakeslee was clearly outstanding—skillful, aggressive and possessing a masterful sense of tactical innovation. For example, the 4th Fighter Group's August 16, 1943 bomber escort mission to Paris: 17 or 18 enemy planes destroyed for the loss of one P-47. This time, instead of becoming involved in the general mêlée, Blakeslee, the mission leader, remained above the main battle force, taking no part in the combat. From his lofty observation post, he watched overall developments closely, directing his pilots to promising targets. The Group would employ this technique frequently, and Blakeslee became the most skillful of all air combat directors.

Of Blakeslee and his methods, Peterson has said, "Don Blakeslee could take a hundred fighters and organize them in the air, tell them what to do and how the battle was being fought, like no one else. He just knew it. He could have had 10 times as many as the dozen or so kills credited to him if he had wanted personal glory. Instead, he just sat there and handled the whole thing and let the other pilots get the credit. He was marvelous."

Long past due for a transfer out of the combat area, Peterson was relieved of command of the 4th on January 1, 1944, and Blakeslee was appointed his successor. Peterson was assigned briefly to Headquarters of the newly activated Ninth Air Force, as combat operations officer for General Lewis Brereton, and then was sent back to the United States for further duties that would lead him up the promotion ladder to the rank of major general.

During January and February, former Eagle pilots now flying P-47s shot down more than 25 enemy planes. The totals included: Beeson, 6; Gentile and Goodson, 4 each; Henry Mills, 3; Vic France and Steve Pisanos, 2 each; and Blakeslee, Paul Ellington, Ray Care and George Carpenter, 1 each.

Meanwhile, in the course of events, an unbeatable combination had been brewing: the 4th Fighter Group, the command appointment of Blakeslee and the advent of the P-51. Now a full colonel, Blakeslee was informed by Major General Kepner, of VIII Fighter Command, that the 4th's P-51s were on the way. On February 14, 1944, each squadron received one Mustang for transition training. Ten days later, a number of P-51s were delivered. The eager new commander told the 4th that they could learn to fly the new planes on the way to the target, if necessary. The first Mustang mission was flown on February 28, an offensive patrol to Compiégne, France. The next day, the P-51s intruded as far as Brunswick, Germany.

On March 4, Blakeslee led the Group on the first American bombing attack on metropolitan Berlin. Paul Ellington had to bail out over the Dutch coast, because of engine trouble, and became a war prisoner. The following day, Steve Pisanos shot down two German planes and was himself shot down. He evaded capture and made his way back to England six months later.

Blakeslee again headed up and supervised the fighter cover for what this time, on March 6, was a 15-mile-long parade of Berlin-bound American bombers. Nazi fighters swarmed up, 100 miles west of the German capital, and fought the Americans all the way into the target and along the homeward flight. Fifteen enemy planes were shot down, one by Blakeslee and another by Hank Mills. Mills had been granted home leave for the first time in three years, but had asked for permission to stay on duty in order to take part in the Berlin assault. As luck would have it, he had to bail out of his damaged plane and became a German prisoner.

A third Berlin show, on March 8, involved almost 2,000 American warplanes. Reporters called it the greatest fire raid on Berlin in history. Few German fighters appeared, but Gentile managed to destroy three, and Clark, France and Fonzo Smith shot down one each. Selden Edner was shot down and taken prisoner. The Americans were astonished that they could bomb Berlin in daylight and encounter almost no resistance. Clearly, the Luftwaffe had come to fear the P-51 for its great range—for its tremendous fuel capacity afforded by bladder tanks in the wings and fuselage, two jettisonable wing tanks and its standard belly tanks—and for its unprecedented combat capability at high and low altitudes. The introduction of the Mustang had changed the character of the air war in Europe.

By mid-March, German fighters had become markedly unwilling to engage in combat unless they found the circumstances to be most favorable. Allied fighter pilots had no recourse but to concentrate more heavily on attacks on ground targets—cargo trains, military trucks and the like. Accordingly, they began to receive kill credit for aircraft destroyed on the ground, and this led into frequent fractional scores. On March 18, Goodson was credited with destroying two Heinkel 111s on the ground. Scores on March 21 were one-half a Ju 88 for Hively, two Me 190s for Vic France and an Me 410 for Goodson, a 190 for Clark, and half a 190 and one-third of a Ju 52 for Carpenter, all destroyed on the ground. On March 27, the ground kills included one and one-half Ju 88s for Beeson, a Ju 88 for Hively, a Ju 52 and Ju 88 for France, two Me 110s for Gentile and also one and one-half Ju 88s for Clark.

In March, 1944, the 4th destroyed 156 enemy planes, the largest number accounted for by any USAAF group in a single month. The cost was 29 fighter planes and pilots. Victories by former Eagles during March included 10 for Gentile, six for Carpenter, four each for Beeson, Clark and Goodson, two each for Pisanos and Hively, two and half a share in a third for Fonzo Smith, and one each for France,

Kenneth Smith and Blakeslee. Kenneth Smith was shot down March 21 and taken prisoner. A similar fate befell Kenneth (Blacksnake) Peterson eight days later. Staff Sergeant Edgar M. Johnson, waist gunner on a B-17 of the 306th Bombardment Group, recounting the event in a combat report, said Focke-Wulf 190s attacked the bomber formation and killed the crew in the forward part of his plane. After bailing out, he watched as Peterson's P-51 closed on one of the 190s and destroyed it, then attacked another and caused it to blow up. Johnson said several members of his crew were trying to bail out, and they owed their lives to Peterson's aggressiveness. "He attacked 12 enemy aircraft alone, with full knowledge that his chance of survival was very small," the Sergeant said. Shortly thereafter the surviving bomber crew members found themselves in jail in Hildesheim, with Captain Peterson.

Gentile and Beeson, running neck and neck, had qualified for home leave but declined to go back to the United States for fear of falling behind in the scoring race. An April Fool's Day mission to the important German river ports of Ludwigshafen and Mannheim, led by Blakeslee, gave both Beeson and Gentile an opportunity to destroy additional 109s, raising their totals to 21 and 22, respectively. The 4th Group total now exceeded 300 enemy aircraft, but the 56th Group was well ahead at about 400. A sweep deep into Germany on April 5 yielded the destruction of 50 and damage of 38 enemy planes on the ground, with credits going to Gentile, Beeson, France, Carpenter and Goodson, among the Eagles. Gentile raised his over-all total to 22 planes shot down and five destroyed on the ground, to collect the Rickenbacker trophy, the case of scotch. Beeson, trailing only one behind his rival, took flak damage to his plane's cooling system, and bailed out. He had planned to serve as best man, in the week ahead, at the wedding of Bud Care and his English fiancee. They had given him a bejeweled bee, and the good luck ornament was swinging from his gunsight on that last mission. Beeson spent the remaining 13 months of war in Stalag Luft I.

"Beeson looked like he should have been selling ice cream, or working as an assistant in a drugstore—anything but a fighter pilot," Lee Gover has remarked. "The Bee" had been a hotel clerk in Oakland, California, before joining the RAF.

Gover continues:

"There were doubts about the accuracy of some pilot combat reports but not those of Beeson and Gentile—they did not exaggerate. Beeson's enemy planes would blow up in his face, and he would have the film to show it. He was the best man we ever had.

"And while some guys would sit around reading magazines, Gentile always wanted to go. He would go on every mission. Don would jump into 50 enemy planes, not think about it beforehand, and after he got in he would yell for help. But he would fight and shoot."

Carpenter led a bomber escort mission over Brunswick April 8, destroying two enemy planes to three for Gentile and one each for Care and Happel. The 4th Group shot down 31 planes that day—an all-time record for a single mission—but lost four Mustang pilots, including Frank Boyles, killed in an air battle near Celle.

General Dwight D. Eisenhower, Supreme Allied Commander, visited Debden and pinned the Distinguished Service Cross on Blakeslee and Gentile. "You seem to be a one-man air force," the future U.S. President told Gentile. In Washington, President Roosevelt called Gentile "Captain Courageous."

On successive missions, Bud Care shot down one enemy plane and Carpenter got two. Newspapers headlined the disclosure that the 4th Group had raised its tally to 403 kills, breaking all records for the European war theater, and that Don Gentile had become the top scorer of both World Wars. Gentile, returning from a successful mission to a base where a small army of newsmen was waiting, jubilantly buzzed the airdrome at too low an altitude, touched the runway, bounced up and over, and came in on the plane's belly. He was hardly hurt, but the Mustang was badly damaged.

"Blakeslee said that anyone who landed wheels up would be kicked out, and he sent Gentile home," Gover recalled. "Gentile at that time was getting his highest scores, and some of the fellows throught Blakeslee acted out of jealousy. Ironically, Blakeslee himself later buzzed a house and came down and landed without his gear—and was sent home."

Bud Care led his last mission to Germany on April 15. His plane was damaged, and he had to bail out and became a war prisoner. Three days later, on a bomber support mission to Berlin, Captain Victor France, a former Dallas, Texas, advertising man who had shot down five enemy planes, was himself shot down and killed. Major George Carpenter, one of the leading aces, shot down his thirteenth and fourteenth Jerries, bailed out of his disabled plane, and became a German prisoner.

During May and June, 1944, and especially around the time of the June 6 D-day Normandy landings, the leadership of combat missions alternated among Blakeslee, Goodson, Blanding, Happel, Hively and Clark. In June one former Eagle, Major Michael G. H. McPharlin, was killed. Goodson belly-landed his damaged plane in Germany and was taken prisoner. In July Major Wilson Edwards, hit by flak near Metz, bailed out and was captured. Major Fonzo Smith suffered a similar fate on an August 3 mission in the Paris area.

In one of the most challenging assignments of his career, Blakeslee was ordered to lead the three squadrons of his 4th Group and one from the 352nd Group over more than 2,000 miles of enemy territory, escorting more than 200 bombers on a shuttle mission from England to Russia and back. The demonstration of the long-range striking range of American air power, and the practicality of launching air attacks from either side of German-held Europe and recovering them from the other, started June 21. Blakeslee, deputy commander Blanding, and Hively and their squadrons guarded the bombers across Germany and Poland into Russia, and landed at Piryatin in the Ukraine while the bombers flew beyond Kiev to Poltava.

After a five-day stay in Russia, the fighters accompanied the bombers to their target in Poland, a refinery at Drohobycy, and then on to a Fifteenth Air Force base at Lucera, Italy, near Foggia. One of the more rebellious and reckless pilots, First Lieutenant Ralph K. "Kid" Hofer, a former boxer and semi-professional football player and the fourth-ranking ace of the 4th Group, had strayed away from the Russia-bound formation to pursue a German plane, and finally had landed at Kiev. He flew from there to Lucera, but found himself in trouble. He reported to Blanding that Blakeslee would have nothing to do with him, and asked if he could fly with Blanding's 336th squadron. Blanding yielded to the young man's entreaty.

On July 2, the visiting Mustangs escorted 15th Air Force bombers from Lucera on an attack against targets at Budapest, Hungary. Hively shot down three attacking planes, but was wounded in one eye. Hofer was missing. Blanding said it later was determined that Hofer had crashed and was killed in Yugoslavia. Blanding himself suffered a fractured skull and other injuries while strafing German planes on a Norwegian coastal airdrome on August 8. Blanding tore strips of his clothing to bandage his wounds. Shepherded by his squadron mates, he managed to fly for two hours to a safe landing at the nearest RAF base, in Scotland. Ground crews lifted him from the cockpit and into an ambulance.

On September 1, 1944, Blakeslee, who had been flying fighters for three years without home leave and had accumulated more than 1,000 hours of combat action, was called back to the States and relieved of his command. He had the satisfaction of knowing that his 4th Group had attained USAAF scoring leadership in April and now, four months later, still held the lead, at 700 enemy planes destroyed. By war's end the 4th was to claim 1,016 enemy aircraft. U.S. top honors for the war.

Another fighter in the American inventory was the Bell P-39 Airacobra. This airplane had a tricycle landing gear, a rearward mounted engine, a nose-mounted cannon and a spotty reception from American pilots in the Pacific. Its reputation in Europe was no improvement.

Bert Stewart recalls that when 400 Airacobras arrived in England, early in the war, "Colonel Jack Hickman said to me, 'Stewart, I want you to sell these P-39s to all these pilots.' That shook me. It was a real bad airplane—a single-seater, and I had never even flown in it.

"So they brought all the young pilots out to see me do my stuff. I got in, and the crew chief showed me which buttons to push. The plane flew nicely at high speed, but down at 150 miles an hour, it was a handful of mush. It had a habit of tumbling if you stalled it upside down, and was hard for the pilot to get out of.

"I put on a one-man show—two or three rolls and splits, always with plenty of speed. I started to land on the 5,000-foot runway and finally got on the ground 30 or 40 miles an hour too fast. I burned up the brakes, and still had to ground loop. It was the first tricycle gear I'd flown. I was scared so badly that I was really sweating. But most of the pilots watching looked impressed. Some even applauded."

Joe Durham, listening to Stewart's account, interjected, "The P-39's the only thing the Russians ever refused in lend-lease."

Later, the 'Cobras again haunted the lives of certain Eagles, some of whom would be among a number of pilots who would fly a small armada of P-39s and close-cousin P-400s to North Africa. Dixie Alexander explains:

"We were told that in the early stages of the lend-lease program, the U.S. had sent a number of P-39s and P-400s to the British. The planes had arrived at Blackpool, and were still there in crates. As desperately as the British needed help—and the lend lease was welcome—they turned thumbs down on the P-39s at any price.

"The Russians came and had a look, the story goes, and found little in the P-39s that they wanted. One Russian colonel was supposed to have commented that the planes did have metal props and thus could be considered 'good for ramming.' Hardly the best way to win a war!

"It was decided that these P-39s, some of them with 20 mm. and 37 mm. guns shooting through the nose, were just what the Allies needed to win in North Africa. The P-39 had a bell shaped 150-gallon belly tank suspended between the wheels of the landing gear. This provided the range to fly nonstop from the south of England to North Africa.

"The P-39s were put in shape at our base, equipped with belly tanks and sent off in squadrons of 16 to Portreath, England. There they would be met by a B-17 and navigated to Berrechid, in French Morocco."

From that decision stems a long, strange tale.

9

WAR AND PEACE
AND WAR

There are times—too many times, some soldiers might say—when the stuff of warriors and the principles of armies do not mix well. If the stuff of warriors means aggressiveness and keen spirits, and the principles of armies demand regulation and discipline, the resulting concoction can mean trouble and bizarre developments for the warriors in question.

A case in point is that of Richard "Dixie" Alexander, an Eagle of merit, mixing with the USAAF. An ingredient: those unwanted P-39s.

Bent on a weekend in London, early in 1943, Alexander and Donald "Mick" Lambert set out in an American AT-6 trainer, planning to land at Northholt Airdrome, where they could take a subway into the West End. Adverse weather forced them to stop at another British base to refuel. The watch officer there, looking at rain reports, refused them permission to take off. Alexander tells the rest.

"Mick and I decided that inasmuch as we had an American aircraft and were now American pilots, we could write our own ticket. We took off for Northholt and London town. We landed safely, and went into town on the tube. I don't know what Mick did, but I came down with the flu and went to the hospital in London for two days. Apparently, the RAF was screaming by then about our unauthorized takeoff, and we were in for it when we got back to Atcham. We were grounded for a day or two, as I remember.

"A lieutenant who had been an instructor in Canada showed up as a pupil at Atcham. I took him in a Master to Debden, where I was to pick up a Spitfire and return it to Atcham while he flew the Master back. When I went to claim the Spit, I found that it was MDJ—my old aircraft, and a good one.

"It felt beautiful on takeoff, after the junk I had been flying at Atcham, so I held it down all the way to the end of the runway, pulled the undercarriage and let it fly off its wheels. I came up fast at the end of the runway almost into a stall turn, and headed back to the officers' mess where Don Blakeslee and a few guys were having a chat. I got back down on the deck and had good flying speed, and was able to yank up the nose and do three quick snap rolls in a row before losing too much flying speed. That shook 'em up a bit.

"On the way to Atcham there was an RDF station, on a wooded hill overlooking a small gully, where I knew some people. I beat up the radar station good, flipped over on my back and glided down the gully and the hill inverted, with throttle back. When I reached the plain area, having righted myself, I eased back to full throttle and flew on. Everyone at the RDF station was sure I had crashed upside-down in the gully, and a prolonged search followed.

"When the RAF reported the incident to the USAAF, all hell broke loose. The inactivity during the past month or two had promoted a bit of other mischief around the Debden area, and Generals Spaatz and Hunter were looking for someone on whom to bestow their wrath.

"Our CO, Mel McNichol, informed me that I was in trouble. He added that his brother, Marv, who was in North Africa, would be glad to have me in his 52nd Fighter Group. This would put me in the Twelfth Air Force and out of the Eighth, where Spaatz and Hunter could work me over. So we volunteered me to lead a flight of P-39s to North Africa.

"As a matter of fact, the flight had already left the day before, and was due out of Portreath in two days. Orders were cut. I grabbed my gear together, took the first available airplane that could be put together, and left for Portreath.

"We were weathered in there for three days, each of which I sweated out, expecting a call that would cancel my flight and summon me back to London. It never came. On April 27, five days after I had landed at Portreath, Airacobra No. 292, piloted by Dick Alexander, took off with 15 other guys in P-39s and P-400s and escorted by a B-17, for Port Lyautey, North Africa.

"The circumstances point to the ineptitude, the lack of consideration for pilots, and plainly the amateur approach to everything we were doing at the time. Portreath was more like a staging area than anything else. During our entire wait there, our information was very limited. Our aircraft sat uncovered on the ramp, and we were not allowed to go near them to run them up, or take care of them in any way.

"Aircraft should not sit out day after day in fog and rain without being run up or looked after. The personnel at Portreath who were responsible for us simply said, 'They flew in; they'll fly out.' This for men who would be flying over water in unknown conditions, into strange territory with no alternate airdromes, for about 600 miles. Everything had to be perfect, or the fuel supply just would not be enough.

"At the airdrome, we were told to wait in our planes for a starting signal. It was overcast behind us, and we had complete cloud cover at Portreath. When the B-17 was overhead they started rolling us off, taking us just as we came, on a single runway which dropped off a cliff at the far end. It was frightening to see each aircraft with its heavy belly tank hit the end of the runway, disappear because of lack of flying speed, and then come staggering up after the drop from the 200-foot cliff, much as Navy planes used to do in the days of the early carriers.

"Of 18 planes that were assigned to the flight, only two did not get airborne. We headed south according to plan, broke out into good weather, and made rendezvous with the B-17.

"Our instructions were that if we should experience mechanical failure or some other difficulty, we were to try to land in Lisbon. Portugal would impound the aircraft and remove it to their flying station in the Azores. As a neutral country, Portugal had the same arrangement with every country involved in the war—the Allies and Axis alike. Pilots would be interned for a reasonable period and then returned home. The Portuguese government was trying to build an air force, and at that time had Italian, German, French, British, and American aircraft—for which, we understood, they made some small payment.

"We were flying at about 18,000 when, more than an hour after takeoff, I detected violent surges in the engine. Finally, the prop ran away, and I had to reduce manifold pressure to bring the RPM down to a respectable figure. This meant that I could not reach the planned destination. With a runaway propeller, it is impossible to conserve on fuel. To complicate matters, the entire electrical system had failed. No prop control, no magnetic compass, no gyros, no radio— nothing. The Airacobra was an electronic whiz, but fortunately, I did have a manual wheels down system.

"England was under complete fog; there was no turning back. Gibraltar was out of reach with my runaway prop. My only choice was to head for Lisbon. I flew east to the coast, hoping not to meet any Fw 190s. I reached the north coast of Portugal at about Porto, flew down the coast to Lisbon, found the airdrome, cranked down my wheels, and after receiving a green Aldis lamp from the tower, landed with wheels down.

"I taxied all the way to the end of the runway, pulled the aircraft off to one side, crawled out on the wing, and blew my IFF as a bunch of Portuguese soldiers with carbines at the ready rolled up to take me prisoner.

"I was to learn later that six others in our flight had to land in Lisbon because of some type of mechanical failure and that two landed in Spain. The flight had formed up under some semblance of a squadron protecting the B-17. In Lisbon, I was told that German intelligence had us as part of a suicide mission escorting President Roosevelt from London to North Africa.

"The assumption was that we were pilots willing to die for our 'Fuehrer.' We would escort him to the last spin of the prop, salute farewell, and crash into the sea.

"There were a few bad moments of rifle waving when I got out of the plane until, through an interpreter, I was able to explain what I had done and to convince the authorities that there was no actual damage to the plane itself.

"I was held under guard that night with two other American pilots. The next day we left by slow train for Elvas, on the

Spanish frontier, where Allied internees were held. Elvas was not what would be considered a beautiful city. It was the headquarters for the Portuguese cavalry, which at that time was about the extent of Portugal's military. The smell of horses and dust was everywhere. But the people were friendly, and the cavalry extended themselves to make us feel at home. The lights at night, the shops crowded with goods, and the low prices of liquor were a wonderful, startling contrast to the blackout and bomb debris of London.

"There were about 20 British and 15 Americans in our group. We were housed in the International, a small three story hotel with good food, a pool table, and bedbugs. The bugs could be kept in check, and the management cooperated grudgingly, upon our insistence. We were allowed the run of the town on the assurance that we would not try to escape, but had to report in daily. We satisfied this by having one person sign in each day for all of the Americans, and another for the British.

"We drank, we read, we loafed, we went sightseeing, we built model airplanes. We took short trips to carnivals and bullfights, and learned to ride under the instruction of the cavalry. I was permitted to compete in the international live pigeon shoot, and finished in a tie for eighth and eleventh against a field of 250 of the best shots in Europe. A lot of people from the Elvas Club, the defending champions, made money betting on me, and I was something of a hero as far away as Lisbon. We received our pay monthly from the United States Embassy. The Portuguese government provided our lodging and subsistence. It was an idle life that palled quickly. We noticed that the British fliers usually left after only three weeks of internment.

"Our entreaties to the embassy brought little but vague promises. In a good-natured tug-and-shove match one day, I fell against a bed and injured myself. A local physician found nothing seriously wrong, but I talked to a couple of the other Americans, and developed a plan to get to Lisbon. The three of us put our gear in a bag and simply caught a bus into Lisbon. We were signed in at the hotel in Elvas as usual, on the group plan. Even if we had been missed, it was unlikely that any action would have been taken.

"In Lisbon we presented ourselves at the American Embassy, the other two as emissaries of the Elvas group, seeking information, and I requesting medical treatment. We had checked into the city's largest hotel and were told we could remain for a few days and then must return to Elvas. As it turned out, we did not have to go. A note from my British doctor won me permission to remain in Lisbon under obser- vation for an indefinite period. The others did not trouble to leave, and the embassy was just too lethargic to do anything about it. On the strength of this, and with information pro- vided by us, the pilots remaining in Elvas soon drifted in to join us. Within two weeks all had arrived in Lisbon.

"In order to account for our presence in Lisbon, the embassy decided that we should become active and designated us good will emissaries attached to the embassy. Our function was to attend breakfasts, luncheons, dinners, parties, and other social functions, representing the United States govern- ment. We were, of course, in civilian clothes.

"A colonel in the embassy, whom I saw frequently but met only once, liked to show off in a uniform of sorts, with riding pants and boots, wearing many ribbons of dubious nature. He would wait for an allied advance in North Africa and then tour the German Embassy area in an open vehicle. It was his decision to withhold .30 caliber ammunition from the Portuguese, under the pretext that it was needed in the war effort. The Portuguese wanted to arm the American planes in their newly formed air force in the Azores. Without the ammunition they could not offer their pilots air firing or gunnery practice. The colonel thought his action gave him the edge in bargaining power. We knew, however, that the Portu- guese were retaliating by holding the American internees. This was the reason for the long delay in our release.

"The air attaché at the American Embassy was a lieu- tenant colonel who proudly displayed the DFC at every op- portunity. Over drinks at Estoril, he told me he and a pilot regularly flew along the coast on a sort of spy mission. They always carried hand grenades, and on one flight sighted a German submarine, dropped the grenades on successive runs, and sank it. Somebody supposedly reported an oil slick. Hence the DFC.

"With some difficulty, I refrained from telling him our group's instructions for handling submarines: A pilot on sea patrol must carry a paint brush liberally dipped in green paint, and on observing a periscope, must fly over and swab it across the glass. The observer in the submarine, seeing nothing but green, would believe himself to be below the water and would continue to surface until the submarine had attained an altitude where it could readily be shot down.

"Lisbon was well lit—festive in a decadent sort of way. The black market was everywhere. Everyone was, or professed to be, a spy or a source of information. There were parties somewhere every night, many of them only sparsely attended. Enterprising diplomats found a good revenue in setting up parties for 400, requisitioning the embassy for supplies, and hoping for 25 guests to show up. The surplus liquor and supplies were easily disposed of in the black market. Although we were more or less detailed to attend these functions, we tired of the charade, knowing that armies were battling across the deserts of Africa and air forces were fighting high above France and Britain.

"As long as the pilot internees remained passive, the American Embassy people were quite content to ignore us and let us pursue our own activities. One day, we discovered a new bar and started talking with a young man who spoke English well and obviously was not Portuguese. It turned out he was an interned Luftwaffe pilot. There were a number of them in Lisbon, all detained under almost the same circumstances.

"In the ensuing days, we met all of the German pilots, and got along surprisingly well with them. For the most part, their gripes, their likes and dislikes and feelings were the same as ours. We were fliers. By mutual consent, we avoided political discussions and loyalties and talked of combat, aircraft, women and other matters of normal interest to young men and pilots. Although we never became real friends, we enjoyed each other, and stood as a united front, in our bar, against the general public. How much this relationship was valued by the Luftwaffe men we were soon to learn.

"We had been hounding the embassy to get us out of Portugal. We insisted that we knew the delay in our release was being caused by our own people, and we began to toss about the names of important persons at home, friends to whom we would complain. The embassy had no way of knowing whether our claims were authentic, but the air attaché and his staff started to worry.

"Rommel was in full retreat in Africa. We were told that plans had been made to fly us out to Ireland or Gibraltar, the routes usually taken by the British. Then, when Rommel counterattacked in the desert, embassy indifference and inefficiency returned, and our hopes for release fell apart.

"One day, two of the German pilots were at the bar when I dropped by. I sensed something guarded in their welcome. After a few words of conversation, one of the Germans said to the other, 'Ask him.' The other turned to me and said, 'We hear you are leaving us, and we were wondering if you would be able to say *auf wiedersehen*.'

"I was amazed. 'Where did you ever hear that?'

"'It's in every bar all over town.'

"He was not joking. 'Do you know how and when?'

"'How, yes; when, almost immediately.'

"We withdrew to a far table.

"'There are three small boats in the harbor loading refugees,' he said. 'I do not know what flag they are flying, but they are going to Gibraltar. It is common knowledge. The German Embassy is fully aware of it.

"'The removal of unimportant refugees was of no great concern to our government until they learned that you Allied airmen are to be aboard. That fact provides an excuse to bomb. The Luftwaffe will be waiting for you. The chance of survival is very small.'

"The look on my face must have been one of shock. 'Why do you tell me this?' I asked. 'It has to be dangerous.'

"His reply was blunt. 'We talked it over and decided we had a duty to you as a kindred officer and flier. We believe you pilots deserve a death in the air rather than what would be in store for you on those boats. We do not blame our government; we blame the stupidity of it all. Do not sail with those ships.'

"'What excuse can we use?' I asked. 'We can't pass on this information.'

"'It is common knowledge by now on the waterfront,' he said. 'When you see the ships, you will have all the excuse you need. No German officer would sail under such circumstances when it was not absolutely necessary.'

"We drank a last toast and said goodbye. Back at the hotel, I confided in two of my fellow Americans, and we went to the waterfront. In a bar, we found a seaman from one of the ships. After a few drinks, he gave us much the same story I had had from my Luftwaffe friends. The seaman added more detail, and said he was not sailing. 'I'll just get drunk and not show up,' he said.

"'How many of your shipmates know and feel this way?' I asked.

"'All.'

"'Then how can she sail?'

"'They will sail. They will get a crew.'

"We returned to our hotel to find that sailing orders had been issued and that our colleagues had been looking for us. We were told to get our things together and to stay in the hotel and not let anyone know our plans. We were, in effect, now in security confinement.

"The three of us called our whole group together and passed along our information about the ships and the danger of German bombing. The others found it difficult at first to believe us. We talked until late in the evening, trying to decide what to do. Certainly we were loyal combat troops, willing to die for our country—but not to die needlessly. As internees, we were treated as civilians, but we definitely considered ourselves military. As officers, we had certain rights and responsibilities; really, we just didn't know what to do. And we had little time to think about it.

"Someone came up with the idea that it should be an individual choice, so that whatever happened could not be construed as mutiny. We decided this was good advice. It would be every man for himself. We would leave on schedule when they came for us, go look at the ships, try to ask questions, and then make our individual decisions.

"The next day we were taken to the pier and directed to the docked vessels. They were tinier than I would have believed. We were told the ships would lie in harbor until dark, and would sail on the evening tide. We would be at sea three days, but we were not given a destination. We would be given C-rations. We would be placed in the holds of the three ships, with the refugees, and would remain there for the entire voyage, with the hatches battened down. Should we be boarded, we must not identify ourselves. We must try to appear as refugees.

"By this time, I had almost made up my mind. I stepped aboard one of the boats and went down into a hold. People were everywhere down there, hollow eyed and unkempt amid human filth and debris. There was water all over the floor, and many persons were lying on wooden pallets or sitting on crates—anything to keep dry. It was a shocking sight, although I lived to see much worse. We were not told how long these people had been waiting to sail. We had no way of knowing why they were fleeing or who pursued them. I hurried to the deck for fresh air, and then climbed back to the pier and started walking toward the city.

"The air attaché saw me and asked me where I was going. When I told him, he asked if I realized the implication of refusing an order to board ship.

"Of the ten Americans who had been ordered to sail, six joined me in refusal. The three who complied with the orders regretted it. One with whom I was reunited later told me of three days of wet, filth and actual horror. German Condor bombers, probably from bases in Spain, attacked three times. One ship was hit and left behind. The other two made Gibraltar. My friend said that had he known what it would be like, he never would have left Lisbon."

The seven Americans were taken by Lisbon police to a prison overlooking the harbor. They were stripped of personal belongings, including belts, shoe strings and shaving gear—and placed in a large cell that was to be their home for the next two weeks.

"The floor on which we were imprisoned contained political prisoners of all nationalities," Alexander said. "It was a privileged area. There were women on the floor above, although we never saw them. On the floors below were the dangerous prisoners and common criminals. Open communal latrines housed the largest rats I have ever seen. I used them only a time or two before we found out that we could get janitor service for this sort of thing, for a fee. From that point on, we had our own facilities, which were emptied regularly by an orderly or a prisoner. Prison fare was grim. We were advised we could have food brought in if we wished to pay for it. Thereafter we had lobster, fish, fowl, steak and eggs— about anything we wanted. After a few days, our room doors were unlocked and we had the run of a corridor, and could visit with prisoners from other rooms. At 10 each evening, we were locked in. Our stay was not pleasant, but it was not bad. It could have been sheer hell. I am sure that for some it was."

The prisoners learned that in Africa, Rommel's last counterattack had been thwarted and that he was in full retreat. In Europe, there were expectations of an invasion of France, as armies massed in England. Supplies were rolling in, and Allied planes were hammering the continent. These developments were reflected in the Lisbon prison. Each day, political prisoners with Allied leanings were released and their places taken by supporters of the Axis cause.

On overnight notice, Alexander and his friends were placed aboard a British ship. When they reached international waters, they were informed they had been returned to military control and were en route to Algiers to be tried under court-martial as deserters. At Gibraltar, they were transferred from the ship to a C-47 transport and flown directly to Casablanca. They went to Berrechid, their original P-39 destination a few miles south of Casablanca and a staging area for air crews, and found their gear, which had arrived on a bomber. They waited there for their orders to Algiers.

"One evening, standing at the bar in the Officers' Club, I was nudged by a fellow who said, 'Drink your drink. We have to leave. I'll explain later,'" Alexander said.

"He informed me that the pilots had placed one member of their squadron in Conventry, and would neither speak to him nor associate with him. When he entered a room, they simply filed out. The story was that he had bailed out on his crew over the Atlantic and that all the others were lost. What's more, this was the second time it had happened with that individual.

"I never questioned the judgment or pursued it further. Whether it was true or fair, I do not know. The man in question had been something of a college football hero. Years later, he worked in radio and on television as a broadcaster."

At Algiers the accused pilots were confined to the military government area while awaiting trial. "But I managed to pitch a game for the quartermaster baseball team," the irrepressible Alexander says. "Won it, too."

This is his account of the proceeding.

"We were assigned, as counsel, a first lieutenant lawyer, from Peoria, Illinois. A very sharp young man. I do not know where he is today, but he has my everlasting thanks. He interviewed all of us at length, but told us little. On the day of the trial, he informed us our plea would be not guilty, but the penalty under such a plea, if we were convicted, could be the firing squad.

"We had the option of pleading guilty to desertion and throwing ourselves on the mercy of the court. 'The plea will be not guilty,' he repeated, and waited. We did not debate the issue. We were with him 100 percent.

"Coming face to face with a court-martial board, when your life is in the balance, is a horrible experience. The grapevine had it that this was the first AAF court-martial of any magnitude to take place during World War II, and that it reached as far as Eisenhower himself. We heard that we were to be made examples of, and that we had little chance of going free. All that stood between us and this and a possible firing squad was a little lawyer from Peoria and our own faith in fair play.

"The board consisted of an infantry general and six other ranking officers of various branches of the service. The prosecution argued simply that we had disobeyed a direct order of the air attaché to sail out of Lisbon. The implication was that we thereby became deserters who wished to remain in Portugal and avoid a return to military duties.

"Our lawyer called only three of us in our defense. He pointed out that all of us were pilots who had asked for combat duty. Three of us had already flown a full tour with the RAF and AAF and could have been rotated home, had we so desired.

"He argued that if the United States were to abide by international laws and accepted rules, we must be regarded as civilians and noncombatants so long as we were on Portuguese soil. Under these circumstances we were not bound by orders from the United States Embassy—at least not as combatants.

"Our lawyer had touched on tricky ground, and well he knew it. He outlined our reasons for refusing to take passage on the ships, and pointed out that after the little convoy left Lisbon, it was bombed on three occasions. That was all. The trial was over before I realized it.

"The officer commanding the board called for a vote, with comments, and noted them all. We were commanded to rise, and were reminded of the charges. Then came the verdict: guilty. Guilty—guilty; the sound of it rang in my ears.

"And then the sentence, in a hushed room. Two weeks of confinement to base at our first place of permanent assignment. The confinement must not conflict with flying duties.

"Wonder of wonders. Afterward we celebrated mildly. The relief was too great to do else."

On August 10, 1943, Dixie Alexander returned to active duty flying Spitfires with the 52nd Fighter Group, 2nd Squadron, at Palermo, Sicily. Palermo had just fallen to the Allies, and the 52nd was moving there from its base near the Mediterranean seaport of Bone, Algeria.

Palermo proved to be relatively uneventful—much convoy patrolling, some interception, little to shoot at. In November, the unit moved 400 miles northward to Borgo airdrome just south of Bastia, near the northern tip of Corsica. The Spitfires were fitted with a 250-pound bomb under each wing, and the group began dive bombing shipping along the Italian coast and intercepting enemy bombers harrassing the Allied shipping supply to the Anzio beachhead.

Alexander was hit badly on January 22, 1944, while shooting up an Italian gun emplacement near La Spezia. He was able to get back to Borgo, where he crash landed, completely wiping out his plane. Wounded, he received a Purple Heart. It was the third time he had had a plane shot up.

The war work of the convicted deserter went on. Alexander was leading a flight of eight planes on February 6, when they encountered Italian aircraft towing gliders, and destroyed them all. Dixie was credited with one of the kills. At that time, the orders were to shoot at all types of enemy aircraft. Two weeks later, leading a 12-plane sweep into Italy, he shot down one of 30 attacking Me 109s. In April, he flew a P-51B for the first time, and on May 24, he destroyed an enemy fighter attacking heavy bombers on a raid over Vienna, an achievement for which he received the Distinguished Flying Cross.

"After several wild passes by everyone, I found myself singled out by a red-nosed 190 trying to stay in a turn with me," Alexander recalls. "I dropped 15 degrees of flaps and was able, after the turns, to come up on him from the rear. He chose to go over on his back and run for it. I followed him through several spirals until we reached the deck, whereupon he headed for the Vienna suburbs, taking me over a number of gun positions. I opened fire at about 300 yards, but first observed strikes at 200 yards. We were shooting .50 caliber, and I imagine he was pretty well riddled. He went directly into the ground in a sort of crash-landing at full speed, scattering himself over the area."

Finally, while escorting B-24s on a bombing mission to Wiener Neustadt, Austria, May 30, 1944, Alexander shot down one of three attacking Me 109s, only to have his own plane so badly damaged that he had to set down in a field. He evaded capture for five days, and was getting close to the Yugoslav border when a group of Hitler Youth discovered him and called German troops. At Stalag Luft III, Charles Cook and other Eagles welcomed him to the fate they had been enduring for a year.

The World War II odyssey of Richard Alexander thus reached its final chapter. After all the battles—the dogfights, the bureaucratic tussles, the court-marital for his life, and again the raging dogfights—the gutsy, irrepressible Dixie waited out victory as a caged Eagle.

10

UNTO THE
BREACH

The Eagles began their service to freedom's cause by helping
the British to contain the German empire and to chip away at
the outer battlements of what had become *Festung Europa*—
Fortress Europe. In time, the nature of the struggle changed. In
North Africa, the British held, and then drove forward to
dislodge, the Germans and Italians from their hold. Eagles
were there.

By early 1943, as the British gained new strength and as
American power began to gather and swell in the Home
Islands, the Allies looked to the Atlantic Wall of Festung
Europa hungrily, determined to breach it. The early intrusion
raids, in which the Eagles had so often participated, were
modest preparations for what was to come. Operation
Jubilee—the Dieppe landings—had been a costly but highly
instructive experiment. The Eagles knew Jubilee, as they
knew Morlaix, all too well. That was another year, 1942,
when the Atlantic Wall was formidable and still in the
building. The year 1943 would be a different matter.

Out of the great assembly line that the United States had
now become, came armadas of planes—Thunderbolts, Mustangs, Lightnings, Flying Fortresses, Liberators, Mitchells,
Marauders, Havocs, and more. From the training camps

came squadrons, wings and whole air forces of pilots and crews. The elements of power to win the skies over Europe and to gouge at the Fortress behind the Atlantic Wall crowded onto the British Isles with the passing months.

The objectives were the successful assault on the Wall—D-Day—and then the overwhelming of German power in Europe. To soften the Fortress for the breaching attempt, cities and installations would be bombed and bombed again. The Luftwaffe would be challenged repeatedly until driven from the battle. For a year before D-Day and for nearly a year after, airmen of the USAAF and RAF would fly sorties virtually without number to prepare the way for and then to support the armies of what General Eisenhower called The Great Crusade.

The air campaign was epic, like nothing ever known before. The statistics—the numbers of bombers and fighters involved, the tonnages of bombs dropped, the miles flown, the missions completed, the kill ratios maintained, the volume of casualties caused and suffered—attested to the magnitude of the effort. The many photographs of devastated cities, crushed installations and dreadful firestorms illustrated the intensity of the onslaught, as did shots of exploding and falling aircraft.

For the airmen, and especially for the fighter pilots, Allied and Axis, the battle of Europe was far more personal; its traces were etched into their faces. Whatever the numbers of victories and losses, each successive day's meaning, for a year and more of days, came down to names—the names of the victors, the names of the survivors, the names of the lost.

Day after day, once more unto the breach.

On May 4, 1943, 4th Group P-47s escorted 79 B-17 Flying Fortresses on an attack against the Ford installation at Antwerp. J. F. "Pappy" Lutz was lost, and one German Fw 190 was shot down.

Pappy Lutz had borrowed a pair of boots from Deacon Hively to wear on the show. Hively's boots, expensive and hand-made in London, were his pride and joy.

On the return from Holland over the North Sea, Pappy's engine failed. He called and said, "Sorry, Deacon; looks like I'm going to get your boots wet." Pappy was seen to bail out and enter the water. Air-Sea Rescue made a thorough search, but found no trace of him.

Lee Gover recalls a May 14, 1943, bomber escort mission to Antwerp, for which he received the first Silver Star awarded to a Fourth Fighter Group pilot.

"Lieutenant Colonel Peterson was leading the Group, and I was leading Blue Section of 336 Squadron. I was at 28,000 feet when I saw four Fw 190s at about 26,000, coming in on the bombers at two o'clock. I broke off and made an attack on one at about 25 degrees head-on, and closed to about 10 degrees head-on.

"I gave a four-second burst, and was getting good hits; but as he passed under me, I could not see the result. I made no claim. I turned sharply to the left and saw another Fw 190 coming in about 500 yards ahead. He turned to the left, and I was then astern.

"At about 300 yards line astern, I fired a short burst, then closed a little and gave a four-second burst. The enemy plane rolled, and pieces started coming off of it, followed by smoke. He went into an uncontrolled spiral. I claimed one destroyed.

"I pulled up to regain my altitude and sighted another enemy fighter to my left and below, going toward the bombers. I dived. The enemy saw me and started a spiral turn to the right. I closed to about 100 yards, allowed deflection, and gave a three- or four-second burst. I saw strikes, and then had to break away. I claimed one damaged.

"Attacked by another Fw 190, I started to dive and turn. The enemy fighter stayed right on my tail, so I pulled up sharply and started a climbing turn to the left. The enemy stayed right on me but wasn't getting deflection.

"I saw that he was starting to mush out of the turn. I closed throttle, and threw stick and rudder to the right, which brought me in line astern on him. I had lost speed, and he pulled away to about 300 years. Then I started to close and fire.

"As I fired, he turned on his back and hung there for two or three seconds. The tracers that designated my last 50 rounds were now coming out, and I saw these strike him.

"Then I was being attacked again. I broke away, and started to rejoin the squadron. The Fw 190 that was chasing me was a little too eager and didn't look behind him. Lieutenant Stanhope shot him down."

On May 16, 1943, Don Young "really blew a good opportunity to score. We were crossing the coast of Holland on a P-47 fighter sweep when about 15 Fw 190s came over the top and bounced us hit-and-run fashion. After a hard turn to avoid the bounce, I saw two 190s at one o'clock below, going to the right. I dove after them, thinking 'Here's a good chance for a double.' I came in range, pulled my sight through the wingman and pressed the trigger. Nothing happened. I tried again, with no results, so I decided to leave the area in a hurry.

"I broke off and suddenly remembered what the crew chief had told me prior to starting my engine. The guns had been rewired to fire from the button on top of the control stick instead of the trigger in front, as we had been accustomed to. I tried the top button and the guns fired normally. By this time the 190s were gone."

On that same day, First Lieutenant Ernest D. Beatie, of Albany, Georgia, claimed an Fw 190 probably destroyed in an exciting encounter over Holland's Walcheren Island: "At 31,000 feet, I saw two Fw 190s flying about 4,000 feet below. My No. 1 and I rolled over and started down, and I attacked one of them from above and astern. He corkscrewed to evade my fire, and I gave him a burst every time he came into my sight. I saw his canopy fly off and other pieces fall off. I followed him to 4,000 feet, when I broke off. I did not see him strike the water. I fired 641 rounds of combat ammunition and used my camera throughout."

Little more than a month later, again over Walcheren, Beatie scored an impressive double victory as German fighters attacked four B-17 stragglers. "I dived into four Fw 190s with my No. 2 man," he reported. "I overshot the last 190 and attacked the one in front of him. I saw strikes and a big ball of black smoke as he snapped over and went straight down. I pulled around and up and blacked myself out. Lieutenant Ellington saw this 190 dive straight into the ground.

"As I came to again, I found myself in the middle of about 10 Me 109s. Three went directly in front of me as I pulled up in a tight chandelle. I dove on the last of a line, and got in a long burst. I saw strikes on his cockpit. He started over in a roll, and went down. I followed him for a way until he started pulling up. I was very close to him, and was just pushing the firing button when he bailed out. I didn't see his chute open, as I was still in the middle of many Jerries, with two of them on my tail. I dived for the deck as fast as possible, with three and sometimes four trying to catch me. They were taking long distance shots at me, and one hit me in the left wing, taking out my landing light and hydraulic lines. I went completely to the deck and started home."

On the day of Beatie's double triumph, Fonzo Don "Snuffy" Smith and James Goodson also scored victories. Four days later Bud Care and Duane Beeson each bagged an Me 109 near Dieppe.

On May 18, on a fighter sweep to Flushing, the P-47s were met at the Dutch coast by 18 Me 109Gs. Duane Beeson and Tom Andrews each shot down a Messerschmitt but saw a teammate, Lieutenant Robert Boock, dive in flames straight into the ground. Three days later, over Ostend and Ghent, the P-47s were attacked at 30,000 feet by Me 109s and Fw 190s. In the series of dogfights, which also involved William O'Regan and Steve Pisanos, former Eagle Gordon Whitlow was killed, and W. Brewster Morgan was shot down. "Damn bad show," Lee Gover wrote in his diary. "Things are getting tougher every day." Morgan survived, as a German prisoner, and later gave this account:

"My wingman (Raymond "Bud" Care, of Angola, Indiana) and I went after two Me 109s below us and hit them both. Mine went down smoking, and Bud's blew up. I followed mine down for additional shots. He finally burned, and hit the ground.

"Four 109s attacked. I tried to dive out to the coast, but about 15 miles from Ostend, they came into range. I turned as they fired, and was nearly on the tail of their No. 4 man. The leader must have called, and they boxed me in. The first shot hit me in the engine. The plane caught fire, and I spun down to within 400 feet of the water. The canopy was jammed, but I got it open. Just before hitting the water, I unstrapped, and was thrown out of the cockpit. I received only two serious wounds—a bullet in my leg and shrapnel in my face.

"The Germans picked me out of the water after nine hours and took me to a dressing station at Ostend. I spent two weeks in a hospital at Brussels, and then was taken to Stalag Luft III."

Unwilling to risk further heavy fighter losses, the Germans adopted a more cautious tactic by drawing their fighters farther from the combat zone and attacking Allied bombers after their fighter escorts, low on fuel, had been forced to turn homeward. The USAAF response was to sling a streamlined belly tank under the P-47s to provide the added range they now needed. Pilots of the 335th conducted the first squadron test flight of external tanks on July 25.

They used the tanks operationally for the first time on July 28, on that initial mission escorting the B-17s all the way into Germany, to Emmerich.

More than 200 enemy aircraft challenged them. Lee Gover shot down an Fw 190 in the scrap, but lost a good friend when Lieutenant Hank Ayres went down, and became a German prisoner. Nine German interceptors were destroyed. Colonel Anderson, Group Commander, who had insisted on being a part of this first belly tank mission, was credited with two enemy planes destroyed shortly after Captain Carl Miley shot down an Me 109. Care, Beeson, Roy Evans, Frank Boyles and Leon Blanding also knocked down enemy planes.

The 4th Group flew to Haldern, Germany, on July 30, 1943, to meet and escort returning B-17s. "I spotted an Fw 190 moving in to attack the Forts from the rear," Don Young reported. "I closed in from a shallow dive and fired a burst, seeing a number of hits. The 190 rolled over and the pilot bailed out. I made a vertical bank to the right to see the parachute below, and noticed tracers from the B-17s passing just below me.

"As I turned out of range of the '17s, I saw an Me 109 at two o'clock below diving away from me at high speed. I fired a burst at long range, with no effect. I looked around for my wingman, Fred Merritt, but he was not in sight. Fred did not return from the mission. Since he was with me just before I attacked the 190, it is possible he was shot down by the B-17s when I was fired at."

Three other Eagles—Boyles, Aubrey Stanhope and Kenneth G. Smith—also shot down enemy planes, along with Pierce McKennon, who thereby became the first non-Eagle in the 4th Group to score. Two weeks later, on August 12, Jim Clark, Steve Pisanos, Bill O'Regan and Cadman Padgett plucked off their German adversaries.

All three squadrons of the 4th Group took part in the fighter cover for 170 B-17s attacking aircraft repair depots and the airdrome at Le Bourget near Paris on August 16,

1943. Forewarned that the area was defended by the hottest Luftwaffe fighter wing, the pilots expected strong resistance, and they got it—and they whipped it. The 4th Group proudly announced that they had shot down 17 enemy aircraft, probably destroyed another, and damaged five more—a new American record for the European Theater of Operations—for the loss of one pilot. That man, Joseph G. Matthews, survived the encounter, escaped from France, and rejoined his squadron two weeks later with the disclosure that he had destroyed the Jerry that shot him down. This raised the day's score to 18. The tally reads as follows.

334 Squadron: Destroyed—Captain James Clark, Lieutenant Henry Mills and Lieutenant F. C. Smith, two each; Lieutenants Deac Hively and Bud Care, one each, with Care credited also with a "probable."

335 Squadron: Destroyed—Captain Don Young, one plus a second shared with Lieutenant Fred Fink; Captain Don Smith and Lieutenants Jim Happel, Aubrey Stanhope and Roy Evans, one each. Damaged—Young, one.

336 Squadron: Destroyed—Lieutenant Jim Goodson, two; Matthews and Major John DuFour, one each. Damaged—DuFour, Lieutenants Don Gentile and Ken Carlson, and Flying Officer Wiggin, one each.

Don Young filed this report:

Leading Blue Section at 27,000 feet, I sighted an Fw 190 approaching the Forts from the rear at about 2,000 yards. I dove after the enemy aircraft, followed by my wingman, Lieutenant Fink. I started firing at about 200 yards with approximately 30 degrees of deflection, continued firing and, closing to 100 yards, saw strikes on the enemy and his canopy flew off. No longer able to hold deflection, I broke off and Lieutenant Fink attacked. The 190 went out of control and crashed.

I opened fire at another Fw 190 at 200 yards and continued firing until he passed across in front. I saw strikes on the trailing edge of the starboard wing.

As another Fw 190 approached the Forts, I went into a shallow dive, closed to 200 yards and opened fire. At 75 yards, I saw strikes, and pieces flew from the plane. The 190 rolled over, went into a spiral dive for about a thousand feet, then entered a violent spin, with large pieces flying off. Gradually, it went into a vertical dive and crashed in a ball of flame in a large square of houses in the northern suburbs of Paris.

John DuFour got strikes on two 109s that were attacking the B-17s, then dove on two more, and saw a foot-long section of wing peel back from one and fall away. Roy Evans went after an Me 109 that was starting to attack a straggling B-17, and got bursts first in the Jerry's tail and then in the fuselage. Evans shot past so close that he could see the German pilot slumped over in the cockpit. The man never got out. Don Smith blasted another 109 from the stern. "I don't think this pilot got out," Smith said. James Happel knocked the canopy off his 109 and watched the plane crash.

The 4th's triumph in the Le Bourget battle was due in good part to the new tactic introduced by Don Blakeslee, the mission leader. Blakeslee deliberately remained for the most part above the main battle force, watching the overall action intently and directing his pilots to vantage points. The 4th Group was to employ this technique frequently, in the months to come, and Blakeslee became one of the most skillful of all air combat directors.

The fact that Blakeslee was orchestrating the fighter defense of the B-17s did not mean necessarily that he would stand off completely from the combat. As the B-17s, their bomb bays emptied, headed homeward and the enemy fighter attack waned, Blakeslee dived toward two 190s that were streaking in toward a bomber. The 190s turned away, and dived. Blakeslee hurtled after them, and began to overtake them.

At this moment Jim Goodson, leading a flight in 336 Squadron, sighted three Fw 190s cutting in after Blakeslee. Goodson called out a warning to Blakeslee, and opened fire on the pursuing planes. Goodson shot the wing off one of the 190s, and then blasted another and saw it crash. Neither German pilot had time to bail out. Goodson, scoring hits on the third 190, seemed near another when his guns stopped firing. Goodson's wing man, Bob Wehrman, approached, and the pilot of the damaged 190 dived away.

One of the enemy pilots on Blakeslee's tail had damaged the P-47's engine, and oil was streaking back from the plane. Two Fws started toward the apparently crippled Thunderbolt but were warded off by Goodson, who maintained the pretence of having ammunition, and Wehrman. As Blakeslee headed for England yet another Fw 190 started after him, then broke off at the sight of the oncoming Goodson and Wehrman P-47s.

Goodson eventually was to become the premier Eagle ace of the 4th Group, outscored in that elite organization only by two men who had not served in the Eagle Squadrons, John T. Godfrey and Ralph K. Hofer. Blakeslee in 1981 had occasion to write to Eagle Squadron Association president E. D. "Jessie" Taylor, in support of Goodson's belated application for ESA membership:

"It would be an honor for the Association to have a member of Jim's caliber. If I sound biased, it's because I am. Jim saved my bacon dramatically."

Into September the raids went on. The Luftwaffe fought back furiously, but the tide of aerial supremacy was turning. 336 Squadron hit Provins, about 50 miles southeast of Paris, with the loss of one American, Lieutenant Dale Leaf. On September 7, they escorted 120 Flying Fortresses to Brussels. More than 20 enemy aircraft came up, with another American loss, the former Eagle, Lieutenant Aubrey Stanhope. A force of 30 German fighters rose to oppose an effective raid over Paris on September 9. Downed were Lieutenant Fred Fink and Lieutenant Vernon Boehle (pronounced Bailey), of 335 Squadron, both Eagle veterans. Boehle was jumped by four Fw 190s, and evaded three of them. He describes it.

"One Jerry pilot nicked me several times. I dived, weaved, and tried everything I knew, but he kept too close and was firing plenty as he came at me. I dived again, almost to the ground. The enemy, perhaps out of ammunition, broke away. I climbed to 19,000 feet and started home.

"I was about 30 miles from Dieppe and could still see the French coast when the engine started running rough. Soon the whole plane was vibrating, tossing me around in the cockpit, and then the entire engine shook itself free. The plane did a couple of tight loops and went into a flat spin. I tried to transmit a distress signal, but the radio was dead.

"I jettisoned the cockpit hood and scrambled out on the wing, expecting to bounce off. The plane was spinning so fast that centrifugal force kept me glued to the wing, sprawled flat for some seconds. I believe I could have stayed there all the way down. I had to shove myself off with my feet."

Boehle parachuted into the water, inflated and climbed into his dinghy, and waited for rescue—and waited, through the day and the night. "They called this the English Channel and I began to wonder where all the English ships were." The second night brought lightning and heavy rains. Around midnight Boehle heard an airplane, and flashed a help signal with his floating light, without result. Several hours later, he heard engines again, and flashed his light above his head until his arm ached. The low outline of a motor torpedo boat loomed up. The craft reduced speed, and edged toward him. Someone called, "Are you okay," and then they lifted him out of the water, after 44 hours of drifting in the channel.

Lee Gover says in his diary that "on September 14, we escorted a newer P-47 group on their first mission. It burned them up to be escorted, and I couldn't blame them one bit." His diary continues with, among other reports, a description of the horrifying bomber losses.

"On the 15th, we took 120 Fortresses to Paris in the evening and saw one of the saddest sights yet. Just as we were taking them in on their bombing run, five Fw 190s came in at them head-on, fired, rolled over and went down. The Forts knocked one of them down. Then the most terrific flak I have ever seen came up. One Fort was hit directly and exploded, went all to pieces and down in flames. Not one chute opened.

"Ten seconds later, another Fort got a direct hit in the wing, caught fire and started down. It began breaking up, and was all on fire. Small dark objects, which must have been the crew, started down. Again, no parachute opened. The explosion probably killed them.

"In about another minute, another B-17 went all to pieces, also with no chutes. God, I felt sorry for those poor fellows. Thirty boys gone, just like that! If it had been fighters after them, we could have done something. But flak—well, we just dodged to beat hell ourselves.

"On the 23rd, we flew down to Warmwell, stayed overnight, and next day escorted B-17s to Nantes, France, twice—seven hours of flying that day, about 2,000 miles. Got the hell shot out of us by antiaircraft fire. Two Forts shot down by flak, which was damned accurate. Landed in the dark at Exeter; stayed the night in an old castle.

"Escorted B-17s to Paris again on the 26th, and 360 B-17s to Emden, Germany, on the 27th. The big boys were really starting to knock hell out of the big cities now.

"In October, we escorted huge numbers of heavy bombers to Emden, Bremen and Munster, Germany. We now had the upper hand on the Krauts for sure, and our fighter losses were getting smaller.

"November started off with a trip to Wilhelmshaven, Germany—400 Forts. Lieutenant Moon and Lieutenant Galleon were shot down when a flock of Me 109s bounced us at the coast. On the 5th, it was 440 B-17s to Geisenkirchen in the very heart of the Ruhr—plenty of flak and fighters. On the 7th, 72 B-26s to Meulan, near Paris. Don Gentile was being shot up by three Fw 190s, and called for help. When asked where he was, he said, 'Down by the railroad tracks.' Hell, there are hundreds of railroad tracks around Paris. He stayed with it, though; shot one down and made it home, all full of holes.

"Meanwhile, Don Blakeslee, who was leading the group, was being clobbered by two Fw 190s. I took my section down to help him out. Jim Goodson, my No. 3 man, was on the inside of the turn, arrived first, and shot down both of the fighters that had Blakeslee in a bad way. When we got back to base, Blakeslee chewed me out for leaving the bombers.

"December found us going into Germany on almost all missions. I was now leading 336 Squadron, and led my last mission December 20, with Gentile and Jim Goodson as flight leaders. Ken Carlson flew my wing, a man you could always count on when things got rough. Johnny Godfrey was on Gentile's wing. Louis Norely, Willard Millikan, and Vermont Garrison were all leading sections. A group of pilots I was grateful and proud to have flown with. All of them became great aces.

"We escorted 600 Forts and Libs—B-24 Liberators—to Bremen. There were many enemy fighters. I got a probable on an Fw 190 near the target. My propeller and electrical system went out over Holland, and I damn near didn't make it back. Ken Carlson came back alone with me.

"I had now finished my tour, as had Roy Evans, CO of 335 Squadron. We went to London to await transportation home. The Jerries put on their last big bombing of London by aircraft. We were staying at the Jules Club when the bombers hit us.

"A bomb knocked the whole side of the building off, and covered me with boards, plaster and rubble. Flying glass cut my face up considerably. I was on the third floor, but managed to get down to ground level by sliding down the elevator cables.

"I found Roy Evans in his room on the ground floor, also covered with debris. I pulled back his covers and he looked up and said, 'What happened?' More than 40 people were killed.

"We went to another hotel and back to bed again. We were in town seven nights, and were bombed five nights. Then we received our orders, and came home on the *Ile de France*."

In the States, Gover flew the Bell P-59, America's first jet fighter, then became Group Commander of a P-40 training unit at Page Field, Fort Myers, Florida. After the war, at March Field, Riverside, California, he flew the new F-80 jet fighter and eventually flew all jet fighter models up through the F-104, winding up his career with 18,000 flying hours, Command Pilot wings, and the rank of a full colonel.

"Those who went home early didn't know what fighting was," he says. "It was much more difficult in the USAAF, flying missions over Germany, than with the RAF, when you were only over England and the edges of France, Holland and Belgium."

Gover also flew in three motion pictures, including all the P-47 stunt flying for actors Edmund O'Brien and Robert Stack in *Fighter Squadron*, which depicted the early days of the USAAF European campaign, the softening up of Festung Europa for Operation Overlord.

"D-Day—June 6, 1944—started off in England black and rainy and bloody awful. The whole group was lined up and ready at 4 A.M. for takeoff from Ashford, in Kent. I was sure they wouldn't send us off in that rain, but they did."

Bill Dunn, now recovered from the crippling injuries that had knocked him out of 71 Eagle Squadron in August, 1941, was back for the show that no one wanted to miss, as operations officer for the 406th Fighter Group. The fighters and the rest of the great invasion force were sent forth into the miserable weather through the agonized decision of General Eisenhower, who gambled everything on enough of a weather break to establish a beachhead on the shores of France.

"We climbed through 20,000 feet of soup, three squadrons of 25 airplanes each, all hoping we wouldn't run into each other. We all made it and broke out on top. After we'd flown about half way across the pond it was clear as a bell all the way to France.

"Our job was to provide close support to the ground troops, if they needed us, and to sweep the area of any enemy aircraft. The sky was absolutely full of airplanes—ours. I understand that only two Krauts showed up, and they strafed the beach once and then beat it for home.

"We did what we called Cab Ranks—flew in sections of four aircraft over designated portions of the front. We were in radio contact with FACs, the forward air controllers assigned to Army units.

"We had code names for our different Cab Ranks, like waiting cabs outside a hotel. If the ground unit needed some close air support, the FAC would call for a Cab, or two or three, to make a strike with bombs, rockets or napalm, or to strafe. That's what our job amounted to—four missions on D-Day, and two or three missions the following days.

"On June 12, we landed in France at A-6 airfield, the first U.S. air unit assigned there. We had a tar-paper and chicken-wire runway right off the beach. If you took off in one direction, you had to turn like mad to keep from hitting the balloons over the convoy ships. If you took off in the other direction, you went right over the bad guys' front lines. It was a little hairy.

"It took the engineers only about a day or so to prepare an advance airfield, using the tar-paper and chicken wire. They used to build an airfield right under the noses of the enemy's 88 mm. artillery guns. Air Force units would occupy the fields before the German infantry had been cleared out of the area.

"When we first landed in France, it was about noon time. The artillery unit near the airfield had lunch ready for us. Roast beef, mashed potatoes, gravy, green peas and dessert—everything all cooked up. It was tremendous."

*   *   *

Three other former Eagle squadron members found themselves operating out of France as part of the Ninth Air Force's 371st Fighter Bomber Group. They were William J. (Jim) Daley, who served as Deputy Commander of the Group from May to September in 1944, Eric Doorly, and Dale "Jessie" Taylor. The 371st had earlier trained at Richmond, Virginia, and then at Camp Springs, Maryland, which became the site of Andrews Air Force Base.

After the Normandy invasion, the 371st's Thunderbolt pilots moved into France, first to Sainte-Mère-Église, at the base of the Cherbourg Peninsula, and then, to keep up with troop advances, to a field near St. Dizier, in the heart of the champagne country.

On October 17, Doorly led a mission out of a concrete runway south of Dole, near Dijon, when the 406th was outnumbered by enemy fighters three to one, yet managed to bring down four German planes and to damage three. Doorly was the top scorer of the mission, accounting for two of the enemy planes destroyed and two of them damaged.

Three days later, Doorly led a strafing mission in which 12 P-47s battled a like number of German aircraft. Four enemy planes were destroyed, one of them by Doorly, who carried with him a particularly sad memory.

He had been a horrified observer on September 10, when a runaway P-47 on a landing-strip at Coulommiers smashed into Jim Daley's plane, killing the extremely popular 24-year-old Texan.

"I was two ships behind Daley when his wingman overran him," Doorly says. "The left wing struck Jim's armor plate and drove it into Jimmy's head, knocking him forward into the gunsight. Jim apparently also hit the throttle, because his P-47 went into a series of wild high-speed ground loops around the field. His wingman jumped out, intercepted him, and managed to close the throttle.

"We had an awful time with the grief-stricken pilot of the runaway plane. A doctor had to help calm him down and cool him off. He was given leave back to the States. He came back later, and proved to be an excellent pilot."

Another Eagle, Red Campbell, describes Jim Daley as "a guy you just couldn't help but like. He was personable, and he was generous. Jim would give you the shirt off his back, and then find some way of making a joke out of it. He was very handsome and had a winning way. Women found him irresistible."

The ground support role in Normandy provided the P-47 pilots with some of their most hazardous assignments—low-altitude fragmentation bombings.

Doorly writes about such missions with little fondness:

"Frag bombs are very delicate things. They go off at the slightest touch.

"On one mission with frags on board, I was so low they hit the trees, and I wound up with 270 holes in my airplane. I had to land my P-47 at a 4,000- or 4,500-foot emergency strip with no flaps or brakes. I ground-looped, put tapes over the holes, and flew home."

After General Patton's Third Army had started its August dash across France, Doorly was in radio contact with some tanks. The tank commanding officer called him up, and asked him to do something about six German destroyers that were off the coast.

"I had eight aircraft, and we dropped some bombs," Doorly said. "When they missed, we went down from 15,000 feet—down to strafe them at 485 miles an hour, and pulled out within 10 feet of the water at about 1,000 yards range. The Germans put up a solid wall of flak—big green balls. They started hitting the windshield. I missed the bridge, tried to get down again, but there was nothing but a sheet of flak.

"The thing that terrorizes you at such a time is that you are committed. The AA looks like it is coming straight in at you. The flak ships are firing and it looks like everything is coming in the windscreen. An 11-inch section of my windshield was shattered, the left side was out, and the machine guns were just lying there. But I got an explosion out of the destroyer. The whole action took only a minute."

That was one of the two scariest missions Doorly could remember. The first had been during his Spitfire days.

"The other time I said 'Oh, God, save me!' was a routine sweep over the French coast at 25,000 feet. The Germans were sending down sucker bait in the form of two 190s at a time diving past our formation. I finally decided that one pair was the last and rolled over after them. In about 10 seconds, I was surrounded by explosive cannon shells and could see six 190s in my mirror. I immediately invented an evasive maneuver that consisted of full forward and left stick and full left rudder, which produced an inverted snap roll followed by a prolonged inverted spin.

"I pulled out at water level and headed home, but one of the Fw's had followed me down, presumably to confirm one destroyed, and he pulled in right behind me. I had two big advantages. I was scared to death, and a Spit will outturn a 190. I dropped down until I could see my wake in the mirror, and watched his guns. As soon as he fired, I yanked into a vertical turn right on the water. He pulled up.

"We did that three times, and then the 190 pulled up and waved goodbye. He was out of ammunition. Ten seconds—60 rounds—of cannon ammunition; just about the scariest thing there is. Don Gentile tried this same thing out two weeks later. 'Say—you know?' he said to me later. 'It works.'"

Doorly and Gentile were part of a band of Eagles and other Yanks who were neither daunted nor jaded nor, apparently, wearied by the grind of war. They accomplished individually, and led their buddies to accomplish, extraordinary feats. Doorly, for example, was irrepressible. Twice in his World War II career, he was shot down. The second time, he bailed out into occupied France and escaped. He was sent back to the States and promptly volunteered for another hitch, which put him back in the European Theater for a long tour with the Ninth Air Force.

Returnee Bill Dunn's 406th Fighter Group was so gung-ho that it achieved the distinction, as Dunn puts it, of being the only outfit in the USAAF to have an entire German army surrender to it. According to Dunn, it happened this way.

"When General Patton went steaming off across France, a German army, cut off on his right flank, started moving up from Issoudun to cross the Loire River.

"We caught these people in a column maybe 15 miles long, and we beat them up in the forenoon, a second time around noon, and a third time in the afternoon. There was just nothing left except burning and destroyed vehicles, and dead and wounded soldiers.

"Quite a few of the enemy vehicles were horse-drawn, and, of course, the horses got shot up, too. It got to the point on the last mission that our pilots stopped shooting up the Germans and started shooting the wounded horses to put them out of their misery.

"The German commander sent word that he and his troops would surrender, but only to the Air Force commander of the fighter group which had destroyed his column. Our group commander was Colonel Anthony Grossetta.

"General Vandenberg, Commander of the XIX Tactical Air Command, came to our airfield and got Tony, and they went down to a bridge over the Loire where the surrender took place. The German general came across first and gave Tony his pistol, and then all the other troops crossed over and put their guns in a big heap.

"That's how Tony accepted the surrender of an entire German army. The 406th Fighter Group got a Presidential Unit Citation for the action.

"That day we must have killed and wounded at least several thousand German soldiers. We could see them clearly on the ground as we beat them up. It was not a pretty sight at all. Some of our boys got sick to the stomach while strafing."

Late in the war, in 1944, one enthusiast unexpectedly renewed contact with an equally spirited old friend. Jessie Taylor was leading two new pilots on a training flight from France to England when one of them had an engine failure and bailed out into the English Channel. Taylor stayed above the downed pilot and repeatedly tried, without success, to arouse Air-Sea Rescue Service by radio:

"I was still yelling into my radio, with only a few minutes of fuel left before I would have to start home, when a calm, clear voice came out of the blue, over the R/T: 'Okay, Jessie; I'll help you.' Instantly I recognized it—a voice I had not heard for two years. Red McColpin, my old Eagle companion from 133 Squadron, was speaking. He had recognized my voice, making that frantic call for help.

"Mac and I had fought together in England for about nine months. I had no idea he was back in this part of the world, and I was happy to turn the rescue-alert job over to him. My pilot was picked up within a few minutes. Later, Eric Doorly and I flew to Mac's base in England, and had a good reunion with the former 133 Squadron leader."

In his Eagle Squadron days, Jessie Taylor had been known as an eager beaver (correction, eager Eagle). His approach to convoy duty has already been described in this book. Most pilots welcomed their days off and could hardly wait to get into London or anywhere else off base. Not Jessie. He would go flying whenever possible on his free days. Repeatedly, he offered to go on missions for other pilots, "just to let them take a rest."

Taylor assumed command of his own Thunderbolt squadron in the Ninth Air Force, and this gave him authority to fly almost whenever he wished. Squadron members noticed particularly that when the unit was supporting ground forces occupying the Cherbourg Peninsula, Taylor would take his P-47 up late in the afternoon, when the Squadron had quit flying for the day. This happened almost every day. Ground crewmen observed that their skipper would go up for what he called a test hop, and 15 minutes later would return, sneaking in just ahead of the evening deadline for flights.

Personnel keeping tab on these so-called gun tests counted more than 30 of them. On 18 or 19 such flights during the Cherbourg campaign, Taylor's plane picked up ground fire. On one of them, returning from an early-morning divebombing and strafing mission, Taylor sighted a convoy of German trucks towing big guns and fuel tanks and carrying troops, halted under a long row of trees.

"I still had some ammo, and decided to make a pass at them," Taylor said later. "Coming in at high speed, it was a successful strafing run. There were three explosions. I couldn't tell whether they were from the trucks or the fuel tanks. As I started to pull out of the dive, I saw for the first time, directly ahead, some large cables strung across my path.

"The Thunderbolt weighed seven tons. Pulling out at high speed, it would nose down and forward. I had a choice of going through the cables—suicide in an all-metal fighter plane—or going under them and through some trees 35 or 40 feet tall. So—look out trees!

"Hitting the trees and touching the ground, did a lot of damage to the plane. The cowling was badly impaired all the way around, with the bottom part missing. The spinner and the base of the propeller blades were damaged. The bottom cylinder was torn off; guns in both wings were knocked loose and broken off; and the right wing was set back four inches.

"The prop ran away, but the plane still flew about 60 or 70 miles back to the Sainte-Mère-Église strip—and then froze up on the final approach. Back safely on the ground, I found that the greatest damage had been casued by a tree trunk about 10 inches in diameter. Amazingly, even though that trunk had knocked off the cylinder, there was not so much as a scratch on any one of the propeller blades—and the prop had been turning at a high RPM at the time.

"Thinking back, I have wondered what those people in the truck convoy must have thought when the big fighter plane charged down out of the sky with eight guns blazing, killed or destroyed everything in sight, knocked down a bunch of trees, bounced off the ground, and then flew off into the morning sunrise.

"My friend, Father John Luongo, told me later that even though mine was a single-seat fighter, it was certain that I had a Passenger with me that day. I was unhurt, and flew other missions the same day."

In part, because of his freedom to roam off on search-and-destroy missions of his own design, Taylor was to count his command of the 406th Squadron the best job in his 20-year career in military flying. By mutual agreement, the master sergeant at the field would patch the holes in the fuselage and engine, and say nothing about the matter. Taylor ducked questions from curious colleagues. A couple of times he invited a trusted friend to go along on a two-plane "gun test." These dual missions were soon discontinued, however. Taylor preferred not to risk getting a pal in trouble. After the 406th moved on to a new base, it became common knowledge that Taylor had been going a-hunting on his own on the mysterious late-afternoon jaunts.

"On his regular operational flights with the squadron each day, Jessie used to map out a flight pattern for after-hours use," one teammate said. "After everyone was through for the day, he'd go up and have a good 10 minutes to fly back over the pattern. He'd fire his guns for only a few seconds—maybe 20 seconds all told—over a period of about two minutes. He had a helluva lot of fun strafing lines of trucks, cars, tanks or artillery—Germans moving materials and troops and guns, setting up gun emplacements. You can't imagine how much damage he inflicted on the enemy, and all on the quiet—probably the way his Indian ancestors used to go on the prowl in the old days. And not one word about it in the squadron records!"

Decades later, Taylor had forgotten the incidents, or preferred that they be forgotten. Asked about them he looked nonplussed and would only chuckle, "No comment."

"We used to call Howard Hively 'Deacon' because after a few drinks he was inclined to preach a lot," says Pete Peterson. "He did monologues, including one in which, sitting on a bar stool, he was the Red Baron flying a Luftwaffe mission—with a broomstick. It was guaranteed to have the audience rolling in the aisles. In another skit, he was a pilot performing evasive action. The scene ended hilariously with the pilot jumping up and running around the cockpit dodging enemy bullets."

Deac Hively, one of the most vocal of the Eagles, used to protest loudly at the RAF's frequently imposed order that "Class A uniforms will be worn." He favored comfort far above elegance when it came to fighting gear, and he didn't mind saying so. When the Eagle Squadron Association was asking the pilots for contributions to its forthcoming informal history, Hively responded, among other comments, with:

"Have you ever tried to wear a Class A uniform in the close confines of a fighter cockpit? Picture yourself dressed up in a tuxedo, sitting in an outdoor john, strapped tight across the lap and shoulders. Then hang on your person 80 pounds of equipment, including a Mae West, backpack chute, oxygen tube, mask, bail out bottle, dinghy, escape kit, large knife, Colt .45, and God only knows what other sundries. Certainly, this order had to come from the brilliant mind of our commanding general."

Hively, who was to shoot down 12 enemy planes before war's end, had to bail out from his P-47 into the English Channel on return from covering a bomber strike against submarine pens at St. Nazaire, France, June 15, 1943.

"First thing I noticed," he said, "were two small streams of blue smoke jutting forward over my shoulders, and an increase in cockpit temperature. When my boots became too hot to be comfortable, I spied flames beyond the firewall on the cockpit floor. Gauges went haywire, temperatures rose out of the green into the red, and the rudders became hot to my feet. The cockpit was no longer feasible."

Another P-47 pilot pulled alongside—Hively identified him as Pierce McKennon, an American who had not been in one of the Eagle squadrons—and said on the radio telephone, "You'd better get out of there, Deac." Hively replied that he might be able to keep on going a bit longer. McKennon assured him that if he had to take to his parachute, his companions would follow him down.

"We were at about 27,000 feet," Hively recalls. "Suddenly, the propeller stopped, frozen into a four bladed apparition. The fire became hotter, so that I had to tuck my feet up under the seat. My boots felt like they were burning."

Hively's narrative, which has also appeared in *Escort to Berlin*, by 4th Fighter Group historians Gary L. Fry and Jeffrey L. Ethell, continues:

"How to get out? Should I merely climb out, step off the wing, and hope—or should I just roll it over, and fall out? Or should I pop out—wind all trim forward until it required a lot of back pressure on the stick to keep the plane level, and then count three, shove the stick forward, and push the plane away.

"I switched the radio over to our emergency channel, D for dinghy, and had all the Maydays going, in my best devil-may-care manner: 'Mayday, mayday; mayday, heyday, pay-day,' which it was.

"Control kept calling for a fix and a long count. The count started off in the proper manner—'1, 2, 3, 4,' but got shorter and shorter as my house got hotter and hotter. At about 7,000 feet I decided the time had come, so I unhooked all the straps and started to roll the plane over. I could not do it. Every time I got halfway over, I'd let loose of the controls and grab the sides to hold on. It is not easy to just give up and fall upside down from an airplane.

"Control called again for a long count. I hurriedly rolled all the trim forward, gave the count '12345678,' said goodbye, popped the stick forward, and departed. I did not pop out, but seemed to float up over my airplane and just hang there. I could look down and see all the straps hanging straight up, and my helmet hanging up from its cord also. I could see the fire, and counted seven bullet holes in the right wing, and was quite concerned about this, for I had not been aware that any enemy plane had come close.

"I seemed to hang there, then all of a sudden—whish—I was free. Falling, yes, but the whole feeling was one of freedom, total unattachment, soft suspension, free of machines and ties of any sort—a wonderful feeling. I found myself yelling, 'Wake up, Deac!' Frantically, I reached for the D ring; it was supposed to be just over the heart, but it was not there. This was a borrowed chute.

"I found the ring around in the middle of my back, almost out of reach, got two fingers around it and jerked as hard as I could. It came loose, but slipped through my fingers and went sailing off into space. I saw the chute coming out, but sideways—not up. It looked old and dirty. I *hope* it opens, I thought, as it kept running out. And then it did open—whoomp! I looked up, and it was beautiful. I looked down, and there right below me, just out of reach, was my D ring. Damn, I thought; there goes a pound. In those days, that meant it was worth $4.04.

"My airplane, some distance away, was heading straight toward the earth. I watched, fascinated. Boom—it exploded, the tail section sailing end over end, and the nose splashing into the water. There was a tremendous rush of hot air that seemed to halt me in midair momentarily. I dropped again with a smaller woomp. Above me, my chute had collapsed on one side. I started to swing, away up almost to the horizontal, and then down again as the other side of the chute collapsed. What a ride! I tried to pull on the risers but that only seemed to make it worse.

"I looked down again, and saw my dinghy hanging on a strap attached to my Mae West. The water was coming close; I knew I was going to have to swim, and I decided to have a last cigarette. This wasn't easy, for the chute straps were so tight I could hardly get at the cigarette pack.

"It was time to get rid of unnecessary weight. I threw away my knife—hated to see it go; dumped my cigarette lighter and cigarette case; pulled out my .38 revolver, a pearl-handled beauty given to me by my father. I had never fired the gun, so I let loose with all six shots before giving it the old heave ho.

"I turned the release dial on the chute harness, ready to drop out just above the water. I was still swinging in a pretty good arc, so it was hard to tell exactly how high I was. Then—swish—across the top of one wave, through the next wave, and splash into the next. I hit the release dial so hard it almost knocked me out. With the wind blowing hard, the waves were enormous. I hit in almost a horizontal position, with the chute directly behind me. As I felt the harness leave, I reached over my shoulder to grab it, but there wasn't a chance. That thing was traveling straight across the water like a speedboat.

"Down I went—deep down. I paddled and kicked until I reached the top, took a big breath, and went down again. The uninflated dinghy was worse than a 180-pound anchor, and I was unable to inflate my Mae West because the pull strings had swelled up with water and were stuck firmly behind the CO_2 bottles.

"The third time I went down, I was frantic. I said to myself, 'Deac, you have to do something.' As I went down for the fourth time, I deliberately opened my eyes, took a careful look at the oxygen bottles, held my breath until I thought I would burst, and managed to free one of the pull strings. When I came up this time, I found I could stay on the surface. I took my time, and got the other one undone, and then it was great.

"I finally hauled the dinghy up, and managed with some difficulty to remove the safety pin and twist the cap to inflate it. Getting into the dinghy was a problem in the rough water, but finally I just reached out and pulled it under me. Once in, I felt the battle was over. It was drier than the Channel—not much, but to some degree. What's more, it was a treasure trove.

"The first thing I found was a little package of six red flares. My buddies were buzzing around, every now and then coming straight over the dinghy just off the water. I was positive they saw me, but knew I should set off a flare to let them know I was all right.

"The first flare buzzed when I pulled the tab, and then— boom!—went sailing up high and beautiful, a big and bright red ball of fire. I tried hitting the guys with the others as they came thundering over me. I never did hit, but I came real close. I missed Jim Clark by a foot or less.

"Afterwards, when we talked about it, none of the fellows ever saw a flare. They did not even see me or the dinghy. I didn't know that then and was happy, thinking all the while that everybody saw me and that a boat would soon be along.

"Soon the flares were all gone, and so were all the guys. There I was, all alone. The dinghy seemed to get smaller and smaller, and the waves got bigger and bigger, and I got colder and colder. I paddled and paddled to get warm. Standing up I could see the English coast in the distance. Right behind me, and even closer, was France. I was making no headway. The little dinghy acted more like a cork than a boat, and every once in a while, if I was standing when I reached the top of a wave, I would fall into the water.

"I was getting sleepy, a bad sign. I knew I must stay awake or I would freeze. I looked through the dinghy for something to keep me awake, and that was when I found the treasure trove.

"First, there was a sea anchor, a little funnel that trailed behind after I threw it out. I found a bright red sail, and rigged it up, and sailed for over an hour. There were also a fishing line and hooks; a waterproof packet containing malted milk tablets, a chocolate bar, dry matches, halazone tablets, two compasses, a saw blade, first-aid kit and 2,000 French francs; plugs, a band pump, a bailer and other items.

"I heard an airplane; my first concern was that it might be German, planning to strafe. Then I saw that it was a Walrus, a British floatplane, coming right toward me. I knew the water was too rough for a landing attempt. Under each lower wing hung a bomb. One of them let loose and came sailing at me. I hit the drink, and when I came up, there it was, six feet away and smoking—a marker, putting out a thick greenish yellow cloud. The Walrus flew away.

"A boat appeared. I stood up, yelled at the top of my lungs, and waved the little flag I had found in the dinghy so hard it went sailing off its stick. A man on deck started swinging a rope, like a cowboy. When he let loose it came sailing across the water like a cannon shot. If I had not ducked, it would have hit me. When I caught hold of the rope, they pulled so hard and fast I could barely hold on. They lowered a sort of net. I clung to it, and climbed. As my head came over the gunnel, hands reached from above and grabbed me.

"Someone threw a shot of rum down my throat. Unable to accommodate anything other than the salt water I had already swallowed, I promptly threw up. My rescuers whisked me below decks, stripped off my clothes, and came at me with towels and rubbed and rubbed until I was raw on both sides. Then came long underwear, thick woolen socks, soft flannel gray trousers, and a white turtleneck wool sweater. And tennis shoes, and blanket after blanket. I lay there getting warmer and warmer.

"Six smiling faces looked down at me. Would I like some medicine—meaning rum? 'I'll try it once more,' I said. 'Will you join me?' The rum was sweet and heavy and good, and did not burn at all. The smiles grew bigger; every face beamed.

"Three ambulances were waiting on the dock at Portsmouth—and a crowd—and there was even a flag flying to show that a man had been recovered. I went ashore in my turtleneck and gray flannels, three sheets to the wind. I felt that I had swum the English Channel—and in Class A uniform at that."

Gilmore "Danny" Daniel and Carroll McColpin were the only two pilots to serve in all three Eagle Squadrons. Daniel flew also in six other RAF squadrons, claiming credit altogether for destroying three enemy bombers and two fighters, probably destroying four other enemy planes, and—in Middle East combat—knocking out two enemy trains, four flak ships and six tanks.

"One might think that, serving in so many RAF squadrons, I set some kind of a record," Daniel has remarked. "Actually, I don't believe it was a record. It was not too unusual to be in units for a short time. Pilots were being transferred quite freely because there was a shortage of them. We kept our kits packed all the time."

Danny was without question the youngest of the Eagles. When he enlisted in the Royal Canadian Air Force in December, 1939, he presented a birth certificate showing that he had become 18 on November 30. Long after the war, he said, a search of records at the Osage Indian Reservation in Oklahoma, where he was born, showed that his birthday was in 1925, instead of 1921, and that he was only 14 when he entered the RCAF.

"Yes, I had a doctored birth certificate that my father had obtained," Daniel says. "Dad would do or get just about anything I wanted, whenever possible. I am sure the RCAF people knew I was not as old as the certificate said, but they knew I could fly because they tested me. And they needed pilots.

"My Indian name is Ku-sha-he—Little Two Shoes, because of the small feet in our family. I was raised by a grandmother until I was eight. My mother died when I was three, and my father was only 19 at the time. He let Grandmother and the Indian Agency take care of me. Dad was a real hell-raiser—racehorses, rodeos and such. He was what white people call an oil-rich Osage Indian.

"The Indian Agency put me in the Oklahoma Military Academy at Claremore when I was eight. It was like a boys' school 12 months a year, and you were promoted on how well you progressed. I remember going from the eighth grade to the tenth in one year, and from the tenth to twelfth. There wasn't anything to do but study, drill and work."

Daniel went to the Spartan School of Aeronautics, in Tulsa, in extension of his work at the military academy, logging 150 hours of flying time and obtaining a limited commercial pilot license and an aircraft-powerplant and mechanic's license. In Canada, he went through the RCAF Instructors' School at Moose Jaw, Saskatchewan, an organization run by the brothers of William J. Hall, whom Daniel was to know well later, in 71 Eagle Squadron. Hall was the first Eagle to become a German war prisoner.

"After a short time in Hurricanes with 121 Eagle squadron at Kirton-on-Lindsey, I went to 129 Squadron at Leconfield flying Spitfires, made several sweeps and Rhubarbs, and shot down a Ju 88 twin-engine bomber making a twilight raid on Hull. Another Eagle, Fred Scudday, was in the squadron with me.

"From 129 I went north to 43 Squadron, flying Hurricanes again. I scored a probable here, and Collier Mize, of Harrison, Arkansas, also shot one down. I also helped in a rescue mission, which later earned me a DFC. I was flying cover and thought it routine, but my fellow Eagles, Mize and Bob Reed, from Lubbock, Texas, wrote it up. Some years later, my father's house was washed away in a flood and we lost that citation. I tried to get another and was told there was no record. There was a notation on my discharge, though, saying the DFC had been gazetted.

"Next I went to 257 Squadron, at Coltishall, where I shot down two Me 109s on sweeps and also shot up many E-boats. Then I was transferred to 242, the squadron commanded by Douglas Bader, the famous pilot who lost both legs in a crash in 1931 and learned to fly again with artificial legs. I was flying Hurricane IIBs in 242 when I was shot down for the first time. A Heinkel 111 twin-engine medium bomber shot my radiator off, but I was credited with probably destroying him.

"I crash-landed in the moor southeast of Norwich but wasn't hurt except for a bump on the forehead. I got back to base three days later, after visiting some very nice people. I can't recall their names, but I do remember the daughter, Violet Barley. She was the reason I didn't report to base sooner.

"From 242 I went across the field to where 133 Eagle Squadron was forming. Scudday, Sgt. Davis Florance and I reported to Squadron Leader George Brown. We had 25 Hurricanes and four pilots.

"I got off on the wrong foot, as usual, with Brown, and he had me posted to 19 Squadron at Fowlmere. I was flying the Spitfire V again.

"The hassles I had were of my own making. I was young, hot-headed, and wouldn't conform. The trouble I had with Squadron Leader Brown was over flying without my jacket or leather helmet or oxygen mask, although I did have my head phones on. He didn't like it that I was wearing a T-shirt with Oklahoma Military Academy on the chest and no jacket.

"I shot down an He 111 off Great Yarmouth. The bomber set my plane on fire. I bailed out into the drink, and was rescued at once by a motor patrol boat from Felixstowe.

"I was transferred to 401 Squadron at Duxford. They were being equipped with the Bell P-39 Airacobra, with all sorts of armament. We were assigned to the Fighter Development unit which had many different types of planes—the German 109, Fw 190, Ju 88, Ju 87, He 111, and Do 217 as well as the U.S. P-40, and P-36, and all current British fighters and night fighters—Whirlwinds, Typhoons, CR-42s— for routine testing of armament and camouflage. We strafed flak ships at Ostend and Calais and into Holland, trying out the American planes. They were no match for German fighters or for British aircraft, either.

"At this time, 133 Eagle Squadron transferred to Fowlmere. I was reassigned to it for three weeks, and received my commission as pilot officer. Then I went to No. 71 Eagle Squadron at North Weald."

Danny Daniel was shot down for the third time on a bomber escort mission over France, October 13, 1941. He had blasted the lead 109F in a formation of three and it had exploded, sending the other two planes down as well. Other enemy planes set Daniel's aircraft afire, and he parachuted into the English Channel. The Germans recovered him and took him to Stalag Luft III to sit out the war. At the time he was still only 15 years of age.

Daniel retired from the RAF in 1946 with the rank of squadron leader—the equivalent of U.S. major—and two years later returned to flying with the USAAF. He flew one of his tours in the Korean action as an Okinawa-based technical sergeant, and the other as a second lieutenant radar observer on Lockheed F-94 Starfire interceptors operating out of K-13 Suwon, often on night patrol above the Yalu River. One such mission with the Fifth Air Force's 319th Fighter Interceptor Squadron north of Chorwon, Korea, August 4, 1952, won him the DFC with this citation:

> Informed that the ground controller had lost contact with the target, he searched the area and made a free-lance contact with a slow moving aircraft flying at extremely low altitude. By skillful interpretation of his radar equipment, Lieutenant Daniel enabled his pilot to maneuver into proper position. During a prolonged chase at dangerously low altitude through twisting valleys, Lieutenant Daniel maintained a careful observation of the surrounding mountains, enabling his pilot to devote his complete attention to the target ahead.
>
> Passing over a small air strip, Lieutenant Daniel found his aircraft to be the object of heavy weapons fire. Calmly continuing his radar surveillance of the target, he directed his pilot in evasive maneuvers which rendered the antiaircraft fire ineffective. During this evasive action the target disappeared and could not be contacted again. Although destruction of the enemy was not effected, Lieutenant Daniel's skillful use of his radar equipment and his coolness in directing his pilot through dangerous terrain, resulted in the enemy abandoning his mission and the prevention of damage to his own aircraft.

Daniel was a pilot once again in the Lebanon crisis of 1958, flying North American F-86D Sabre Jets with the 512th Fighter Interceptor Squadron covering landings by U.S. Marines. Later, he served as Base Operations Officer in Beirut.

In Vietnam, as staff officer at Seventh Air Force Operations in 1966 and 1967, he directed covert operations, including all strikes in North Vietnam with fighter-bombers from Thailand. He received the Bronze Star medal with a citation which declared that:

> During this period, Major Daniel consistently demonstrated outstanding professional knowledge, ability, and unswerving devotion to duty. Major Daniel's superior performance and expertise were instrumental in the translation of general operational concepts and strategy into well defined fragmentary orders for conduct of strike missions into North Vietnam.

After retiring from the Air Force in 1969, Daniel became a corporation pilot for two companies in Tulsa.

It is fitting to conclude this narrative by looking from the youngest of the Eagles to their "elder statesman." Harold Strickland, who first joined their ranks at an age many would consider old for a fighter pilot, was exemplary as the steady, reliable comrade warrior, the inspiration by example, committed to duty and ready to serve.

After transfering from the RAF to U.S. service, he became a captain, returned to the States, and flew as a test pilot at Eglin Field, in Florida. One of his first test flights there, in February 1943, was in a P-47 equipped with an oversize, long-range belly tank, the sort that made possible the invaluable fighter escort penetrations deep into Fortress Europe. Shortly after the Normandy landings, he arrived as a lieutenant colonel at the IX Tactical Air Command advanced headquarters, in France. The unit lived with and supported the advance of the First Army in Normandy, Northern France, the Ardennes and the Rhineland.

"Strick" Strickland rounded out the course of the war in which the Eagles had fought so long, and, with characteristic brevity, voiced the warrior's acceptance of further duty expected on the other side of the world, where there was another, unfinished war to be concluded:

"On VE-Day, May 7, 1945, about 11 months after Normandy, the Allied tactical forces, with their thousands of tanks, airplanes, guns, trucks, jeeps, rifles and mortars, came to a weary halt deep within the wreckage of Hitler's Germany.

"Then, at IX Tactical Air Command, we began preparing to load on ships and embark for the invasion of Japan.

"However, the Japanese signed their formal surrender on September 2, 1945. When we boarded our ships in the Mediterranean soon after VJ-Day, the destination was good old U.S.A."

EPILOGUE

MOTIVES AND MONUMENTS

Thus, the story of the Eagles, as told by the Eagles themselves, the remarkable true history of a brotherhood as gallant as ever took wing in support of a great cause.

Woven through the reminiscences, the narratives, the letters is the common theme of military personnel engaged in combat in distant parts, facing the fear, the loneliness, the physical pain of wounds, the anguish of loss, and the longing of men for their families and their native land.

"Home! We're still alive. We're going home," Eddie Miluck wrote in his diary on a glorious New Year's Eve, when the campaign was finished and successful and his close buddy had just turned up, out of nowhere, out of captivity.

They had chosen to leave their loved ones and their native land. There was "someone else's war" to be fought, because, as so many of them sensed, it was in truth their country's war but neglected by their country. And there was glory to be sought, by some, though the glow faded as an attraction, as it tends to do in our khakied times.

And there was *flying* to be done. At home, there were Wacos and Staggerwings and Spartans and similar civilian craft. In England, there were Hurricanes and Spitfires—*hot ships*—to be followed by Thunderbolts and Mustangs. Perhaps it takes a pilot to understand the allure of such opportunities. To fly as a fighter pilot flies—the pinnacle, first-rate!

In view of that, what of the idea that the pilots of the RAF Eagle Squadrons were mercenaries? Were they essentially soldiers of fortune, cashing in on Britain's need for pilots, to make good money?

Two of the three Eagles who became U.S. Air Force generals, Chesley Peterson and Carroll McColpin, even after 40 years had definite feelings on the point of whether the Eagles were mercenaries.

Peterson: "Negative. We were not mercenaries or soldiers of fortune—not one of us was. For two major reasons: one, the pay; two, pure ideology. We just were not that type."

McColpin: "We could not have been mercenaries. Even officers got only $87 a month, less taxes—about $15 a month—and food. By the time we got through paying our mess bills, there was nothing left."

Reade Tilley, survivor and ace of Malta and past president of the Eagle Squadron Association: "Mercenaries? No; the word has an unpleasant connotation. It implies a motley bunch fighting for money. Soldier of fortune? That has a romantic ring to it and aptly applies to the Eagles, who were blithe spirits seeking adventure, which they found fighting for Britain in the RAF."

Dixie Alexander: "I don't like being called a mercenary, but in the dictionary sense of 'a soldier serving for pay in a foreign army,' within those limits, we were mercenaries. But the broader meaning—men out to make a bundle, willing to fight for any country that paid enough—no, that did not apply to us."

Of the Eagles who survived the war, only one, Leo Nomis, went on to fight another country's war: Israel's War for Independence, in 1948. Ironically, for a while, Nomis flew Me 109s over Palestine. Of the others, several flew combat again —for the United States in Korea and Vietnam.

Most of the Eagles went back to more peaceful pursuits, some in aviation, others in entirely different areas.

As they prepared to assemble in the autumn of 1982 in Victoria, British Columbia, for the fortieth anniversary of the transfer of their three squadrons from British to American command, the surviving Eagles were hard at work on two projects, in addition to the informal written accounts, to preserve a record of their accomplishments. In London, they had won tentative approval for the erection of an Eagle Squadrons monument in one of that city's famous squares. They still were short of the funds required, however, and the design, a beauty by some American standards, had run up against objections by certain British advocates of more traditional architecture. In spite of the temporary disagreements among good friends, the debate and the feeling were in the service of history, with pride and gratitude.

In the United States, through their association, the Eagles agreed with the International Aerospace Hall of Fame, in San Diego, California, to establish an impressive memorial to the Eagle Squadrons, including the acquisition, it was hoped, of one of the Spitfires the Yanks had flown.

Among the participants of these ventures there was a sense of urgency. Three of the aging Eagles died in 1980, and three more in 1981. The press of time is as it must be, but these former pilots, these hot bloods of World War II, could be confident that they would long be remembered in Great Britain as well as at home.

From Leslie Graves, of Harrow, Middlesex, England, who had been a photographer with 71 Squadron, comes a clipping, a letter to the editor of the London *Sunday Express*, signed by one W. R. Hemming:

> A party of tourists was being escorted around St. Paul's Cathedral, but an elderly couple remained behind when their friends moved from the American Memorial Chapel behind the High Altar. They told me that their son had been killed while with the Eagle Squadron in the early days of the war. They had last seen him in 1940, when he left for Britain, and as he was shot down in the Channel, no grave existed for them to visit. But they understood that a list of American War Casualties was kept in the chapel.
>
> I led them to a large glass case containing a volume of 28,000 names inscribed who died on active service while based in Britain. A page is turned in this book each day. The volume lay open—at the page on which their son's name is listed.

APPENDIX A

FLIGHTS OF IMAGINATION: CHRONICLE OF A HOAX

If the idea of a bunch of brash young Yanks making their way overseas to defy the Nazis for the RAF seems romantic today, it certainly was no less so at the time the events occurred. Officially, America was neutral, but the public was intensely involved, isolationist or interventionist. Newspapers, magazines, newsreels and dramatic films soon brought the Eagles and their derring-do home to the USA. Book publishers were no less interested, although getting enough material about the Yanks in the RAF to fill a book was not easy to do—unless the right source came along.

For a glory-hungry entrepreneur who was in the right place at the right time to be, or appear to be, the right source, there was hay to be made in the sunshine of public curiosity and adoration.

Of a young man named Byron "Jack" Kennerly, the girl who married him when she was but 17 and he 27 said, "Jack wanted to be Lawrence of Arabia. He was off like a skyrocket in every direction."

Like many of the young American men in 1940 who wanted to fly and help Britain defeat Nazism, Byron Kennerly was restless at home, bored with unpleasant jobs at poor pay, ever on the lookout for glamor and excitement. From wages earned as a truck-driver in Arkansas, a lumber mill hand in Oregon and an oilfield roustabout in southern California, Kennerly had managed to save enough money to buy flying lessons. He had run away from home four times by the time he was 16, and 10 years later, when he learned that England needed pilots and that he could qualify for the RAF, he was ready to run again. Since his Royal Air Force pay would be at a mere subsistence level, his young wife, whom he had married when she was three months out of high school, would have to struggle along as a counter clerk in a five-and-dime store, in Pasadena, California.

Kennerly was one of the early Eagles. The day of his arrival was a red-letter one for the brand new 71 Squadron. On November 7, 1940, the new unit at Church Fenton gained its first combat-ready fighters, nine Hawker Hurricanes, and to fly them Chesley G. Peterson, Mike Kolendorski, James L. McGinnis, Edwin E. Orbison, Dean Satterlee, Richard Arthur "Jim" Moore, Gregory "Gus" Daymond, and "Jack" Kennerly.

These men were added to a nucleus of earlier arrivals and were soon followed by more volunteers. Later in the month, 71 Squadron moved to a somewhat larger base at Kirton-in-Lindsey. The young Eagles were eager to fly and fight, and their high spirits showed. Squadron Leader Bill Taylor knew that such was to be expected, but, as he said of Kennerly afterward, the tall, huskily-built, frequently belligerent Californian was a problem from the very beginning of his tenure with 71.

On February 3, 1941, almost three months after his arrival, the 71 Squadron Operations Record Book, which listed all operational flights of each pilot, mentioned Byron Kennerly for the first time, only to note that he had been sent back to America because of "unsuitability." Taylor explains why:

"He was an SOB whom I tried to have court martialed but whom the RAF, not wanting any bad publicity, sent home steerage class. His almost nightly conduct in the mess was such that the hefty Station Commander told me one morning that he had to sock Kennerly and send him to bed."

On another occasion, Kennerly started making "filthy remarks" to the Station's non-flying and older officers in the mess, and smashed phonograph records over the heads of some of the them. Some of his flying was also less than satisfactory. On one occasion, Kennerly loudly accused the leader of his three-plane section of trying to spin him in. "After landing, he raised bloody hell with the section leader and with me," Taylor said.

"His offenses were cumulative and they added up to the fact that he certainly was not officer material. It became quite evident that he had to go.

"My suggestion that he be court-martialed was made over the Station Master's head to the kindly Irish AOC—Air Officer in Command—of 12 Group. His decision was, perhaps wisely, to ship Kennerly quietly back to the States. Kennerly left long before the Squadron became operational. The book he wrote later was a real hoax."

Kennerly went home in disgrace, but no word of this leaked to the public. Interviewed when his ship reached Ottawa in mid-March, 1941, Kennerly said he was home on furlough because of eardrum damage sustained in a five-mile-a-minute power dive. He also said that he planned to help recruit RAF cadets before he returned to combat.

As perhaps the first American volunteer to return from Britain, Kennerly found on arriving back in Pasadena that he was an immediate celebrity, presumed to be a war hero. He submitted to a number of interviews and talked about plans for a book about his experiences. Ten days after a flattering profile appeared in the Los Angeles *Times*, the Warner Brothers Studio said in a news release that Kennerly had been signed as technical advisor on a motion picture, *The Flight Patrol*, co-starring Ronald Reagan and James Stephenson as American pilots in the RAF.

Reagan was at the peak of his movie popularity. He had been in films for only four years but had worked in more than 30 pictures. His salary was $1,650 a week, and the studio said his fan mail was second only to that of Errol Flynn. Kennerly boasted freely of his friendship with the star of *Kings Row*, the dying George Gipp—the "Gipper"—of *Knute Rockne—All American*. It pleased him to be referred to banteringly, now and then, as Reagan's Eagle.

A month after its first press release on Kennerly, Warner Brothers, now identifying the former Eagle as having been "injured in action," announced that Kennerly would portray himself in a scene in *The Flight Patrol*, with Reagan and

Stephenson. As with many other films, the title changed, and the picture had its trade showing in Hollywood August 12, 1941, as *International Squadron*.

The film fared well enough with critics and with the public. "For all its flaming crashes and for all its shots of helpless planes spinning clumsily earthward," said the *New York Times*, "credit *International Squadron* with a neat three-point landing at high speed. . . . It breezes along with dash and bravado and not too much self-importance. . . . Ronald Reagan is excellent as the slap-happy hell-diver who finally pays for his moral failures with his own death in combat."

The Warner Brothers film made its way into theaters well ahead of a rival, Universal Pictures' *Eagle Squadron*, a Walter Wanger production, which was ridiculed by many Eagles as being silly and unreal. Kennerly was happy to disclaim any participation whatever in that film.

Meanwhile, a book, *The Eagles Roar!* by Byron Kennerly "as told to Graham Berry," an Associated Press reporter in Los Angeles, was taking shape, under a contract with Harper & Brothers Publishers, of New York and London. Kennerly's marriage, however, was falling apart. He asked his Catholic wife to get a divorce, and she reminded him that she was working at a Kress store for $15 a week, while he was making $250 a day at the studio. "You get the divorce," she told him. He did so, in Las Vegas.

The Eagles Roar! came out in 1942, as part of a flood of war stories. It soon sank from view with hundreds of other books that failed to make it into the movies. So far as could be determined, many of the Eagles were unaware of its existence. An exception was Vic Bono, who said he encountered Kennerly late in the war.

"Jack said, 'I did a book, but you don't have to believe everything you read,'" Bono recalls.

"And I told him, 'I've read it—and I don't believe any part of it.'"

In the opening chapter of his first-hand account of the Eagle Squadrons, Kennerly writes, "This is not fiction. Since truth is stranger than fiction, you may run across some incidents that are hard to believe."

A casual reader might have no suspicions about *The Eagles Roar!*, and any historian using the book as a reference would have to be careful about checking primary sources to detect the booby traps of misinformation the book contains. Anyone who reads the 71 Squadron ORB—the Official Operations Record Book maintained meticulously from day to day by a very thorough squadron staff—would soon come to feel that there was something amiss with Kennerly's accounts.

For example, Kennerly wrote that while he was leading a three-plane section in battle formation, his wingmen, Leckrone and Orbison, collided. Orbison managed to land safely, but Leckrone slumped forward in his seat as though he were unconscious. Kennerly added that he called over the radio telephone, "Phil! Phil! Bail out! Jump! You're in danger." Kennerly says that he followed the man down as closely as possible, to within a few hundred feet of the ground, yelling and pleading all the way. Leckrone failed to respond, and his plane smashed into the ground. Kennerly then says that he climbed to 2,000 feet, made a dive over the scene, pulled up and performed a roll as "a final salute to the first casualty of the Eagle Squadron."

Following is the RAF's official report for January 5, 1941, from the ORB:

> Today the squadron lost one of its best pilots, P/O (Pilot Officer) P. H. Leckrone, who was killed in a flying accident. Flying in a formation of three with P/O V. C. "Shorty" Keough and P/O E. E. "Bud" Orbison, Phil collided with Orbison at over 20,000 feet and, going into a gradual dive, crashed just outside Scunthorpe. Keough followed him down all the way, shouting to him over the R/T, but Phil never replied and made no attempt to bail out. It appears that either he was knocked unconscious by the collision, or was unconscious before the collision through the lack of oxygen. Orbison did very well to manage to land safely, as his left wing was badly torn in the collision.

There was no mention whatever of P/O Kennerly. Asked about this matter, Chesley "Pete" Peterson, the Eagle ace who was to command 71 Squadron throughout most of its combat period, said: "Kennerly never led a flight at any time while in the squadron. He was always a wingman. The Ops Record is correct regarding this accident."

The Operations Record Book entry for February 9, 1941, said: "Today the squadron had its second fatality, P/O E. E.

Orbison being killed while on an operational patrol. While flying through thick cloud he must have lost his bearings and spun from about 4,000 feet."

Orbison was killed six days after Kennerly was sent home. Yet in his book, Kennerly gave an eye-witness account of the accident and said that "when we reached the aircraft, we found Bud dead."

Kennerly also described a February mission in which he, Keough and Andy Mamedoff attacked six Ju 88 bombers and damaged them, and received damage in turn. In his account, Keough's fin and rudder were almost completely shot away, and an exploding cannon shell had missed Kennerly by a scant foot. In dogfights with some Me 110s, Keough disappeared and Kennerly barely made it back to base. Keough was found to have landed at another field.

A few days later, Kennerly said, he and Keough and Maranz intercepted a Dornier bomber over the North Sea and poured bullets into its fuselage. He said Keough failed to pull out of a vertical dive, called in a choking voice that he was going in, and plunged into the water, apparently hit by a bullet or cannon shell.

Later, Kennerly said, three Hurricanes from the squadron flew over the crash scene, dove toward the water and dropped wreaths "in final tribute to a gallant little officer."

The ORB report for February 15, 1941, said:

> P/O V. C. Keough did not return from a scramble when a section of this squadron was ordered to protect a convoy just off the coast. We have given up hope that he will return safely. P/O Maranz, who was with him, broke formation with Keough at 7,000 feet in cloud when they were in a steep dive. We have heard, although it has not been confirmed yet, that the Coast Guard Station in that section heard what might have been a plane crashing into the sea.

Keough's death occurred 12 days after Kennerly had left the Squadron. Pete Peterson had this to say:

"The Ju 88/Me 110 story is pure fantasy, as is also the Dornier story. Keough and Maranz were scrambled after a bogey. No contact was made. Weather tops were above 20,000. At about 18,000 Keough spun out because he hadn't turned on his oxygen, according to the findings of the accident investigator.

"There were never any wreath-dropping ceremonies ever in the RAF. Just out of character for the British! Kennerly was never combat ready, nor ever flew a combat mission except possibly an air defense scramble without contact."

Kennerly said in his book that in March he took part in a three-plane mission that forced some Me 109s to jettison their bombs and turn back. On return to base, he said, the Eagles learned that Jim McGinnis had just been killed in a takeoff crash.

McGinnis in fact was killed April 26, 1941—almost three months after Kennerly's departure—while leading a section of two planes on a scramble. "The cause of the accident was never determined," Peterson says. "I believe it probably was power loss, as Jim was a pretty good pilot. Even though the weather was bad, he could usually cope.

"Bill Taylor suspected sabotage at the time, and we had some RAF C.I.D. (intelligence) types stay with us a while. I discount any such idea."

Kennerly said that on three occasions he flew in such close formation with a British flight lieutenant that he felt bumping and scraping, and afterward found paint from the other plane on his own wing tip. An encounter with a Dornier 17 heavy bomber was so close, he said, that he could see the tense face of the enemy gunner, his lips parted and his teeth clenched. He said he saw the gunner fall back, arms upraised, and watched two other members of the German crew drag the gunner's body from his seat. Kennerly said three Heinkel 113 fighters attacked but were driven off, and when he landed, he found that an enemy shell had burst not six inches from where his forehead had rested against a gunsight.

In a dramatic concluding chapter Kennerly described an attack by six Americans in Hurricanes and six British pilots in Spitfires on a formation of 15 Ju 88 bombers escorted by 50 Messerschmitts. Kennerly said he put bullet bursts into one bomber and probably destroyed it, fired at another at almost point-blank range, and then took a cannon shell through the hatch just above his head. He said he tried to bail out, but finding the hatch jammed, stayed in the plane and flew it back to an English field.

Kennerly also told in his book of firing at Heinkel 111 and Junkers 88 bombers on a night attack against Coventry as early as November, 1940. Yet RAF records showed that:

1. Eagle pilots pursued an enemy aircraft for the first time on April 13, 1941, when McGinnis and Sam Mauriello chased a Ju 88.

2. An Eagle pilot got close enough to the enemy to shoot, for the first time, on April 17 when Gus Daymond fired ineffectively at a Dornier.

3. The first enemy kills by Eagles occurred July 2, 1941, when Squadron Leader Paddy Woodhouse, Bill Dunn, and Gus Daymond each shot down a Messerschmitt 109. One pilot, Bill Hall, was shot down then, to become the first Eagle prisoner of war.

Harold Strickland said in 1974 that he was at first rather favorably impressed by the book, since it was lucidly presented and did not seem overly boastful. Early in 1975, when he learned of its many variations from truth, he said in a note, "Wow! Looks like the whole book is phony, although some of the 'literary license' could be reasonably accurate if other unmentioned sources were identified."

Did any of the Eagles complain to the publisher or anyone else, or were they all too busy to care? "Except in personal letters home, no complaints were made regarding Kennerly's book in any official manner," Pete Peterson said. "Frankly, we just ignored it, as we did the innumerable magazine and newspaper articles written by some other characters."

The attractiveness of the material and Kennerly's manner may have helped to impress an aura of authority upon Kennerly's stories. Graham Berry, his collaborator on the book, says that he found Kennerly to be a decent person, and had no reason to doubt the flier.

Eagle Bill Dunn points out: "You've got to remember that Kennerly's book was published in the first part of the war, when publishers would print anything that sounded first hand. We can't blame Kennerly too much. He wasn't the only guy with a loose pen in those days."

The Eagles Roar! resurfaced in 1981, offered for sale by a mail order publisher.

After the war, Kennerly's fortunes declined. In February 1951, he held up a Los Angeles bank, making off with $1,600. Quickly apprehended, he pleaded guilty to a charge of bank robbery. Imposition of a sentence was suspended, but he was on probation for five years. He died some years later, in a Veterans Administration hospital, of lung cancer.

APPENDIX B

ROYAL AIR FORCE AWARDS

In grateful appreciation for outstanding achievement, the Royal Air Force awarded 40 decorations to 31 members of the Eagle Squadrons. It happened that the awards were distributed equally by nationality: 20 to 14 Englishmen and 20 to 17 Yanks. Many of the American pilots who transferred into U.S. service went on to win further honors from their own government.

Thirty-four of the RAF awards were the Distinguished Flying Cross. Three pilots—American Chesley Peterson and British Walter M. Churchill and Eric Hugh Thomas—received the Distinguished Service Order in addition to the DFC. Thomas, in fact, was the only Eagle to win three awards, garnering a second DFC in 1943.

There were five other double winners of the DFC: Britons Peter Powell and H. A. S. Johnston, and Americans Peterson, Gus Daymond and John J. Lynch. R. C. Wilkinson, an Englishman, won the double award of the Distinguished Flying Medal in May, 1940, when he was still an enlisted man. The other RAF award was the Military Cross, presented in July, 1943, to H. F. Marting, one of the American pilots.

Other winners of the DFC include: *British*—C. F. Ambrose, W. D. Williams, S. T. Meares, Henry Woodhouse, George A. Brown, H. T. Gilbert, Hugh Kennard, Gordon Brettell, and E. R. Bitmead. *American*—C. W. McColpin, A. G. Donahue, J. E. Peck, Reade Tilley, W. J. Daley, O.H. Coen, Don Blakeslee, John A. Campbell, J. B. Mahon, S. R. Edner, S. A. Mauriello, A. F. Roscoe, James A. Gray.

APPENDIX C

ROSTER

How many true Eagles were there—how many pilots who actually flew as members of Royal Air Force Eagle Squadrons 71, 121 or 133 during their operational phases in World War II? For 35 years after the war the answer to this question usually was: "Around 300." In mid-1980 a research team headed by James A. Gray, Adjutant of the Eagle Squadron Association, came up with a definitive reply.

There were 243 American Eagle pilots, 16 British Eagle pilots and 28 Special Duty Officers.

Gray said he and his colleagues drafted a list after careful assessment of all available records. The sources of information included the following.

In England: Air Historical Branch, Ministry of Defence, London; Public Record Office, Kew, Richmond, Surrey; Commonwealth War Graves Commission, Maidenhead, Berks.

In Canada: Canadian Forces Records Centre, Ottawa, Ontario.

In the United States: Albert F. Simpson Historical Research Center, Maxwell Air Force Base, Alabama; National Air and Space Museum, Washington, District of Columbia; Spartan School of Aeronautics, Tulsa, Oklahoma.

Two of the Eagle pilots, Carroll McColpin and Gilmore Daniel, saw service in all three squadrons. A number of others served in two Eagle Squadrons. In the roster compiled under Gray's direction, however, each pilot is identified only with the squadron with which he primarily was associated.

Roll of American Eagle Squadron pilots

J. K. Alexander, 71; R. L. Alexander, 133; L. E. Allen, 71; T. W. Allen, 121; F. E. Almos, 121; N. Anderson, 71; P.R. Anderson, 71; S. M. Anderson, 71; T. J. Andrews, 71; W. A. Arends, 133; R. H. Atkinson, 71; F. C. Austin, 121; J. B. Ayer, 71; H. L. Ayres, 133.

W. H. Baker, 133; C. S. Barrell, 133; C. E. Bateman, 71; E. D. Beatie, 121; R. N. Beaty, 133; D. W. Beeson, 71; J. L. Bennett, 133; E. H. Bicksler, 133; D.J.M. Blakeselee, 133; L. M. Blanding, 121; C. O. Bodding, 121; V. A. Boehle, 71; V. R. Bono, 71; R. A. Boock, 71; D. E. Booth, 121; F. R. Boyles, 121; R. G. Braley, 133; W. O. Brite, 71; R. V. Brossmer, 121; H. C. Brown, 133; J. I. Brown, 121; G. R. Bruce, 133.

J. A. Campbell, 121; R. C. Care, 71; G. Carpenter, 121; N. R. Chap, 121; L. A. Chatterton, 71; J. A. Clark, 71; O. H. Coen, 71; C. A. Cook, 133; F. M. Cox, 121; J. G. Coxetter, 133; S. H. Crowe, 133.

W. J. Daley, 121; G. C. Daniel, 71; G. A. Daymond, 71; B. P. DeHaven, 133; A. G. Donahue, 71; E. Doorly, 133; F. P. Dowling, 71; B. C. Downs, 121; W. R. Driver, 71; J. G. DuFour, 71; W. R. Dunn, 71; J. E. Durham, 121.

S. R. Edner, 121; W. V. Edwards, 133; G. E. Eichar, 133; P. M. Ellington, 121; J. E. Evans, 71; R. W. Evans, 121.

H. S. Fenlaw, 71; M. W. Fessler, 71; G. B. Fetrow, 121; F. M. Fink, 121; D. R. Florance, 133; J. Flynn, 71; W. K. Ford, 133; P. J. Fox, 121; V. J. France, 71; R. W. Freiberg, 121.

C. O. Galbraith, 71; T. A. Gallo, 133; F. A. Gamble, 121; D. Geffene, 71; W. D. Geiger, 71; D. S. Gentile, 133; J. D. Gilliland, 121; J. R. Goodson, 133; L. Gover, 133; J. A. Gray, 71; J. E. Griffin, 121; C. P. Grimm, 121; D. D. Gudmundsen, 133.

H. C. Hain, 133; W. I. Hall, 71; G. O. Halsey, 121; F. Hancock, 133; J. R. Happel, 121; C. A. Hardin, 121; C. W.

Harp, 133; J. C. Harrington, 71; J. F. Helgason, 71; H. D. Hively, 71; K. L. Holder, 121; W. J. Hollander, 71; A. H. Hopson, 71.

W. B. Inabinet, 71; M. E. Jackson, 133; W. L. C. Jones, 121.

J. L. Kearney, 121; J. M. Kelly, 71; W. P. Kelly, 121; B. F. Kennerly, 71; V. C. Keough, 71; K. K. Kimbro, 133; C. C. King, 133; S. M. Kolendorski, 71.

D. E. Lambert, 133; L. L. Laughlin, 121; P. H. Leckrone, 71; L. S. Loomis, 133; J. F. Lutz, 71; J. J. Lynch, 71.

J. B. Mahon, 121; A. B. Mamedoff, 133; R. L. Mannix, 71; N. Marans, 71; C. H. Marcus, 121; C. L. Martin, 121; H. F. Marting, 71; E. W. Mason, 121; J. G. Matthews, 133; S. A. Mauriello, 71; G. S. Maxwell, 71; B. F. Mays, 71; H. H. McCall, 133; C. W. McColpin, 133; T. P. McGerty, 71; J. L. McGinnis, 71; R. E. McHan, 121; D. W. McLeod, 121; R. D. McMinn, 71; M. G. H. McPharlin, 71; C. E. Meierhoff, 133; G. H. Middleton, 133; C. H. Miley, 133; E. L. Miller, 133; H. L. Mills, 71; E. T. Miluck, 71; D. E. Miner, 133; G. E. Mirsch, 133; J. Mitchellweis, 133; C. Mize, 121; J. J. Mooney, 121; R. A. Moore, 71; W. B. Morgan, 71; M. S. Morris, 133; R. S. Mueller, 133.

H. T. Nash, 121; D. D. Nee, 133; J. C. Nelson, 133; G. P. Neville, 133; W. H. Nichols, 71; L. S. Nomis, 71.

L. D. O'Brien, 121; V. W. Olson, 71; G. I. Omens, 133; E. E. Orbison, 71; W. T. O'Regan, 71; J. M. Osborne, 121.

C. V. Padgett, 121; V. A. Parker, 121; R. F. Patterson, 121; R. G. Patterson, 121; J. E. Peck, 121; W. Pendleton, 71; C. G. Peterson, 71; K. D. Peterson, 133; R. L. Pewitt, 133; S. N. Pisanos, 71; E. M. Potter, 71; R. L. Priser, 71; P. B. Provenzano, 71; H. A. Putnam, 133.

L. F. Reed, 121; C. H. Robertson, 133; A. F. Roscoe, 71; D. H. Ross, 121; G. C. Ross, 71; L. T. Ryerson, 133.

J. M. Sanders, 121; D. H. Satterlee, 71; R. O. Scarborough, 71; S. M. Schatzberg, 133; F. Scudday, 133; A. J. Seaman, 71; W. V. Shenk, 121; N. D. Sintetos, 121; L. A. Skinner, 121; W. C. Slade, 133; J. T. Slater, 121; G. J. Smart, 133; B. Smith, 121; D. D. Smith, 133; F. C. Smith, 121; F. D. Smith, 121; K. G. Smith, 121; R. E. Smith, 133; F. J. Smolinsky, 121; W. G. Soares, 133; G. B. Sperry, 133; R. S. Sprague, 71; A. C. Stanhope, 121; A. J. Stephenson, 133; M. L. Stepp,

121; H. L. Stewart, 71; R. N. Stout, 133; H. H. Strickland, 71.

B. A. Taylor, 121; E. D. Taylor, 133; J. L. Taylor, 121; K. S. Taylor, 71; W. D. Taylor, 71; W. E. G. Taylor, 71; G. Teicheira, 71; C. R. Thorpe, 121; R. F. Tilley, 121; E. Q. Tobin, 71; C. W. Tribken, 71; T. H. Tucker, 121.

F. R. Vance, 121; M. S. Vosburg, 71.

T. C. Wallace, 71; W. R. Wallace, 133; R. C. Ward, 71; J. W. Warner, 133; V. E. Watkins, 121; J. W. Weir, 71; S. F. Whedon, 133; W. J. White, 133; G. H. Whitlow, 71; W. C. Wicker, 133; D. K. Willis, 121; R. L. Wolfe, 133; G. G. Wright, 133.

D. A. Young, 121; N. D. Young, 121; F. G. Zavakos, 71.

Roll of British Eagle Squadron pilots

C. F. Ambrose, 71; E. R. Bitmead, 71; E. G. Brettell, 133; G. A. Brown, 133; W. M. Churchill, 71; H. T. Gilbert, 71; H. A. S. Johnston, 133; H. C. Kennard, 121; S. T. Meares, 71; R. P. R. Powell, 121; G. W. Scott, 133; E. H. Thomas, 133; R. E. Tongue, 71; R. C. Wilkinson, 121; W. D. Williams, 121; H. D. C. Woodhouse, 71.

The following are Eagle Squadron Special Duties officers, all British except for three Americans in 71 Squadron and an Argentinian in 133 Squadron.

71 Squadron: E. Brookes and F. H. Tann, and American R. V. Sweeny, adjutants; F. N. B. Bennett, R. F. Collin, B. J. Hudson and American W. A. Becker, engineering; F. A. Binks and D. G. G. Jones, and American A. S. Osborne, medical; J. R. Robinson and P. T. Salkeld, intelligence; W. J. Smith, ground defence.

121 Squadron: M. D. Assheton-Smith, intelligence; C. L. Bessey, C. D. Sorrie and C. E. Wood, engineering; H. H. R. Browne, H. E. Wilson and P/O Wright, adjutants; D. Laing, medical.

133 Squadron: T. C. Beswick and R. T. Wood, engineering; F. J. S. Chapman, medical; J. G. Staveley-Dick, adjutant; J. M. Emerson, Argentinian, intelligence.

INDEX

Numbers preceded by *p* indicate photograph insert page.

940.54 Haugland, Vern
HA
    The Eagles' war